# LITERARY HISTORY OF SANSKRIT BUDDHISM

# LITERARY HISTORY OF SANSKRIT BUDDHISM

G. K. NARIMAN

GYAN

*Published by*

Gyan Publishing House
5, Ansari Road
Daryaganj, New Delhi-110002
Phone: 011-47034999, 9811692060
E-mail: books@gyanbooks.com

*Distribution Network*
gyanbooks.com
India, USA, Canada, UK, Australia, France



ISBN: 978-81-212-8562-9 (PB)
First Published, 1920

2nd Impression 2023

*Printed at:* Gyan Press, Delhi.



**LITERARY HISTORY OF SANSKRIT BUDDHISM**

Author: G.K. Nariman

# LITERARY HISTORY

OF

# SANSKRIT BUDDHISM

(FROM WINTERNITZ, SYLVAIN LEVI, HUBER)

BY

G. K. NARIMAN

(*Author of Religion of the Iranian Peoples; Iranian Influence on Muslim Literature.*)

Bombay:

D. B. TARAPOREVALA SONS & Co.

1920

Printed by Mr. Dhanjibhoy Dosabhoy, General Manager, **The Bombay Printing Works, Ltd.**, at **The Commercial Printing Press**, 11, Cowasji Patell Street, Fort, Bombay, and published by Messrs. D. B. Taraporevala Sons & Co., Bombay.

**OFFERED**

AS A TRIBUTE OF APPRECIATION

TO

**Sir RABINDRANATH TAGORE**

THE POET SCHOLAR

OF

AWAIKENING ORIENT.

# CONTENTS.

## CHAPTER V.



## CHAPTER VI.

## CHAPTER VII.



## CHAPTER VIII.

PAGE.



## CHAPTER IX.

## CHAPTER X.



## CHAPTER XI.



## CHAPTER XII.



## CHAPTER XIII.

## APPENDIX V.



## APPENDIX VI.



## APPENDIX VII.



## APPENDIX VIII.



## APPENDIX IX.

APPENDIX X



APPENDIX XI



APPENDIX XII

## ABBREVIATIONS.

BEFEO—Bulletin de l'Ecole française d'Extrême Orient.

Bibl. Ind.—Bibliotheca Indica.

Ep. Ind.—Epigraphia Indica.

ERE—Encyclopaedia of Religion and Ethics, edited by James Hastings, Edinburgh.

GGA—Gottinger Gelehrte Anzeigen.

Grundriss—Grundriss der indo-arischen Philogie und Altertumskumde, founded by G. Buhler, continued by F. Kielhorn, edited by H. Luders and Wackernagel, Strassburg, Trubner.

Ind. Ant.—Indian Antiquary (Bombay).

JA—Journal Asiatique.

JAOS—Journal of the American Oriental Society.

JASB—Journal of the Asiatic Society of Bengal.

JBRAS—Journal of the Bombay Branch of the Royal Asiatic Society.

JPTS—Journal of the Pali Text Society.

NGGW—Nachrichten von der K. Gesellschaft der Wissenschaften zu Gottingen.

OC—Orientalistenkongresse (Verhandlungen, Transactions, Acts).

PTS—Pali Text Society.

RHR—Revue de l'histoire des Religions, Paris.

SBA—Sitzungsberichte der Berliner Akademie der Wissenschaften.

SBE—Sacred Books of the East, edited by F. Max Muller.

SWA—Sitzungsberichte der Wiener Akademie der Wissenschaften.

WZKM—Wiener Zeitschrift fur dir Kunde des Morgenlandes.

ZDMG—Zeitschrift der Deutchen Morgenlandischen Gesellschaft.

## FOREWORD.

The works with which our standard literary histories of Sanskrit literature deal are almost exclusively confined to Brahmanic texts. Weber, Barth and Hopkins and after them even Barnett and Keath have scarcely assigned its due place in the history of Sanskrit literature to the contribution made by the Buddhist authors. The brilliant and outstanding exception in English is still the Renaissance chapter of *India: What can it teach us* by Max Muller. That there was a vast literature embodied in Sanskrit by Buddhist thinkers is attested even by the sparce references in classical Sanskrit to them and by an occasional find of a Buddhist work in a Jain *bhandara*. The late Dr. Peterson came upon the *Nyayabindutika* in a Jain library, and the various papers read before the Bombay Branch of the Royal Asiatic Society by Telang and Professor K. B. Pathak demonstrate the deposits of Buddhist works in extensive quotations, if not in entire texts, to be found in the libraries of the Jainas of Kanara. The Mahavyutpatti in one place (p. 51) mentions thirty-eight famous writers, the names even of some of whom have grown strange to us. The works of others have perished and there are hardly any, of the lives and complete literary remains of whom we have positive knowledge. For a search of Sanskrit Buddhistic texts in Jain libraries the public may look up to enlightened Jain religious preceptors like the Jainacharya Vijayadharmasuri who combines ancient traditional practices,—the Jain saint did all his journies to Benares, Calcutta and other sacred places in Northern India on foot from Surat,—with a broad religious outlook and a Western method of organised research.

Thus there is a gap in our knowledge of Sanskrit literature which this book is intended to supply. I have entirely depended upon Winternitz in the first thirteen chapters. It was my intention to bring up-to-date the work which appeared originally in 1913; but commercial Bombay has evinced small care for literary research and the best of its libraries are yet innocent of the learned series like the SBA. SWA. and *toung pao*, not to mention a host of other continental periodicals, without which it is impossible to continue Winternitz's laborious history. Winternitz is by no means a new name to English readers. He prepared for Max Muller the voluminous index to the forty-nine volumes of his *Sacred Books of the East*. I have endeavoured to embody all his valuable notes and cite all the authorities which he has most industriously collected; but it is possible that some may have been left out since the chapters were first prepared for the literary columns of the *Bombay Chronicle* which had naturally to be kept free from learned overloading.

Next after Winternitz the reader will have to feel grateful to M. Sylvain Levi, of the College de France, of some of whose charming studies I have attempted to produce a faint reflex. The "Constitution of the Buddhist canon," was turned by me into English for the *Rangoon Gazette* as soon as I received a copy of it from the distinguished savant. It created a mild sensation in the Asiatic seat of Pali learning where my efforts at the appreciation of Buddhism as incorporated in Sanskrit literature were combated with a fury familiar to those who have a practical acquaintance with *odium theologicum*. The romance of *Sutralankara* is a brilliant essay of Sylvain Levi's for the accidental defects in which the responsibility must be borne by myself. The Appendix (III) on the Pali canon gives a foretaste of the splendid pages of Winternitz which I hope it will not take me long to bring out in English. As a supplement to the history

I have added as Appendix IV the weighty contribution to the Buddhist drama by Winternitz (VOJ. 1913, p. 38). While these chapters will more or less appeal to the specialist, Appendix V on the "Treasures of ancient literatures" by Luders will interest any one susceptible to the importance of the revival and resuscitation of a dead past and, in some cases, of a past neither the existence nor the death of which was suspected. It was prepared in the first instance for one of Mrs. Besant's literary periodicals. The number of works which have been brought again to unanticipated light from Central Asia includes not only Sanskrit and Buddhist texts, but Iranian and especially Pahlavi documents of prime value. The Appendix (VII) on the sources of the *Divyavadana* is inserted as a proof of the great importance of Chinese for Sanskrit Buddhism. The contribution by Ed. Huber (Appendix VIII) is believed to be his last. The death at the early age of thirty-five of this French genius is a loss not only to Buddhist scholarship in its difficult ramifications of Chinese Tibetan, Sanskrit and Pali but to that exceedingly rare branch of learning which links Mahayana Buddhism to Persia through the intermediary of Tibet. (Mełanges, Sylvain Levi, p. 305). As the literary activities of the Buddhists have perhaps not been fully represented in the work of Winternitz in respect of grammar, lexicography,—Amara was most probably a Buddhist,—astronomy and medicine, I have inserted the condensed remarks of J. Jolly on medical science of the Buddhists from the *Grundriss*. Much concise information in English on Vasubandhu has been supplied by Sylvain Levi and the Japanese scholars in the various articles in the *Encyclopaedia of Religion and Ethics*; but I hope the few pages from Burnouf will not be held antiquated (Appendix X). The *Abhidharma Kosha Vyakhya* may yet possibly attract the leisure and the attention of an Indian lover of learning in a position to have it edited. References to Buddhism in

Brahmanical and Jaina writings (Appendix XI) and Appendix XII represent a portion of the notes made by me for a Sanskrit Buddhist literary record which must be effaced in the presence of Winternitz's work. My thanks are due to all the editors of the periodicals in whose journals the chapters in this collection appeared in the first instance.

Some inconsistencies in the matter of spelling have to be explained. They relate generally to the *ch*-sound and the *sh*-sound. The consensus of Orientalists is inclined to assign to the English *c* the phonetic value of *ch* in church. However, old associates like Panchatantra will no doubt long appear in their time-honoured shape. There is much to be said in favour of the exclusive phonetic value of *c* especially as it never now represents the *k*-sound. Various devices have been adopted to do away with the *h* and at the same time to represent *sh*. Here the general agreement of scholars is less pronounced. I do not think many, if any, scholars will agree with me in my insistence on avoiding Sarvastavad*in* and Chandragom*in* which are to me alien importations such as at least Indian Sanskritists should unhesitatingly reject. If we speak of our friend Trivedi there is no reason why we should adopt the European exotic Yajurved*in*. I adhere to Mula Sarvastivadi.

I have to thank the Commercial Press, Bombay, for promptness and care and to deprecate in advance a certain amount of overlapping of material due to my having had to deal with several authors working on the identical themes. My own notes are indicated by N. at the end of each.

THE AUTHOR.

*Bombay, November 1919.*

# LITERARY HISTORY OF BUDDHISM.

**Introductory**

Buddhism rose in India and it is all but dead in India; but the zeal of the early Buddhist missionaries spread the faith far beyond the boundaries of its native land. There is no lack of authentic histories of Buddhism but up to now no systematic history of the Buddhist literature in Sanskrit has appeared. Buddhism has had an immense literature. The literary productions of the Buddhists fall into two divisions. The sacred language, however, of Buddhism has not been one. The religion had early branched into several sects and each of them had a sacred tongue of its own. It is yet a moot question what the original language of Buddhism was and whether we have descended to us any fragments of the tongue employed by the Buddha himself. Whatever that original language was it is now certain that Pali has no claim to that distinction. Strictly speaking there are only two sacred languages of the Buddhists, Pali and Sanskrit. Pali is the hieratic language of the Buddhists of Ceylon, Siam and Burma who observe a prosaic and more ancient form of Buddhism. The sacred language of Tibet, China and Japan is Sanskrit and although very few books on Buddhism written in Sanskrit have ever been discovered there, it is unquestionable that at one time there was an immense Buddhist literature, a vast amount of which was translated into Tibetan and Chinese and latterly scholars have succeeded in recovering a portion of the Sanskrit canon which was believed to have perished beyond recall. The history of Buddhism will have a sufficient amount of light thrown on it when we have accessible to us in a European language the essence of the Chinese and Tibetan Buddhist works. But Pali Buddhism has the merit of being compact and has been studied more or less vigorously in Europe. The Sanskrit Buddhism has had the disadvantage of being looked upon with suspicion. It was believed to be a later production. Very few scholars are now sceptical regarding some of the texts which this Sanskrit Buddhist literature embodies and which date from an antiquity as respectable as any of the Pali texts.

**Plan of the work**

The following chapters were intended to be published in English with the collaboration of the distinguished scholar who first conceived and executed the plan of a history of Buddhist literature in Sanskrit. The War interrupted the design. At the suggestion of Indian scholars interested at once in Buddhism and in Sanskrit I have undertaken to publish these chapters which, unlike my studies on *Parsis and Early Isl.m*, lay claim to no originality. The merit of these pages devoted to an elucidation of the historical data comprising the Buddhist literature, that has survived in Sanskrit, consists in a lucid marshalling of every available source which makes the study as valuable as it is original. It is at once a pioneer and a perfected enterprise. In the original scheme due regard is had to the Pali branch of Buddhism as well as Sanskrit. I propose, however, in view of the deserved sanctity attached to Sanskrit first to lay before brother Pandits the section on Sanskrit. The original work is supported throughout by authorities and references. The extent of these notes covers almost as much space as the text itself.

G. K. N.

## CHAPTER I.

**Two Schools of Buddhism.**

However extraordinarily rich and extensive the Pali literature of India, Ceylon and Burma may be, still it represents only the literature of one sect of the Buddhists. Alongside of it in India itself and apart from the other countries where Buddhism is the dominant religion, several sects have developed their own literary productions, the language of which is partly Sanskrit and partly a dialect which we may call the mid-Indian and which is given the designation of "mixed Sanskrit" by Senart. Of this Sanskrit literature there have remained to us many voluminous books and fragments of several others while many are known to us only through Tibetan and Chinese translations. The major portion of this literature, in pure and mixed Sanskrit, which we for brevity's sake call Buddhist Sanskrit literature, belongs either to the school known as that of the Mahayana or has been more or less influenced by the latter. For an appreciation, therefore, of this literature it is necessary in the first place to make a few observations on the schism in Buddhism which divided it early into two schools, the Mahayana and the Hinayana.

The most ancient Buddhist school, the doctrine of which coincides with that of the Theravada, as perpetuated in Pali tradition, sees in salvation or Nirvana the supreme bliss and in the conception of *Arhatship*, which is already in this life a foretaste of the coming Nirvana, the end and goal of all strivings,—a goal which is attainable only by a few with the help of a knowledge which is to be acquired only in ascetic life. This original objective of early Buddhism has not been rejected by the adherents of the later or Mahayana school. On the other hand it has been recognised as originating with the Buddha himself. It is characterised as the Hinayana or the "inferior vehicle" which does not suffice to conduct all beings to cessation of sorrow. What the later doctrine teaches is the Mahayana or the "great vehicle," which is calculated to transport a larger number of people, the whole community of humanity, over and beyond the sorrow of existence. This new doctrine. as is claimed by its followers, rests upon a profounder understanding of the ancient texts or upon later mystical revelation of the Buddha himself and it replaces the ideal of the Arhat by that of the Bodhisattva. Not only the monk but every ordinary human being can place before himself the goal to be re-born as a Bodhisattva, which means an enlightened being or one who may receive supreme illumination and bring salvation to all mankind. If this goal is to be made attainable by many there must be more efficient means for making it accessible to all than are to be found in the Hinayana doctrine. Therefore, according to the doctrine of the Mahayana, even the father of a family occupied with worldly life, the merchant, the craftsman, the sovereign,—nay, even the labourer and the pariah—can attain to salvation on the one hand, by the practice of commiseration and goodwill for all creatures, by extraordinary generosity and self-abnegation, and on the other, by means of a believing surrender to and veneration of the Buddha, other Buddhas and the Bodhisattvas. In the Pali canon the Buddha is already sometimes shown as a superman but he becomes such only because of his attainment to supreme illumination which enables him to perform miracles and finally to enter Nirvana. What has remained for us as an object of veneration after his passing away is only his doctrine or at any rate his relics. The school of the Lokottaravadis, which are a special sect of that Hinayana, go further and decline to see in the Buddha an ordinary man. For the Buddha is a superhuman being (Lokottara) who comes down for a limited period of time for the succour of all mankind.

Essence of Mahayana.

In the Mahayana, on the other hand, the Buddhas from the first are nothing but divine beings and their peregrinations on the earth and their entry into Nirvana no more than a freak or thoughtless play. And if in the Hinayana there is the mention of a number of Buddhas, predecessors of Shakyamuni in earlier æons, the Mahayana counts its Budddhas by the thousand, nay, by the million. Moreover, innumerable millions of Bodhisattvas are worshipped as divine beings by the Mahayana Buddhists. These Bodhisattvas who are provided with perfections (Paramitas) and with illumination, out of compassion for the world renounce their claim to Nirvana. Furthermore, there are the Hindu gods and goddesses especially from the Shiva cycle who are placed on a par with the Buddhas and Bodhisattvas who contribute to the amplification of the Buddhist pantheon. This newly formed mythology, this new Bodhisattva ideal and the much more vigorously prominent worship of the Buddha or Buddha-bhakti together form the popular phase of Mahayana. So far this process was already extant in the Hinayana, it developed itself under the influence of Hinduism; and similarly the philosophical side of Mahayana is only a further evolution of the doctrine of Hinayana under the influence of Hinduism.

The ancient Buddhism denied the Ego and saw in the knowledge of the non-Ego a path to Nirvana, to extinction of the Ego. The Mahayana schools went still further and taught that not only there was no Ego, but that there was nothing at all,– only a blank, *sarvam shunyam*. They professed a complete negativism or *shunyavada* which denied both Being and non-Being at the same time or believed in idealistic negativism or *Vijnanavada* which at least recognises a Being comprised in consciousness. As Max Wallaser has put it, negativism is a better characterisation of the Mahayana philosophy than nihilism.

The Sanskrit literature in Buddhism, however, is by no means exlusively Mahayanist. Before all the widely spread sect of the Sarvastivadis, which belonged to the Hinayana and which is indicated by its designation of positivists, possessed a canon of its own and a rich literature in Sanskrit. Literally the doctrine of Sarvastivada means the doctrine of All-Exists.

## CHAPTER II.

**Sanskrit Buddhist canon.**

Of this Sanskrit canon no complete copy is to be found. We know it only from larger or smaller fragments of its Udana-varga, Dharmapada, Ekottaragama and Madhyamagama which have been discovered from the zylographs and manuscripts recovered from Eastern Turkistan by Stein, Grunwedel and Le Coq, as well as from quotations in other Buddhist Sanskrit texts like the Mahavastu, Divyavadana and Lalitavistara and finally from Chinese and Tibetan translations.

The literature of Central Asian discoveries has already assumed great proportions. The more important references are: Pischel, Fragments of a Sanskrit Canon of the Buddhist from Idykutsari in Chinese Turkistan, SBA 1904, p. 807. New Fragments, *ibid* p. 1138; The Turfan Recensions of the Dhammapada, SBA 1908, p. 968. What, however, Pischel regarded as the recensions of the Dhammapada are in reality fragments of the Udanavarga of Dharmatrata, the Tibetan translation of which has been rendered into English by Rokhill in 1883, and the Sanskrit original of which Luders is going to edit from the Turfan finds. Vallee Poussin has discovered fragments of the same work in the collection brought from Central Asia by Stein and there is found *Udana* corresponding to the Pali Udana (JA, 1912, p. 10, vol. xix, p. 311). Levi, JA, 1910, p. 10 vol. xvi, p. 444. On the other hand the ancient Kharosthi manuscript discovered in Khotan by Dutreuil de Rhins, important equally from the standpoint of palæography and literary history, represents an anthology prepared after the model of the Dhammapada in Prakrit (Comptes rendus de l'Academie des inscriptions, May 1895 and April 1898; Stein, Ancient Khotan, 1188; Senart

OC XI, Paris, 1897, i, i, seq. JA 1898, p. 9, vol. XII, 193, 545; Luders NGGW 1899, p. 474; Rhys Davids JRAS. 1899, p. 426, and Franke ZDMG 60, 1906, p. 477).

Buddhist Sutras in Sanskrit inscribed on bricks have been found by V. A. Smith and W. Hoey in the ruins of Gopalpur along with inscriptions ranging between 250 and 400 A.D. (JASB proceedings, 1896, p. 99). For translations into Chinese and Tibetan see Oldenberg ZDGM 52, pp. 654, 662; Anesaki *Le Museon*, new series xx, vi 1905, pp. 23-37. On a Chinese translation of a "Nirvanasutra," see JARS 1881, p. 66.

To the Vinayapitaka of the same canon belongs probably also the fragment of a ritual for the initiation of monks written in Sanskrit which was found in Nepal by Bendall as well as the *Pratimokṣhasutra* which is inferred from one Tibetan and four Chinese translations, Album Kern, p. 373, and OC xiii, Humburg, 1902, p. 58. S. Levi discovered the fragment of a Vinayapitaka of the Sarvastivadis in the Tokharian (JA 1912, p. 10, vol. xix, p. 101. Oldenberg ZDMG 52, p. 645.)

The principal texts of the canon of the Mulasarvastivadis—this is the designation of the Sanskrit canon according to tradition—were translated from Sanskrit into Chinese in 700-712 by the Chinese pilgrim I-tsing.

(J. Takakusu, a record of Buddhist religion by I-tsing, translated, Oxford 1896, p. XXXVII. See Anesaki JRAS 1901, p. 895; Ed. Huber in DEFEO VI 1906, p. 1, Sylvain Levi in the Toung Pao, V. 1904, p. 297; VIII, 110).

A sub-division of the Mulasarvastivadis are the Sarvastivadis who had a Vinaya of their own just as the other three sub-divisions of the same school, *viz.*, the Dharmaguptas, Mahishasakas and Kashyapiyas (Levi ibid p.114 1907). But the Chinese "Tri-pitaka" does not mean the same thing as the Pali Tipitaka but contains also many non-canonical texts and even philosophical treatises of Brahmanism (Takakusu, JRAS 1896, p. 415.)

Likewise in the Tibetan Kanjur which is also denominated "Tripitaka," there is much which has no comparison with the Tipitaka of Pali and which doubtless does not belong to the ancient canon. As in these so also in the Chinese and Tibetan, there are the sub-divisions into Vinaya, Sutra and Abhidharma.

This Sanskrit canon in its Chinese rendering betrayes in the texts and in the arrangements of its component books many coincidences with the Pali canon and on the other hand many deviations from it. This is to be explained by assuming that the Pali canon was first translated in some part of India first from a common source, probably the lost Magadhi canon and later on in another province the Sanskrit canon branched itself off.

According to Sylvain Levi (Taung Pao 1907, p. 116) the Vinaya of the Sanskrit canon was first codified in the 3rd or 4th century after Christ. In the Sanskrit canon the Agamas correspond to the Nikayas in Pali, the Dirghagama answering to the Dighanikaya, the Madhyamagama to the Majjhinanikaya, the Ekottaragama to the Anguttaranikaya and the Samyuktagama to the Samyuttanikaya. There was also a "Kshudraka" corresponding to the Khuddakanikaya. Whether in this latter all those texts were included which in the Pali canon are embodied in this Nikaya we do not know but we know that in the Sanskrit canon also there were corresponding to the Pali texts of Suttanipata a Sutranipata, Udana corresponding to Udana, to Dhammapada a Dharmapada,, to Theragatha a Sthaviragatha, to Vimanavatthu a Vimanavastu and to Buddha Vansa a Buddha Vansha. It is doubtful whether the collection of the "seven Abhidharmas" which stands translated in the Chinese Tripitaka was also derived from the ancient canon in as much as these Abhidharmas have nothing in common with the Abhidhammapitaka of the Pali canon except the numeral seven and a few titles.

J. Takakusu, J.R.A.S. 1905, p. 138 and J.P.T.S. 1905, p. 67.

Thus if the canon of the Mulasarvastivadis has been preserved only incompletely, the other Sanskrit Buddhist sects likewise give no closed canon, each having only one or more texts to which was accorded special sanctity as a kind of Bible and which assimilated the older texts of a Tripitaka recognised as such in principle and rejecting others.

## CHAPTER III.

**Mahavastu.**

As belonging to the old school of Hinayana we have in the first place to mention the Mahavastu " the Book of the Great Events."

*Le Mahavastu*, Sanskrit text, was published for the first time with introduction by E. Sanart with a detailed conspectus of contents in the Introduction, Paris 1882-1897. A Barth in RHR., 11, 1885, p. 160 ; 42, 1900, p. 51 and *Journal des Savants* 1899, p. 459, p. 517, p. 623. E. Windisch, the *Composition of the Mahavastu*, Leipzig 1909. A conspectus of the contents is also given by Rajendralal Mitra in his *Nepalese Buddhist Literature*, pp. 115-161.

The book gives itself the title of: " The Vinayapitaka according to the text of the Lokottaravadis belonging to the Mahasanghikas." These Mahasanghikas, that is, the adherents of the Mahasangha or the Great Order are according to concurrent reports the most ancient Buddhist schismatics.

This is the only thing positive which we can ascertain regarding the rise of Buddhist sects from the contradictory and confused accounts. (Compare Kern *Manual of Buddhism*, p. 105).

A sub-division of theirs was the Lokottaravadis, that is, those according to whose doctrine the Buddhas are Supra-Mundane or Lokottara and are only externally connected with worldly existence.

" Nothing in the perfectly Awakened Ones is comparable to anything in the world but everything connected with the great Rishis is exalted above the world." (Mahavastu V. 1, 1. p. 159,2). They wash their feet although no dust attaches to them, they sit under the shade although the heat of the sun does not oppress them, they take nourishment although they are never troubled with hunger, they use medicine although they have no diseases. (Windisch loc. cit. p. 470.) According to the Mahavastu, the Lokottaravadis belong to the Madhyadesha or the 16 countries lying between the Himalaya and the Vindhya mountains, (Mahastu V. 1, p. 198.)

Entirely in keeping with this doctrine, the biography of the Buddha which forms the principal contents of the Mahavastu is related as an "Avadana" or a miraculous history. It is clearly not thereby differentiated much from the texts of the Pali canon which are devoted to the life of the Buddha. Here in this Sanskrit text just as in the Pali counterpart we hear of miracles which accompanied the conception, the birth, the illumination, and the first conversions brought about by the Buddha. The Mahavastu harmonizes with the Pali Nidanakatha in this that it treats of the life of the Buddha in three sections, of which the first starts with the life of the Bodhisattva in the time of the Buddha Dipankara (V. 1, 193) and describes his life in the time of other and earlier Buddhas. The second section (in V. 2, 1) takes us to the heaven of the Tushita gods, where the Bodhisattva who is re-born there is determined to seek another birth in the womb of Queen Maya and relates the miracle of the conception and the birth of the prince, of his leaving the home, his conflict with Mara, and the illumination which he succeeds in acquiring under the Bodhi Tree. The third section (V. 3), lastly recounts, in harmony with the principal features of the Mahavagga of the Vinay apitaka, the history of the first conversions and the rise of the monastic order. And this is also one reason why the Mahavastu is described as belonging to the Vinayapitaka, although barring a few remarks on the initiation of the Order it contains next to nothing about the Vinaya proper or the rules of the Order.

Note: The Mahavastu does not contain the Pali technical expressions, Durenidana, Avidurenidana and Santikenidana. See Windisch loc. cit. p. 473, 476 ff.

When we, however, say that the Mahavastu recounts the main outline of the life of the Buddha for the Lokottaravadis, that by no means implies that this exhausts the contents of the work; nor does it give an adequate idea of its composition. Far from being a literary work of art, the Mahavastu is rather a labyrinth in which we can only with an effort discover the thread of a coherent account of the life of the Buddha. This account is constantly interrupted by other material, specially by the numerous Jatakas and Advanas and also by dogmatic Sutras. We find no order. Sometimes an attempt is made to put together in a loose fashion the various component parts of the work. Moreover, the same story is frequently repeated whether it be an episode in the life of the Buddha or a Jataka, being related twice one after another, first in prose and then in verse, although in a more or less diverging version. But in several passages the same episodes recur with a trifling difference. Thus the legend of the Buddha's birth is recounted no less than four times (Windisch, *Buddha's Birth*, p. 106, 124 ff.). Again the language is also not uniform. No doubt the whole work, both the prose and verse, is written in what we call "mixed Sanskrit," but this dialect makes a varying approach to Sanskrit. The more disparate it is from Sanskrit, the more ancient it appears. (Oldenberg ZDMG 52, 663).

**Importance of Mahavastu.**

Despite this and notwithstanding the circumstance that out of this book we learn hardly anything new on the life of the Buddha or of the Lokottaravadis, it is of the greatest importance because it preserves for us many ancient traditions and old versions of texts which also occur in the Pali canon. Thus the setting out of his home by the Prince Siddhartha, the celebrated *abhinishkramana* of Sanskrit books, is related, as in the Pali Majjhimanikaya (26 and 36) in the most archaic fashion (V. 2, 117). As an instance of the various strata of the book we may mention another version of the same episode in the life of the Buddha and belonging to a later period which follows immediately after the first and more ancient recital in the Mahavastu. Similarly we find early versions of the celebrated "Benares sermon" and presentments of the following well-known texts in the Pali canon:—The Mahagovinda Sutta (Dighanikaya 19) the Dighanakhasutta (Majjhimanikaya, 74) the Sahassavagga of the Dhammapada, the Khuddakapatha, the Pabbajja, the Padhana and the Khaggavisana Suttas belonging to the Suttanipata, and pieces from the Vimana Vatthu and the Buddha Vansha (Oldenberg ZDMG 52, 659 f. 665 f. Windisch *Mara and Buddha*, 316 f, 322 f). There are poems, moreover, on the birth of the Buddha and vestiges of ancient Buddhistic ballads which we so often come across.

**Its Jatakas.**

Quite of special value is, however, the Mahavastu as a mine of Jatakas and other stories. These have been separately treated by Serge d'Oldenberg (JRAS 1896, p. 335 f.) and by Barth (*Journal des Savants* 1889, p. 625 f.) Charpentier has discussed a few of the Jatakas in the Mahavastu in his history of the Pacceka Buddhas (p. 2 f. 12 f, 25 f.). A good half of the book consists of Jatakas which are related partly in prose with verses inserted, or first in prose and then again in verse. Further we see the Bodhisattva now as a universal sovereign, now as the son of a merchant, then as a Brahman, again as a Naga prince as a lion, as an elephant, etc. Many of the Jatakas are versions of the same story which we find in the Pali book of Jatakas. They harmonize word for word with the Pali and many a time show more or less divergence. Thus, for instance, the Shyamakajataka (V. 2, p. 209 f.), the pathetic story of the Brahman's son who is shot dead with his arrow by King Peliyaksha is only a version of the Shyamakajataka so well known to us. The Kinnarijataka (V. 2, p. 94 f.) corresponds in character, though not in contents to the Kinnara legend in the Jataka book. Kushajataka appears once (V. 2, p. 420 f.) in a recension which is tolerably divergent from Pali, a second time (V. 1, p. 3 f) in metrical form which betrays resemblances with the Pali *gathas*. The story of Amara, the smith's daughter, (V. 2, p. 836) answers to the Pali Jataka No. 387. The Markatajataka (V. 2, p. 246 f.) is the fable of the monkey and the crocodile and is known to us as No. 208 of the Pali Jataka book. The history of Nalini, who is seduced by Eka Shringa, grows into a highly developed legend in Mahavastu (V. 3, p. 143 f.). But it retains some of the more ancient features which have disappeared in the prose Pali Jataka of Isisinga (Luders, NGGW 1901, p. 20 f.).

**Mahavastu and Puranas.**

There are, however, many Jatakas and Avadanas in the Mahavastu which have nothing corresponding to them in Pali. In these are especially glorified again and again the extraordinary propensity to self-sacrifice and generosity on part of the Bodhisattva. Thus as King Arka, for example, the Bodhisattva bestows upon the Buddha of the age 80,000 grottoes or cave temples fashioned out of the seven kinds of precious stones (1, 54). On another occasion he surrenders his wife and child only to learn a wise maxim (1, 91 f.). As a beggar he is more pious than King Kriki, for he kills no living being and places his pots on crossways in order that they may be filled with rice and grain for the hungry; and when he hears that his parents in his absence have given away to the Buddha the straw with which he had shortly before embellished his hut he rejoices over it for a month (1, 317 f.).

Many of the narratives bear the impress of a Brahmanic or Puranic character. Such is for instance the history of Brahmadatta, who is childless and betakes himself to the Rishis upon which three birds are borne to him which speak with a human voice and utter many sapient proverbs. This story reminds us of the beginning of the Markandeya Purana. And incidentally it may be observed that the portrayal of hell in the beginning of the Mahavastu has points of contact with the same Purana. It is, however, in the Pali tradition that we find the foundation of the visit of Maudgalyayana to the 8th Inferno as well as his sojourn in the world of beasts and the world of Pretas, the Asuras, and various kind of deities. For in the Pali tradition also Moggalana is a saint who roams through heaven and hell and all the worlds. However the Rajavamsha or the History of the Kings to whose dynasty Shakyamuni belonged begins entirely after the fashion of the Puranas with an account of the creation (1, 338 ff.). The spirit of the Puranas is also breathed by the Jataka (1, 283 ff.), in which a Rishi named Rakshita who is the Bodhisattava, attains to such miraculous powers as an ascetic that he touches the sun and the moon with his hand. The spirit of the Puranas is very similar to that of the Mahayana and many of the stories in the Mahavastu betray the same partiality for the phantasmagorial—astounding sorcerers to perform the miracles of saints, so peculiar to the Mahayana texts. To this class belongs "the Story of the Umbrella" (Chattravastu I, 253 ff.) After the Buddha had freed the city of Shravarti of a terrible plague caused by Yakshas, gods or spirits hold up umbrellas over the Buddha to do him honour. The latter however with his usual compassionateness makes one Buddha to appear under each umbrella by virtue of his supernatural powers so that each god believes that the Buddha is seated under his own umbrella.

**More Mahayana affinities.**

And, although the Mahavastu belongs to the Hinayanâ and has contacts with much which may or actually does occur in the Pali texts of the Theravadis, it embodies a good deal which makes an approach to the Mahayana. Thus, for instance, we find in the first volume (1, 63-193) a large section on the ten *bhumis* or places which a Bodhisattva has to go through and the description of the virtues which he must possess in each of the ten stages. In this section has been interpolated a Buddhanusmriti (1, 163 ff.) that is, a hymn to the Buddha who in no way is here different from Vishnu or Shiva in the *stotras* of the Puranas. It is also in keeping with the idea of the Mahayana when it is said that the power of the Buddhas is so great that the adoration of the Exalted One alone suffices for the attainment of Nirvana (II, 362 ff.) and that one earns for oneself infinite merit when one only circumambulates a *stupa* and offers worship with flowers and so forth. That from the smile of the Buddha proceed rays which illuminate the whole Buddha field (Buddha Khetra) occurs innumerable time in the Mahayana texts (III, 137 ff). It is also a Mahayanist conception when mention is made of a great number of Buddhas and when it is stated that the Bodhisattva is not generated by father and mother, but springs directly from his own properties (*Windisch, the Buddha's Birth*, p. 97, Note, p. 100 f. and p. 193 f.)

**Antiquity of Mahavastu.**

The nature of the composition of the Mahavastu entails the difficulty that the period when it was composed is very hard to determine. Many circumstances point to a high antiquity, for instance, the fact that it belongs to the Lokottaravada school and its language. That the work is entirely written in "mixed Sanskrit" while in the Mahayana texts this dialect alternates with Sanskrit, is a mark of its greater antiquity. For, as Barth says, Sanskrit is in Buddhist texts only an interloper (*Journal des Savants*, 1899, p. 459). Certainly old are those numerous pieces which the Mahavastu has in common with the Pali canon and which go back to ancient Pali sources. The *gathas* of the Khadgavishna Sutra (I 357,) may be even older than the corresponding Khaggavisana Sutta in the Pali *Suttanipata*. When, however, in the Mahavastu these verses are sung by five hundred dying Pratyeka Buddhas then' in their mouth they refrain. "He wanders lonely like a unicorn" sounds peculiarly incongruous and it becomes improbable that the prose portion should be as old as the *gathas*. To the time of the first century after Christ likewise point the Mahayanist features already indicated as well as a few passages which seem to have been influenced by the sculptors of the Gandhara art. When, for example, in the scene of the flower miracle, the lotus flowers in the form of a circle fall round the halo of the Buddha, it may be noted that the halo was first introduced into India by Greek artists (see A. Foucher JA 1933, p. 10, part II, p. 208, and his *L'art greco-bouddique du Gandara*, vol. I, p. 622; besides, the many Buddhas under the umbrellas remind us of the sculptured monuments) The reference in the Mahavastu to the Yogacharas brings us down to the fourth century (I, 120); and so do the allusions to the Huns and the most interesting ones to the Chinese language and writing and the characterisation of astrologers as "Horapathaka" (III, 178). But the core of the Mahavastu is old and probably was composed already two centuries before Christ; although it has been expanded in the fourth century after Christ and perhaps even at a later period. For it is only the embellishment that has been borrowed from the Mahayana, while on the other hand, it is merely a feeble admixture of the Mahayana doctrine proper and not of the Mahayana mythology which we find in the Mahayavastu.

## CHAPTER IV.

**Lalitavistara.**

The Mahavastu describes itself as a work belonging to Hinayana, although it has assimilated some of the Mahayana features. The Lalitavistara on the contrary is regarded as one of the most sacred Mahayana texts, as a Vaipulya Sutra. It is a text-book of voluminous contents and given the usual designation of a Mahayana Sutra and yet originally the work embodied a descriptive life of the Buddha for the Sarvastivadi school attached to the Hinayana.

The Lalitavistara is edited by S. Lefmann who also brought out a translation of the first chapters In Berlin in 1875. The great Bengali scholar Rajendralal Mitra prepared an English translation for the Bibliotheca Indica of which 3 fasciculi have appeared. (Calcutta, 1881 to 1886.) He has also brought out an incomplete text. A complete French translation by Foucaux appeared in Paris in the Annals du Musee Guimet, vol. vi, xix, (Paris, 1887-1892.) The Chinese tradition as to the Lalitavistara makes it a life of the Buddha representing the Savastivadi school (Beal, the Romantic Legend of Sakya Buddha from the Chinese Sanskrit, London, 1875, Introduction. Also Foucaux's French translation of Lalitavistara introduction, vol. II., Beal's Romantic Legend is an abbridged translation from the Chinese version of the Abhinish-Kramana Sutra which has not been preserved in the original Sanskrit, but was translated into Chinese so early as 587 A.D. It appears to have been a biography of the Buddha representing the sect of the Dharmaguptas.

The Mahayana idea however corresponds already to the very title of the Lalitavistara which means the "exhaustive narrative of the sport of the Buddha." Thus the life work of the Buddha on the earth is characterised as the diversion (Lalita) of a supernatural being.

In the introductory chapter the Buddha appears as an exalted divine being, although the chapter starts after the mode of the ancient Pali Suttas with the words: "So have I heard. Once upon a time the master was sojourning at Sharvasti in the Jeta Park in the garden of Anathapindada."

But while in the Pali texts the Master is introduced with these or similar stereotyped initial phrases and is surrounded by a few disciples or at the most his suite of "500 monks," and then immediately the Sutta proper begins, in the Lalitavistara, as in all the Vaipulya Sutras of the Mahayana, the picture that is outlined of the Buddha is a grandiose one encircled by divine radiance. He is surrounded by twelve thousand monks and by no less than thirty-two thousand Bodhisattvas, "all still in the trammels of only one re-birth, all born with the perfections of a Bodhisattva, all enjoying the knowledge of a Bodhisattva, all in the possession of an insight in magical charms" and so forth. While in the middle watch of the night the Buddha sits sunk in meditation, from his head issues forth a stream of light which penetrates into the heavens and sets all the gods in commotion. These latter forthwith chant a hymn of praise to the exalted Buddha and soon after appear Ishvara and the other divinities before the Master, throw themselves at his feet and implore him to reveal the excellent Vaipulya Sutra called the Lalitavistara for the salvation and blessing of the world. While they panegyrize in extravagant terms the excellences of the text revealed by this and even earlier Buddhas, the Buddha expresses his assent by silence. Only after these circumstantial introductions, which fill a large chapter commences the biography proper of the Buddha which forms the contents of the work. And it starts indeed just from where in the Pali Nidanakatha, the second section, (avidure-nidana) begins.

**Extravagant imagery.**

The Bodhisattva abides in the heaven of the Gratified (Tushita) gods in a glorious celestial palace. The Bodhisattva is the recipient of over a hundred honourific epithets and the celestial palace in which he resides of over a dozen.

**Conception and Birth of Buddha.**

Under the sound of eighty-four thousand drums he is called upon to descend to the earth to commence his work of salvation. After long consultations in which the excellences and the deficiencies of a large number of princely families are weighed the Bodhisattva finally decides to be re-born in the house of King Shuddhodana in the womb of Queen Maya. She alone possesses all the qualities of a Buddha's mother. Perfect like her beauty, which is described to minutest detail, are her virtue and chastity. Besides, of all the women of India she is the only one in a position to bear the future Buddha since in her is united the strength of ten thousand elephants. The conception proceeds with the assistance of the gods after the Bodhisattva had determined to enter the womb of his mother in the form of an elephant. The gods prepare not only a celestial residence for Maya during her lying in, but construct a palace of jewels in her womb so that the Bodhisattva may not remain soiled there for ten months. In this palace of jewels he sits in his marvellous tenderness. But his body shines in glorious sheen and a light expands itself for miles from the womb of his mother. The sick come to Maya Devi and are cured of their diseases as soon as the latter places her hand upon their head. "And whenever she looks towards her right she sees the Bodhisattva in her womb just as a man beholds his own face in a clear mirror." The yet unborn Bodhisattva in his mother's womb delights the celestials by pious sermons and the god Brahma obeys his every suggestion.

This part is comprised in chapters 2 to 6. The beginning of the sixth chapter has been translated by Windisch in his *Buddha's Geburt*, p. 162 ff.

As the conception so also the Bodhisattva's birth. It is accompanied by miracles and portents. In the Lumbini Park he is born in the manner well known to us through numerous sculptures though not like an ordinary human but as an omniscient Exalted Being, as a Mahapurusha, "The Great Spirit." Lotus flowers are strewn under every step of his and the new born child announcing his greatness takes seven steps towards each of the six cardinal points.

The creator Prajapati is characterized as Purusha and Mahapurusha in the Brahmanas and Upanishads and subsequently also Brahma and Vishnu. The seven steps of the new born child Buddha are also to be explained from the myth of the march of Vishnu.

**Sin of unbelief.**

Here the narrative is interrupted by a dialogue between Ananda and the Buddha in which vehemence is shown towards every unbeliever who does not credit the miraculous birth of the Buddha (chapter vii, p. 87 to 91). Faith in the Buddha is taught as an essential component of religion. And we are reminded of Krishna in the *Bhagavadgita* when the Buddha says:

> "To all who believe in me I do good. Like friends are they to me who seek refuge in me. And many a friend the Tathagata has. And to those friends the Tathagata only speaks the truth, not falsehood. . . . . To believe Ananda should be thy endeavour. This I commend unto you."

Why this dialogue should appear just here is certainly not due to accident, but is based on the fact that it is with reference to the legends relating to the conception and the birth of the Buddha that the Lalitavistara diverges very strikingly from other Buddhist schools in its extravagance as to the miraculous. It is no longer so in the further course of the narrative. Indeed there is here very often an extraordinary harmony with the most ancient Pali account, *e. g.*, that of the Mahavagga of the Vinayapitaka, although, it may be noted incidentally, that the Gathas of the Lalitavistara appear more ancient than those in the corresponding Pali texts. (The relation of the Pali tradition to the Lalitavistara is treated of by Oldenberg in OC, V 1882, vol. 2, p. 1017 to 122, and Windisch in *Mara and Buddha* and *Buddha's Birth* as well as by Kern in SBE, vol. 21, p. xi ff, and last but not least by Burnouf *Lotus de la Bonne Loi*, p. 864 f.)

**Pali and Sanskrit go back to an older source.**

The two texts in such cases are not dependent upon each other; but both go back to a common older tradition. But even here the Lalitavistara has much that is wanting in the older accounts. Two episodes in particular are noteworthy. One of these recounts (chapter 8) how the Bodhisattva as a boy is brought by his foster mother to the temple and how all the images of the gods rise up on their pedestals to prostrate themselves at his feet. The other episode (chapter 10) relates the first experience of the Bodhisattva at school.

**The Buddha at school.**

With a suite of ten thousand boys with immense pomp in which the gods participate—eight thousand heavenly damsels for instance scatter flowers before him—the small Bodhisattva celebrates his admission into the writing school. The poor schoolmaster cannot bear the glory of the divine incarnation and falls to the ground. A god raises him up and tranquillizes him with the explanation that the Bodhisattvas are omniscient and need no learning, but that they come to school only following the course of the word. Then the Bodhisattva amazes the schoolmaster with the question as to which of the 64 scripts he was going to instruct him in. And he enumerates all the sixty-four in which are included the Chinese symbols and the script of the Huns,—alphabets of which the teacher did not know even the names. Finally with the ten thousand boys he commences his study of the alphabet. With every letter of the alphabet the Bodhisattva pronounces a wise maxim.

According to E. Kuhn, *Gurupuja Kaumudi* (p. 116 f.) these two legends of the child Buddha may have served as models for the Gospel Apocrypha which relate similar stories of the child Jesus. The chapters 12 and 13 also contain episodes which are wanting in the other biographies of the Buddha. (Winternitz WZKM 1912, p. 237 f.).

**Acts of the Budha.**

On the other hand in its further course the Lalitavistara narrative (chapters 14-26) deviates only a little from the legend known to us from other sources; the principal events in the life of the Buddha being the four meetings from which the Bodhisattva learns of old age, disease, death and renunciation; the flight from the palace; the encounter with King Bimbisara; Gautama's years of instruction and his futile ascetic practices; the struggle with Mara; the final illumination and the enunciation of the doctrine to the world at large at the request of god Brahma. But even here the Lalitavistara is remarkable for its exaggerations. While Gautama, for instance, passes the four weeks after his illumination, in our most ancient account, in meditation under various trees (Mahavagga, 1, 1-4, Dutoit *Life of the Buddha*, p. 66), in the Lalitavistara (p. 377), in the second week, he goes out for a long promenade through thousands of worlds and in the fourth week takes a small walk, which stretches only from the eastern to the western ocean. The last chapter (27) however is once again after the fashion of the Mahayana sutras, a glorification of the book of Lalitavistara itself, and is devoted to the enumeration of the virtues and the advantages which a man acquires by its propagation and reverence.

**Component elements of Lalitavistara.**

From all these it is quite probable that our Lalitavistara is a redaction of an older Hinayana text expanded and embellished in the sense of the Mahayana,—a biography of the Buddha representing the Sarvastivada school. This assumption also explains the nature of the text which is by no means the single work of one author, but is an anonymous compilation in which very old and very young fragments stand in juxtaposition. The book moreover consists, according to its form, of unequal sections, a continuous narrative in Sanskrit prose and numerous often extensive metrical pieces in "Mixed Sanskrit." Only rarely these verses constitute a portion of the narrative. As a rule they are recapitulations of prose narration in an abbreviated and simpler and some times also more or less divergent form. Many of these metrical pieces are beautiful old ballads which go back to the same ancient sources as the poems of the Pali Suttanipata mentioned above. The examples are the birth legend and the Asita episode in chapter VII, the Bimbisara history in chapter XVI and the dialogue with Mara in chapter XVIII. They belong to the ancient religious ballad poesy of the first centuries after the Buddha. But several prose passages also, like the sermon at Benares in the XXVIth chapter, are assignable to the most ancient stratum of Buddhistic tradition. On the other hand the younger components are to be found not only in the prose but also in the Gathas, many of which are composed in highly artistic metres. Such are the Vasantatilaka and Shardulavikridata which are tolerably frequent (see the index to metres in Lefmann's edition VII, p. 227 f, and Introduction, p. 19 ff).

**Translation into Chinese and Tibetan.**

We do not know when the final redaction of the Lalitavistara took place. It was formerly erroneously asserted that the work had already been translated into Chinese in the first Christian century. As a matter of fact we do not at all know whether the Chinese biography of the Buddha called the Phu-yau-king which was published in about 300 A. D., the alleged "second translation of the Lalitavistara," is really a translation of our text (Winternitz, WZKM 1912, p. 241 f.). A precise rendering of the Sanskrit text is in the Tibetan, which was only produced in the 5th century. It has been edited and translated into French by Foucaux. It may be taken for certain that a version little different from our Lalitavistara was known to the artists who about 850-200 decorated with images the celebrated temple of Boro-Budur in Java. For these magnificent scriptures represent scenes in the legend of the Buddha in a manner as if the artists were working with the text of the Lalitavistara in the hand. And Pleyte has simply recapitulated the entire contents of the Lalitavistara as an explanation of the sculptures (*The Buddha legend in the sculpture in the temple of Boro-Budur*, Amsterdam, 1901. See also Speyer *La Museon*, 1903, p. 124 ff).

**Relation to Buddhist Art.**

But the artists who embellished the Greco-Buddhistic monuments of Northern India with scenes from the life of the Buddha are also already familiar with the Buddha legend as related in the Lalitavistara. They worked no doubt not after the text, but in accordance with living oral tradition. The harmony, nevertheless, between the sculptures and the Sanskrit text is not rarely of such a character that we must assume that the literary tradition was at times influenced by the artist. Upon art and literature there was mutual influence.

The authorities to be consulted here are *L'art Greco-bouddhique du Gandhara*, part 1,324 f. 666 ff; Grunwendel *Buddhist art in India*, p. 94, 104, f, 134; Senart O C XIV, 1905, 1,121 ff; and Bloch ZDMG 62, p. 370 ff.

**No image in primitive Buddhism.**

While the ancient Buddhistic art in the time of Ashoka, in the reliefs of Bharhut, Sanchi, etc., knows of no image of the Buddha but only a symbol (*e.g.*, the wheel) for the person of the Founder of the religion, a representation of the Buddha is the principle object of the Gandhara art. Can it not be connected with this that in the intervening centuries the Buddha became an object of *Bhakti* and the adoration of the Buddha was pushed into the central point of his religion?

Thus there is concurrent testimony that the age of the Gandhara art, the *floruit* of which falls in the second century after Christ, was also the period of Mahayana texts which treat of the Buddha legend.

"On the grounds of style derived in the first instance from Greco-Roman art the period of the development can only be the period from the birth of Christ to the fourth century." Grunwendel Buddhist Art in India, p. 81. According to Foucher *L'art Greco-bouddhique du Gandhara*, part 1, p. 40 ff. the flourishing period of the Gandhara art coincides with the second half of the second century A.D.

General estimate of Lalitavistara.

It is, therefore, but natural that we should have preserved in the Lalitavistara both the very old tradition, and accounts younger by centuries, of the legend of the Buddha. An important source of old Buddhism it is only there, where it coincides with the Pali texts and other Sanskrit texts like the *Mahavastu*. But it is erroneous to regard the Lalitavistara in its entirety as a good old source for our knowledge of Buddhism as does Senart in his ingenious and unsuccessful *Essai sur la legende du Buddha*, (p. 81 f., 456 f.). Nor does the Lalitavistara give us a clue "to popular Buddhism" of older times as is claimed by Vallee Poussin. It is rather a key to the development of the Buddha legend in its earliest beginnings, in which only the principal events of the life of the great founder of the religion have been adorned with miracles, down to the final apotheosis of the Master in which from start to finish his career appears more like that of a god above all the other gods. But from the standpoint of literary history the Lalitavistara is one of the most important works in Buddhist literature. It is not indeed a Buddha epic proper, but it embodies all the germs of one. It was from the ballads and episodes which have been preserved in the oldest elements of the Lalitavistara, if probably not from the Lalitavistara itself, that the greatest poet of Buddhism, Ashvaghosha, created his magnificent epic called *Buddhacarita* or life of the Buddha.

# CHAPTER V.

**Ashvaghosha and his school.**

Authorities: Sylvain Levi, Le *Buddhacarita d'Ashvaghosha*, JA 1892 p. 8, vol. XIX, p. 201 ff. When Levi at p. 202 characterises the *Buddhacarita* as " a substantial abridgment of the Lalitavistara " he is in the wrong. At least the Lalitavistara in its present redaction could not have been the model of Ashvaghosha. The *Buddhacarita* has been edited by Cowell, Oxford 1893, and translated by him in SBE, vol. XLIX. On Ashvaghosha and his importance to Indian literature, Sylvain Levi deals in his comprehensive study *Ashvaghosha le Sutralankara et ses sources*, JA 1908, p. 10, vol. XII, p. 77. ff. Anesaki in ERE, vol. II, 159 f. We now know from the discoveries of Luders that Ashvaghosha was also a dramatic poet, as the author of the Shariputrapakarana SBA, 1911, p. 388 ff. A biography of Ashavaghosha by Kumarajiva was translated into Chinese between 401 and 409 A.D. It is given as an excerpt by Wassiljew in his *Buddhism* though it is a wholly legendary account.

Down to the year 1892 when the French scholar Sylvain Levi published the first chapter of the Buddhacarita, people in Europe knew little of Ashvaghosha beyond his name. To-day he is known to us as one of the most eminent poets of Sanskrit literature, as the masterly model of Kalidasa and as the author of epic, dramatic and lyrical poems. Unfortunately, however, we know very little of his life. All tradition agrees that he was a contemporary of king Kanishka (about 100 A.D.) and that he was one of the leaders, if not the founder, of the Mahayana doctrine of Buddhism.

On the uncertainty of the age of Kanishka see above vol. I, p. 437; Franke and Fleete independently come to the conclusion that Kanishka came to power in 5153 B.C. On the contrary, R. G. Bhandarkar (JBRAS XX ff 19,385 ff ) is of opinion that Kanishka lived in the third century A.D. Boyer in JA 1900, V. XV., p. 526 ff. makes it probable that he lived at the end of the first and the beginning of the second century A.D. In his latest investigation on the æra of Kanishka, Oldenberg comes to the conclusion that he is to be assigned to the close of the first century A.D (NGGW 1911, p. 421-427). To the same result arrives on other ground Pandit Haraprasada Shastri (Sundaranandam Kavyam, p. 427) He would also identify the poet with Ashvaghosha Raja occurring in an inscription of the times of Kanishka (Ep. Ind. VIII, 171 f.) which however Vogel considers to be an unsuccessful attempt.

**Life of Ashvaghosha.**

Quite positively Ashvaghosha came of a Brahman family and had a sound Brahmanic education before he went over to Buddhism. As a Buddhist he joined, we may surmise, at first the Sarvastivada school but laid great stress on *Buddha Bhakti* and thus prepared for the Mahayana. As his birthplace or home is mostly mentioned Saketa or Ayodhya, modern Oudh. But Benares and Patna are also mentioned in this connection. His mother's name was Suvarnakshi. The Tibetan life of Ashvaghosha says of him: "There was no question that he could not solve, there was no objection which he would not remove; he threw down his opponents as fast as a strong wind breaks down decayed trees."

According to the same account he was a distinguished musician who himself composed music and with his troupe of minstrels, male and female, roamed through market towns. There he played and sang with his choir melancholy ditties on the nullity of existence and the crowd stood charmed with his entrancing melody. In this way he won many over to his religion. According to Vasubandhu he assisted Katyayaniputra in the preparation of his commentary on the Abhidharma.

The Chinese pilgrim I-tsing, who journied through India in 671-695 speaks of the learned monks who successfully combated the heretics, furthered the religion of the Buddha and were consequently esteemed higher than gods and men by the people. And he adds that in each generation there are only a couple of such men—men like "Nagarjuna, Deva and Ashvaghosha of antiquity."

Hiuen-tsiang calls Ashvaghosha, Deva, Nagarjuna and Kumaralabdha "the four suns which illuminate the world" (SBE V, XLIV, p. IX.) The same I-tsing relates how in his time in India was read in front of Buddhist shrines *inter alia* a manual of sacred texts prepared by Ashvaghosha. He also knows him as the author of hymns, of *Sutralamkara* and of the *Buddhacarita* (I-tsing *Record* translated by Takakusu, p. 152 f. 165, 181).

**Ashvaghosha's great work: the Buddha's biography.**

Of the *Buddhacarita* I-tsing says that it was a voluminous poem which recounted the life and the work of the Buddha "from the time when he was still living in the royal palace till his last hour in the park of the *sal* trees." He adds: "It is extensively read in all the five parts of India and in the countries of the South Sea (Sumatra, Java and the neighbouring islands). He clothed manifold notions and ideas in a few words which so delighted the heart of his reader that he never wearied of perusing the poem. Moreover it was regarded as a virtue to read it inasmuch as it contained the noble doctrine in a neat compact form" (I-tsing p. 165 f.). From what I-tsing says it follows that he knew the *Buddhacarita* in the form of its Chinese translation in which the epic consists of 28 cantos and the narrative is brought down to the Nirvana of the Buddha.

It is the Fo-sho-hing-t-tsan translated from Sanskrit into Chinese between 414 and 421 by Dharmaraksha and by Beal from Chinese into English in SBE XIX. Rhys Davids (JRAS 1901, p. 405 f.) has rightly emphasized that this Chinese work is no translation in our sense. Much more accurate is the rendering of the 7th or 8th century into Tibetan (Leumann, WZKM 7, 1893, p. 193 ff.).

Now since the Tibetan translation also contains 28 cantos we must indeed suppose that in the Sanskrit text which comprises only 17 cantos and terminates with the conversions in Benares we have only a torso; and in fact it is but a torso. For out of these 17 cantos only the first 13 are old and genuine. The concluding portion was supplied by one Amritananda, who lived as a copyist in the beginning of the 9th century, because he himself admits he could find no complete manuscript. Even the manuscript of the *Buddha-carita* discovered by Haraprasada Shastri reaches down only to the middle of the 14th canto (JASB V. V. 1909 p. 47 ff.).

And what the Chinese pilgrim says in eulogy of the *Buddhacarita* we can completely substantiate on the basis of the torso we possess. Here we have in reality for the first time a proper Buddha epic created by a true poet,—a poet who, permeated with the love and reverence for the exalted person of the Buddha and profound reverence for the verity of the doctrine of the Buddha, represents the life and the teaching of the master in noble language of art which is not artificial. The *Buddhacarita* is technically called a Mahakavya or great poem,– a courtly epic in art, and it is composed in the style appropriate to Kavya, the beginnings of which we find in the Ramayana. Valmiki and his immediate followers were the predecessors of Ashvaghosha just as the latter himself was a forerunner of Kalidasa. All the three great poets, however, agree in this that in the employment of Alamkaras or poetic embellishment they are throughout moderate. And moderate as to language and style is Ashvaghosha also in the presentment of the miraculous in the Buddha legend. He eschews the extravagance such as we find for example in the Lalitavistara. In contrast with the chaotic disorder of the text of the Mahavastu and the Lalitavistara we find in the *Buddhacarita* a considered and artistic arrangement of the material. And although the poet is at home with the older sacred texts he stands independent of them. Not that he has in any way altered the tradition: he understands how to invest with a new poetic garb the legend known of old and to lend originality of expression to the doctrine of the primitive Buddhistic sutras. Always is Ashvaghosha more of a poet than a monk,—at least in his *Buddhacarita*. As Windisch observes, Ashvaghosha seems to have diligently avoided the ring of the phraseology of the older texts—(Mara and Buddha, p. 205).

**Buddhacarita and Kalidasa.**

Quite differently poetical for instance from that of the Lalitavistara is the picture of the young prince going out for a walk in cantos 3 and 4:

Here in a charming way is depicted how when the news arrives that the prince had gone out the ladies of the city in their curiosity hasten from their chambers to the roofs of the houses and to the windows, hindered by their girdles which fall off, and rush forward with the greatest haste pressing on and pushing each other, frightening by the clank of their waistbands and the ring of their ornaments the birds on the roofs. The faces of the beauties, charming as lotus, gleaming out of the windows appear, as if the walls of the houses were really decorated with lotus flowers. As Cowell has already noticed in the preface to his edition of the *Buddha Charita*, Kalidasa has imitated this scene from Ashvaghosha (Buddha Charita, iii 13/24) in his Raghuvamsha (vii, 5/12). The meeting with the old man whom the gods cause to appear before the prince is charmingly described. In his astonishment the prince asks:

> "Who is the man coming this side, oh charioteer?
> With white hair, eyes sunk deep in their sockets,
> Bending over his staff, his limbs quavering?
> Is that Nature's course or a sport of Chance?"

To this the charioteer replies :

"Old age it is that has broken him,—age,
The thief of beauty and the destroyer of strength,
The source of sorrow and the end of joy,
The foe of intelligence and the disappearance of memory.
He too sucked at his mother's breast,
As a child learnt to walk in course of time.
Slowly he grew big and strong,—a youth,
By degrees has old age crept on him."

After the prince had learnt, on his three walks out of his palace, of old age, disease and death, no more could he find any joy in life. It is in vain that the family priest by order of the king calls upon the women and maidens of the palace to bend their energies on their seductive art to soothe the prince and turn him from his distressing thoughts. The prince remains untouched by the soft distractions. He only thinks of the unthinking ways of these women and cries out (iv 60 f.):

"How senseless the man appears to me whose neighbour ill and old and dead he

Sees and yet holds fast to the good things of this life and is not thrilled with anxiety.

It is as if a tree divested of all flower and fruit must fall or be pulled down.—

Unaffected remaining the neighbouring trees."

**Statecraft, erotic art and warfare.**

The presentment of the love scenes belongs to the indispensable element in the poetic art as an appanage to the court. And the poet satisfies this demand in depicting the sports of the lovely maidens who endeavour to draw the prince towards themselves (iv, 24/53) just as well as in the vivid portrayal of the night scene in the ladies' chamber which causes the prince to fly from the palace. These themes give Ashvaghosha the opportunity for the display of his erotic art. It may be noted that the description (v, 48/62) in its primitive shape is recounted by the young Yasa in the Pali Vinayapitaka. We have already had occasion to remark that a similar scene in the Ramayana (v, 9/11) has been copied from this Buddhist poet Ashvaghosha. The court poet, however, must also be familiar with the doctrine of the *nitishastras* or statecraft. And the world-wise principles are unfolded to the prince by the priest attached to the royal household in order to divert his mind from his meditations (iv, 62/82). Finally, belonging to the same species of court poetry is the delineation of the battle scene. Here our poet rises to the occasion in that in the thirteenth canto he conjures up a vivid scene of the struggle of the Buddha with Mara and his hordes.

**Love and religion.**

Ashvaghosha was the author of another poem to be classed in the category of court poetry *viz.*, *Saundarananandakavya*. The lucky discoverer and editor of this poem is Pandit Haraprasada Shastri (A. Bastion, JA 1902, vol. xix, p. 79 ff and F. W. Thomas JRAS 1911, p. 1125). It also turns round the history of the Buddha's life, but limns especially those scenes and episodes which have been either lightly touched upon or not treated at all in the Buddha-charita. Thus in the first canto is exhaustively described the history of the finding of the city of Kapalivastu. The actual content of this poem, however, is constituted by the history of the loves of Sundari and Nanda, the half-brother of the Buddha who is initiated into the Order against his will by the latter:

"Just as Sundari, the lovely bride of Nanda, weeps and wails over her lost husband so does Nanda suffers for his beloved. Vain are the attempts of the brother monks to tranquillize him. Even the word of the Buddha is impotent to reconcile him. Then the Master takes him by the hand and rises with him to heaven. On their way they see in the Himalayas a hideous one-eyed female monkey and the Buddha asks Nanda if Sundari was more charming than she and Nanda naturally says "Yes" with energy. Soon after, however, they see in the heaven the *upsaras* or celestial nymphs and Nanda finds that the difference between them and his wife is as great as that between the latter and the one-eyed ape. From this moment onwards he is possessed with a passionate longing for the fairies and returning on earth gives himself up to serious ascetic practices in order to be able to attain to the paradise. Thereupon Ananda, the favourite disciple of the Buddha, teaches him that even the joys of paradise are vain and nugatory. Nanda is finally convinced and goes to the Buddha to say that he had no longer a desire for the beauties of heaven. The Buddha is greatly pleased and preaches to him in several cantos the cardinals of his doctrine. Nanda now retires into the forest, practices the four great meditations and becomes an *arhat.* Gratefully he betakes himself to the Buddha and does him reverence but the Master calls upon him now that he has attained his object, out of compassion for others to preach the doctrine of salvation and conduct others to emancipation.

The reference to the forcible conversion of Nanda occurs also in our older sources: Mahavagga, i. 54; Nidanakatha p. 91; Rhys Davids Buddhist Birth Stories, p. 128. As is pointed out by Haraprasada Sastri (p. xiii) a strongly divergent version of this legend is to be found in the Pali commentary on the Dhammapada. See also Spence Hardy, *Manual of Buddhism;* Kern, *History of Buddhism*, i, 155; Foucher, *Greco-Buddhist Art* (i, 464).

**Synthesis of Schools.**

Whilst in the Buddha Charita there is no express doctrine emanating from the Mahayana school, the concluding portion of the Saundarananda-kavya already begins to betray a leaning towards the Mahayana. It is not sufficient for it that Nanda himself should become a saint who attains to Nirvana. He must also be an apostle of the faith, although it must not be forgotten that even in the Hinayana the obligation of the propagation of the faith and proselytism is highly praised, as in a Sutra in the Anguttaranikaya. Besides in the third great work of Ashvaghosha, entitled the *Sutralankara*, which we up to now knew only from a French translation of the Chinese version belonging to about 405 B.C., many of the semi-legendary stories are based on a Hinayanic foundation. From this Sutralankara translated into French from the Chinese version of Kumarajiva, Huber was able to trace three stories to the *Divyavadana* (BEFEO, 1904, pp. 709-726) but fragments of the Sanskrit original have more recently been discovered at Turfan and studied by Luders in an old palm leaf manuscript, (see Fragments of Bhuddhist Drama, Berlin, 1911, and Vallee poussin *Le Museon*, 1909, p. 86.)

**Sutralamkara.**

Sutralamkara or "Sutra-Ornament" is a collection of pious legends after the model of the Jatakas and Avadanas which are narrated in prose and verse in the style of Indian poetic art. Many of these legends are known to us of old, *e. g.*, that of Dirghavus or prince Long-life and of king Shibi. Others already show more of the spirit of the Mahayana or at least a reverence for the Buddha which is more Mahayanistic in its tendency. An illustration is furnished by story No. 57, which happens also to be one of the most charming in the collection.

A man comes to the monastery and desires to be initiated into the Order. The disciple Shariputra examines him and finds that the candidate in none of his previous existences for æons had done the smallest good deed and pronounces him unworthy of admittance. The man leaves the monastery in tears. Then the Buddha himself meets him and the Buddha's heart being full of compassion he strives to convert all mankind with the love that a mother bears to her son. He lays his hand on the head of the rejected one and asks "Why dost thou cry"? And the latter relates to him how Shariputra had dismissed him. Thereupon the Buddha consoles him "in a voice that resounded like distant thunder" and adds that Shariputra was not omniscient. The Buddha himself then brings the man back to the monastery and relates before all the monks the *karma*, which was a good act whereby the man had acquired right to emancipation. Once upon a time in his previous birth this person was a poor man who was wandering in a hill forest to collect wood, when a tiger rushed at him. Filled with terror he cried out "adoration to the Buddha." On account of these words the man must partake of deliverance from sorrow. The Buddha himself initiated him and presently he became an Arhat.

An example of a real Mahayanistic Buddha-bhakti is also furnished by No. 68, where Gautami, the foster mother of the Buddha, attains to Nirvana through the grace of the Buddha.

That the Sutralankara is of later origin than the *Buddha charita* is proved by the fact that the latter is quoted in the former. (Huber, page 192, 222). Since in two of the stories of the Sutralankara a part is played by king Kanishka, Ashvaghosha must have lived at the time of the composition of the book as an old man at the court of the king. But it is much to be deplored that up to now we have only Chinese translations of the *Sutralankara.* The Sanskrit text so far has never been discovered. Not only is it in itself a literary work of importance the merits of which impress themselves upon us through two translations, first Chinese and then French, as has been appropriately observed by Levi, but it is not of trifling significance for the history of Indian literature and culture inasmuch as it mentions the epics of the Mahabharata and Ramayana, it combats the philosophical doctrine of the Sankhya and Vaisheshika schools just as forcibly as it opposes the religious views of the Brahmans and the Jains and refers in a variety of ways to the scripts, to the arts and to painting. Still more is uncertainty a matter for regret with reference to a few other books which are attributed to Ashvaghosha. It is a question whether they really belong to him. This applies especially to the *Vajrasuchi* or Diamond Needle, which is in any case an interesting little book in which there is a vehement polemic against the caste system of the Brahmans.

**Vajrasuchi: polemic against caste.**

The Vajrasuchi or Refutation of the Arguments upon which the Brahmanical institution of the caste is founded by the learned Buddhist Ashvaghosh (edited by Lancelot Wilkinson) also the Tunku by Soobajee Bapoo, being a reply to the Wujra Soochi, 1839. A. Weber, Uber die Vajrassuci (Abdhandlungen der Preu ss. Akademie der Wissenschaften phil.-hist. Kl. 1859, S. 295 ff. und Indische Streifen 1, 116 ff.) B. H. Hodgson Essays on the Languages, Literature and Religion of Nepal and Tibet, London 1874, p. 126 ff. and S. Levi J. A. 1908, s. 10, t. XII p. 70 f.

Here the author very effectively takes up the Brahmanic standpoint and demonstrates on the authority of Brahmanic texts and citations from the Veda, the Mahabharata and Manu the invalidity of the claims of castes as recognised by Brahmanas. When in 1829 Hodgson published a translation of the book and Wilkinson in 1839 published an edition they astonished scholars by the democratic spirit of Europe displayed in the book. In this tract the doctrine of equality of mankind has been advocated ; for all human beings are, " in respect of joy and sorrow, love, insight, manners and ways, death, fear and life, all equal." Did we but know more about the author and the time when the book was composed it would be of much greater importance for the literary history of India on account of the quotations from Brahmanic texts. It speaks for the authorship of Ashvaghosha that in Sutralamkara No. 77 the Brahmanic institutions are arraigned with the help of quotations from Manu's law book just as in the Vajrasuchi. On the other hand the Vajrasuchi is enumerated neither in the Tibetan Tanjur nor among the works of Ashvaghosha by I-tsing ; and further in the Chinese Tripitaka Catalogue the Vajrasuchi, which is said to contain " a refutation of the four vedas," is described as translated into Chinese between 973 and 981 and is ascribed to a Dharmakirti. (Bunyo Nanjio, Catalogue of the Chinese translation of the Buddhist Tripitaka, No. 1303). The Chinese term "fa-shang" is the translation of the Sanskrit proper name Dharmakirti.

**Other works of Ashvaghosha.**

It is altogether undecided whether other books the authorship of which is assigned to Ashvaghosha by Chinese, Japanese and Tibetan writers were actually composed by him. The fame of Ashavaghosha as a teacher of the Mahayana is founded on his *Mahayana Shraddhotpada* or the Rise of the Mahayana Faith, a philosophical treatise studied in the monasteries of Japan as the basis of the Mahayana doctrine. " The poet of the *Buddhacarita*," says Levi, " shows him here as a profound metaphysician, as an intrepid reviver of a doctrine which was destined to regenerate Buddhism." However, it is anything but certain or rather highly improbable that it is in reality the product of Ashvaghosha since it embodies teaching which is assignable to a later date. So long, however, as the Sanskrit text of the book is denied us a final judgment regarding the age of the author is impossible.

The Shraddhotpada was translated first in 534 and then in 710 A.D. into Chinese. From the second Chinese translation T. Suzuki prepared an English version, "Discourse of the awakening of Faith in the Mahayana." Suzuki holds Ashvaghosha the poet to be the author and asserts on the basis of the book itself, the Mahayana Shraddhotpada, that he was the actual founder of the Mahayana sect. The doctrine which the book incorporates is, however, that of the Vijnanavada as taught by Asanga and the teaching of the Tathagatagarbha and the Tathata which occurs in the Lankavatara. Professor Takakusu, who holds the authorship of the poet Ashvaghosha as altogether out of the question, says that the older catalogue of the Chinese texts does not contain the name of Ashvaghosha as the author. In the Tibetan Tanjur Ashvaghosha is also described as the composer of the *Shatapancasha'ika-namastotra*, the panegyric in 150 verses, which according to I-tsing, is the work of the poet Matriceta. In fact I-tsing cannot say too much regarding the renown of this Matriceta, who at all events belongs to the same school as Ashvaghosha and is accordingly confused with him.

**Matriceta.**

To follow the Tibetan historian Taranatha, Matriceta is only another name of Ashvaghosha, (F.W., Thomas OC XIII, 1902, p. 40). One dare not decide whether our Matriceta is identical with the Matriceta, the author of the *Maharajakanikalekha*, (Thomas Ind. Ant., 1903, p. 345 ff. and SC Vidyabhushana JASB, 1910, p. 477 ff.) "It is entrancing," says I-tsing, "in the congregation of the monks to hear recited the hymn in 150 verses or the hymn in 400 verses. These fascinating poems are like heavenly flowers.

in their beauty and the exalted principles which they contain emulate in dignity the height of mountain summits. Therefore all the composers of hymns in India imitate his style regarding him as the father of literature. Even men like the Bodhisattva Asanga and Vasubandhu greatly admire him. Throughout India every monk, as soon as he is able to recite the five or ten commandments, learns the psalms of Matriceta.' The legend would have it that in a previous birth he was a nightingale which eulogised the Buddha in charming melody. I-tsing himself traslated from Sanskrit into Chinese the hymn of 150 verses (*Record*, p. 156, 666). Now, however, most fortunately we have discovered in Central Asia fragments of the Sanskrit originals of the hymns of Matriceta and from the mutilated manuscripts discovered at Turfan, to which we already owe so much, Siegling has succeeded in reconstructing almost two-thirds of the text. The verses are in the artistic, but not the extravagant Kavya, style. Besides Dr. Siegling who has been preparing an edition for the press similar fragments discovered in Central Asia have been published by Levi (JA 1910, page 455, and Vallee Poussin 1911, page 764) F. W. Thomas translated one of Matriceta's poems, the *Varnanarthavarnana*, from the Tibetan rendering into English (Ind. Ant. vol. 34, p. 145).

**Buddhist poet Shura.**

Better known is the poet Shura or Aryashura, probably issuing from the same school, although of a considerably younger date whose *Jatakamala* strongly resembles the Sutralamkara in style. The *Jatakamala* or the Garland of Jatakas is, however, only the name of a species of composition. Several poets have written jatakamalas that is, they have treated with a free hand in an original poetic speech in mixed verse and prose selections of the Jatakas. It was also not Aryashura's business to discover new stories but to reproduce ancient legends in artistic and elegant idiom. His diction in prose as well as verse is of the *kavya* class, but noble and elevated, more artistic than artificial. So far as the jatakas are designed to be employed by the monks in their sermons, the jatakamala also serves this purpose for the preacher. Only the poet who was probably himself a preacher at the court, has none but monks before his eyes, who held their religious discourses in courtly circles where Sanskrit poesy was understood and appreciated. The book contains 34 jatakas which, like the 35 jatakas of the Pali *Cariyapetaka*, illustrate the Paramitas or the excellences of the Bodhisattva. Nearly all the stories appear also in the Pali Book of Jataka and twelve are to be found likewise in the Cariyapatika. Many of the Sanskrit verses harmonise with the Pali jatakas. (See Speyer's translation, p. 337.) To the few stories which are wanting in the Pali collection belongs the first in which is related how the Bodhisattva sees a hungry tigress about to devour its young and sacrifices himself to be her nourishment. It is a highly characteristic story and may be reproduced here as an example of the anecdotal literature designed to convey the Mahayana doctrine of universal compassion.

This most characteristic story runs as follows:—

**Master's selfless love.**

" Already in his earlier births the Master displayed a selfless love for all creatures and allowed himself to be absorbed into other beings. Therefore must men cherish for the Buddha, the Lord, supreme attachment. For the following miracle on the part of the Lord in one of his previous births is recounted—a deed which was celebrated by my venerable teacher, one of the adorers of Three Jewels, who gave satisfaction to his preceptor by his insight and truth and became himself an eminent master in the search for virtue. In those days the Bodhisattva, who is now the Lord, in keeping with his extraordinary promises by virtue of his charity, love, succour to the poor conferred grace on the world out of compassion issuing from the immaculate stream of insight and love, was born in a Brahman family devoted to their duties and pre-eminent for character, learned and powerful." As he grew up he presently acquired mastery over all the arts and sciences. He obtained much wealth and honour. However he found no pleasure in worldly life and soon withdrew into retirement. As a pious ascetic he lived in the forest. One day he was wandering accompanied by a single disciple in the mountains. He saw in a cave a young tigress exhausted with hunger and about to devour her own young, trustfully approaching her to feed on her milk.

" As the Bodhisattva saw her

Trembled he, brave as he was,

Filled with compassion for the sorrow of the nearest,

Like the prince of mountains in an earthquake.

How strange! The compassionate remain intrepid even under great personal grief.

But when a stranger is smitten, however small, they quail."

He sent out his disciple to fetch meat. But this was only a pretext in order to be left alone. He was already determined to hurl himself down the precipice in order to save the life of the creature and to serve as food to the mother tiger. He based his resolve on this that this futile earthly life has no value except as an offering for others. Moreover, he would give a heartening example unto those who would benefit the world, put to shame the self-seekers, point the path of heaven to the benevolent and himself attain to supreme illumination. Nothing else he desired:—"Not out of covetousness, nor in search of renown, nor joys of Heaven or kingly rule to acquire; not for the sake of my eternal weal; but only to do good to my neighbour, do I act thus. As surely as this is truth, so may it be granted unto me to remove the tribulation of the world and to bring salvation to it, even as the sun brings it light when darkness swallows it up."

With these words he hurls himself down the cliff. The tigress has her attention called by the noise, leaves her young and throws herself upon the body of the Bodhisattva to devour it. When the disciple comes back and beholds the spectacle, he is profoundly moved and utters a few verses of veneration for the exalted Master. Men, demi-gods, and gods express their admiration for the Lord by strewing garlands of flowers and precious stones over what is left of his bones.

The inexhaustible sympathy of the Bodhisattva has also been glorified in most other stories. I-tsing extols the Jatakamala or Jatakamalas among the works which in his time were great favourites and were much read in India. Among the frescoes in the caves of Ajanta there are scenes from the Jatakamala with inscribed stophes from Aryashura. The inscriptions belong palæographically to the sixth century A. D. and since another work of Aryashura had already been translated into Chinese in 434, the poet must have lived in the fourth century.

I-tsing, Tr. Takakuku, p. 166 f.; H. Luders, NGGW 1902, p. 758 ff. B. Nanjio, Catalogue of the Chinese Tripitaka, No. 1349; The Zachariæ, GGA, 1888, p. 850, F. W. Thomas in Album Kern, p. 405, ff. The Chinese translation of the Jatakamal mentions Aryashura as the author. It has only 14 stories, see Ivanovski in RHR, 1903, V. 47, p. 298 ff.

## CHAPTER VI.

**Literature of Avadanas.**

The Jatakamala is also called Bodhisattva Avadanamala, for Bodhisattva Avadana is synonymous with Jataka. The Jatakas are consequently nothing but Avadanas having the Bodhisattva for their hero. Consequently works like the Sutralankara and the Jatakamala have much in common with the texts of the Avadana literature. On the other hand numerous Jatakas are to be found in the collections of Avadanas.

On the Avadana literature in general see Burnouf, Introduction to the History of Buddhism, p. 207; Feer in the introduction to his translation, and Speyer, Foreword to his edition of the Avadanashataka.

**Veneration for the Buddha.**

Like both the books of Buddhist story literature, the Avadana texts also stand, so to say, with one foot in the Hinayana and the other in the Mahayana literature. And I-tsing (Takakusu, p. xxii f. and 14 f.) lets us know that the line of demarcation between the Hinayana and the Mahayana was often anything but rigid. The older works belong entirely to the Hinayana and yet they display the same veneration for the Buddha which is not wanting likewise in the Pali jatakas and *apadanas*; but they eschew the hyperbole and the mythology of the Mahayana, while the latest avadana books are permeated with the Mahayana.

**What is Avadana?**

The word 'avadana' signifies a great religious or moral achievement, as well as the history of a great achievement. Such a great act may consist in sacrifice of one's own life, but also may be confined to the founding of an institution for the supply of incense, flowers, gold and jewels to, or the building of, sanctuaries,—*stupas*, *chaityas*, and so forth. Since these stories as a rule are designed to inculcate that dark deeds bear dark fruits, white acts beget fair fruit, they are at the same time tales of *karma* which domonstrate how the actions of one life are intimately connected with those in the past or future existences. They are to be regarded as legends only from our modern standpoint. To the Buddhist they are actualities. They have indeed been related by the Buddha himself and are warranted to be the word of the Buddha,—Buddhavacana—like a Sutra. Like the jatakas the avadanas also are a species of sermons. It is accordingly usually related by way of an introduction where and on what occasion the Buddha narrated the story of the past and at the close the Buddha draws from the story the moral of his doctrine. Hence a regular avadana consists of a story of the present, a story of the past and a moral. If the hero of the story of the past is a Bodhisattva the avadnna can also be designated a jataka. A particular species of avadanas are those in which the Buddha instead of a story of the past relates a prognostication of the future. These prophetic anecdotes serve like the stories of the past to explain the present *karma*. There are besides avadanas in which both the parties of the stories are united and finally there is a class in which a *karma* shows good cr evil consequence in the present existence. All these species of avadanas occur sporadically also in the *Vinaya* and the *Sutra pitakas* They, however, are grouped in large collections with the object of edification or for more ambitious literary motives. A work of the first variety is the *Avadanashataka* which is most probably the most ancient of its kind. It is a collection of a hundred avadana legends.' Since it was already rendered into Chinese in the first half of the 3rd century and since it makes mention of the *dinara* we may with tolerable certainty assign it to the second Christian century. That it belongs to the Hinayana is indicated already by the character of the anecdotes; but this is likewise corroborated by the circumstances that in the stories relating to the present there are fragments embodied from the Sanskrit canon of the Sarvastivadis relating to the Parinivana and other sutras. In these legends the worship of the Buddha plays a great part. There is no trace in them, however, of the Bodhisattva cult or of any Mahayanistic mythology.

**Avadana-shataka.**

The *Avadanashataka* consists of ten decades, each treating of a different theme. The first four contain stories designed to show the nature of acts, the performance of which enables a man to become a Buddha or a Pratyeka buddha. The division into *vargas* (Pali *vagga*) of ten components each is a favourite with Pali texts and accordingly would appear to date from the older Buddhist period. All the tales of the first and nearly all of the third decade are of a prophetic nature.

Here an act of piety is related by which a person,—a Brahman, a princess, the son of an usurer, a wealthy merchant, a gardener, a king, a ferry man, a young maiden and so forth,—makes adoration to the Buddha which usually leads to the occurrence of some kind of miracle, and then the Buddha with a smile reveals that the particular person in a future age will become a Buddha or (in the Third book) a Pratyekabuddha. On the other hand the histories in the Second, and in the Fourth decades are Jatakas. With regard to the saintly virtues and astounding acts, it is explained that the hero of these tales was no other than the Buddha himself in one of his earlier births. A kind of *Pretavastu*, corresponding to the Pali *Petavatthu*, is represented by the Fifth book. A saint,—usually it is Maudgalyayana,—proceeds to the world of spirits and observes the sorrows of one of its denizens, (pretas) male or female. He questions the spirit regarding the cause of his tribulation. The spirit refers him to the Buddha, and the latter then narrates the history of the " black deed ",—the refusal to give alms, offence to a saint, etc.—which this creature perpetrated in his previous birth. The Sixth book relates histories of men and beasts that through some pious act are born as deities in heaven. The last four decades narrate stories purporting to show the nature of acts which lead to Arhat-ship. The Arhats of the Seventh book are all derived from the Shakya clan; those of the Eighth book are all women; those of the Ninth are persons of irreproachable conduct; and those of the Tenth are men who in former days committed evil deeds and suffered in consequence and subsequently owing to an act of virtue attained to the state of an Arhat.

**The fixed model.**

Now these stories in our collection have not only been arranged after a definite plan and system, but are related according to a set model. This process of working according to a pattern is carried to the extent of perpetual reiteration of phrases and descriptions of situations in unaltered strings of words. Thus following the rigid pattern every one of our tales begins with the protracted formula:

"The Buddha, the Lord, venerated, highly respected, held in honour, and lauded by kings, ministers, men of wealth, citizens, artisans, leaders of caravans, gods, Nagas, Yakshas, Asuras, Garudas, Kinnaras and gigantic snakes, adored by Devas, Nagas, Yakshas, Asuras, Garudas, Kinnaras and gigantic snakes, the Buddha, the Lord, the Renowned, the Served, betook himself, accompanied by his disciples and provided with all the necessaries in clothing, food, bedding, covering, refreshments and medicaments in the shape of alms to.. ........and was sojourning at......"

Similarly every one of these tales ends with:

"Thus spake the Lord and with ecstacy in their hearts the monks applauded the speech of the Master."

Finally when the moral of the story is pointed out the process is invariably described in these words :

" Therefore, Oh monks, is the fruit of wholly dark deeds wholly dark ; that of wholly white deeds is wholly white ; that of mixed deeds is mixed. Wherefore, Oh monks, you shall abandon the dark and the mixed deeds and take your pleasure only in fair acts."

**Culture evidences.**

A pious man, an opulent personage, a mighty sovereign, a happy wedding, the up-bringing of a young man, the appearance of an earlier Buddha and similar recurring phenomena are ever described in stereotyped terms. Nor is this applicable only to a few brief sentences. It holds good of extensive pieces covering several pages of print. One of the longest of these fixture pieces describes the smile of the Buddha with which the latter lays down that every one can attain to the state of a Buddha. The Buddha always is moved to a smile before he prophesies the future. When he smiles from his mouth issue rays of blue, yellow, red and white. One of these beams of light go down to the depths of inferno, the others are darted heavenwards. After encircling thousands and thousands of worlds they return back to the Buddha and disappear into some one or the other of the parts of the Buddha's body according to the nature of the vaticination ; and all this is delineated to the minutest particular. This circumstantiality and the minutiæ are characteristic of the narrative mode of the *Avadanashataka.* However, together with much that is banal and wearisome we always get edifying stories and many valuable anecdotes and noteworthy variants to other stories accessible to us from other portions of Buddhist narrative literature. We can cite only a few examples in order to give an idea of the character of this remarkable collection of Buddhist folklore.

Here are some characteristic stories in which the true social life of India is mirrored.

**Maiden disciple: Story 28.**

A poor girl smears the feet of the Buddha with sandal paste. This fills the whole city with the fragrance of sandal. At this miracle the maiden is exceedingly delighted, falls at the feet of the Buddha and prays that in her future birth she may be born a Pratyeka-Buddha. The Buddha smiles and prophesies that she shall be a Pratyeka-Buddha named Gandhamadana, (Fragrance-Delight).

**Extreme Compassion: Story 34.**

This story is a version of the tale of King Shibi who has given away all his goods and possessions in charity. He, however, is not content with merely making men happy; he would show kindness to the smallest creature. He cuts off his skin with a knife and exposes himself in such a manner that flies feast on his blood. This is seen by Shakra (Indra) in his heaven and he comes forward to put king Shibi to a further test, appearing before him in the form of a vulture ready to pounce upon him. The king looks at the bird only with benevolence and says, "Take, my friend, what you like of my body I present it to you." Thereupon the god metamorphoses himself into a Brahman and asks of the king both his eyes. Shibi says "Take, Great Brahman, what thou wouldst; I will not hinder thee." Next Shakra reassumes his true form and promises to Shibi that he shall attain to perfect enlightenment.

**Disinterested pity: Story 36.**

This is the legend of Maitrakanyaka representing the Sanskrit version of the Pali Jataka of "Mittavindaka." But the story here takes quite a different turn from the Pali inasmuch as the hero is the Bodhisattva. He gets here also his penalty for offending his mother and undergoes the hot wheel torture. But while he is subjected to the fearful torment he is informed that he will have to suffer it for sixty-six thousand years till another man guilty of a similar sin appears. He feels compassion for the creature and resolves to bear the wheel on his head for all eternity so that no other being may have to endure the agony. In consequence of this thought of compassion the wheel disappears from on his head.

**Princess devout: Story 54**

At the suggestion of his princess, king Bimbisara set up a Stupa in his seraglio over some hair and nails presented to him by the Buddha. The Stupa was worshipped by the women with incense, lamps, flowers, etc But when prince Ajatashatru assassinated his father Bimbisara and himself ascended the throne, he gave strict orders that no lady of his harem should, on pain of death, venerate the shrine. Shrimati, however, who was one of the ladies in the harem, did not obey the command and laid a garland of lights round the Stupa. The infuriated king put her to death. She died with the thought of the Buddha in her mind and was immediately translated to heaven as a divinity.

**Guerdon of service to Buddha : Story 100**

While the heroes of all the Avadanas are the Buddha's contemporaries, the hero of this last story is a person who lived in the times of king Ashoka. The connection with the time of the Buddha is established by the insertion of an account of the decease of the Buddha. This narrative piece is extracted from a *Parinirvanasutra* and is in tolerable accord with the celebrated Pali *Mahaparinibbanasutta*. (Another passage from the *Parinirvanasutra* serves as an introduction to Story No. 40).

A hundred years after the passing of the Buddha lived king Ashoka. He had a son named Kunala who was so charming that the king thought he had no equal in the world. One day, however, he learnt from merchants from Gandhara that there were still more handsome young men than the prince in their country. According to the merchants there was living a youth called Sundara who was not only of irreproachable beauty, but wherever he turned there sprang up a lotus pond and a garden. The astonished king Ashoka sent a messenger and invited Sundara and satisfied himself about this wonder. The king asked to what *karma* the youth owed his excellence and the Elder Upagupta gave the explanation. At the time that the Buddha had just attained to complete Nirvana the present Sundara was an impoverished peasant who prepared a refreshing bath and revived with food Mahakashyapa and his suite of 500 monks who had performed the obsequies of the master, who were depressed with sorrow at the passing of the Lord and who had been exhausted with the long journey. Sundara was now enjoying the fruit of this his good deed.

**Avadanashataka and cognate tales.**

A number of the stories in our Avadanashataka turn up in other Avadana anthologies and a few also in the Pali *Apadanas.* Thus the legend of Rashtrapala which is No. 90 in our collection corresponds partly to the *Ratthapalasutta* of the Pali *Majhimanikaya* and partly the *Ratthapala Apadana.* But the correspondence stops short of the titles in the Sanskrit and the Pali and the Pali Apadana displays great divergence (Feer, Avadanashataka, pp. 240 f., 313 f., 335, 340 ff., 354 f., 360 f., 372 f., 439 f.).

**Tibetan and Chinese analogues.**

An old work which bears a great resemblance to the Avadanashataka and has a number of stories in common with it is the *Karma shataka* or Hundred Karma Stories. This work, however, is unfortunately preserved to us only in a

Tibetan translation. (Feer pp. XXIX f., 442 ff.; V. V, 382 ff., 404 ff. and JA 1901 V. XVII, pp. 50 ff., 257 ff., 410 ff; Speyer p. XIX f.). Translated from Sanskrit but no longer preserved in the original language is also the Tibetan collection of Avadanas now celebrated in the literature of the world as the story book of Dsanglun under the title of *The Wise Man and the Fool.* It has been translated into German by J. Schmidt. Takakusu points to a Chinese version of this work (JRAS 1901, p. 447 ff.)

**Divyavadana.**

A collection younger than the Avadanashataka but one which has incorporated in it exceedingly old texts is the *Divyavadana* or the Divine Avadana. The original Sanskrit has been edited by Cowel and Neil of Cambridge. Large extracts from it had already been translated by Burnouf (Introduction to the History of Indian Buddhism). The title of the work is not certain; it is only found in the chapter headings of some manuscripts. Rejendralal Mitra described a manuscript entitled *Divyavadanamala* which greatly deviates from our printed edition (Nepalese Buddhist Literature, pp. 304-316). Also a Paris manuscript which is described in the Cambridge edition (p. 663 ff.) harmonizes only partially with our Divyavadana.

**Characteristics.**

This collection of stories, of great importance for the history of Indian sociology, begins with the Mahayanistic benediction, "Oh, reverence to all the exalted Buddhas and Bodhisattvas" and contains a few obviously later accretions in the Mahayanistic sense. As a whole, however, the book decidedly belongs to the Hinayana school. As the example of the Mahayanistic interpolation we may mention chapter XXXIV which is noted in the collection itself as a Mahayanasutra (p. 483). In chapter XXX there occurs the *shadakshara vidya* or the well-known Tibetan formula of *om mani padme hum* (Poussin, Boudhisme p. 881). The Sanskrit canon of Buddhism is repeatedly mentioned and individual canonic texts are quoted such as *Dirghagama*, *Udana*, *Sthaviragatha* (Oldenberg, ZDMG 52, 1891, pp. 653, 655 f., 658, 665). It mentions the four Agamas (p. 333). Many of the stories commence and terminate exactly as in the Avadanashataka. And finally a number of stereotyped phrases and descriptions, so characteristic, appear again in self-same words in the Divyavadana. In all probability they are derived from the common source,—the *Vinayapitaka* of the Sarvastivadis. As a matter of fact, more than half of the anecdotes have been borrowed from the latter but several have been loans from the *Sutralankara* of Ashvaghosha which we discussed above (Huber BEFEO IV, 1904, 709 ff.; VI, 1906, 1 ff;—Sylvain Levi T'oung Pao, V. VII, 1907, 105 ff., and Speyer Avadanashataka II, preface p. XVI f.).

**Analysis of components.**

The Divyavadana is composed of very varied materials. It has no principle of division, nor is it uniform with regard to language and style. Most of the legends are written in good simple Sanskrit prose which is only here and there interrupted by Gathas. But in some passages we find also elaborate poetry of genuine Kavya style with long compounds. The editor of this collection of legends appears, therefore, to have simply pieced together a variety of stories from other texts. From this also follows that the several component elements of the work are assignable to different periods of time. If our collection, as has been alleged, was already translated into Chinese in the third Christian century it could not have been published in the original long before that date. At the same time we have to bear in mind that because some of the Avadanas in the *Divyavadana* were translated into Chinese in the third century (Cowel Neil, p. 655), therefore it does not necessarily follow that the work as a whole was rendered into Chinese

(Kern Manual, p. 10 Barth, RHR 889, V. 19, p. 260). Not only there is the mention of the successors of Ashoka, the kings of the Shunga dynasty down to the Pushyamitra (178 B.C.) but there is the repeated occurrence of the *dinara*, which brings us down to the second century. And some period after Ashvaghosha must have elapsed before a compiler could take extracts from his Sutralankara for his own anthology. The Divyavadana, therefore, was redacted rather in the third than in the second century. Nevertheless it is remarkable that just one of the most interesting legends in the Divyavadana, the story of Shardulakarna, was translated into Chinese in 265 A.D. The contents of this Avadana noteworthy in many respects, are as follows :—

**Shardulakarna: love of the untouchable.**

The Master was sojourning in Shravasti and Ananda was wont daily to repair to the town on his begging round. Once upon a time, as he was returning from the town, he became thirsty and saw a Chandala maiden, named Prakriti, fetching water from a well. "Sister," said he to her, "Give me some water to drink." Prakriti replied, "I am a Chandala girl, Revered Ananda." "Sister," said Ananda, "I do not ask you about your family and your caste, but if you have any water left, give it to me and I will drink." (Note that so far the similarity with Jesus and the Samaritan woman is surprising, John 4, 7 ff., but the whole course of the narrative further down in the Gospel is so different that we can scarcely think of any connection between the Buddhist and Christian Scriptures.) The maiden hands him the water to drink and falls deep in love with the Saint. She tells her mother that she will die or have Ananda for her husband. The mother, who was a powerful witch, prepared a potent philtre and attempted her sorcery on Ananda with *mantras*. The process is described in a way similar to the incantation in the Kaushikasutra of the Atharvaveda. The charm is successful. Ananda comes into the house of the Chandala where the joyful Prakriti has prepared a bed. But in the moment of supreme danger, Ananda breaks out into tears and supplicates the Buddha in his distress. The latter hastens to his succour with his own counter *mantras*. Ananda leaves the Chandala home and returns to his monastery. The great witch declares to her unfortunate daughter that the necromancy of Gautama is superior to her own. But Prakriti, the Chandala maiden, was yet not cured of her love. She went into the town and followed Ananda day after day as he went forth on his mendicant's circuit. Once more Ananda in his sorrow turned to the Master for help. The latter summoned Prakriti to himself and ostensibly consented to her desire that Ananda should be her husband. Soon, however, he brings her to a frame of mind in which she takes the vow of spinsterly chastity and turns a nun. She not only has her hair shaven and dons the nun's weeds, but dives into the profundity of the four Noble Truths and understands the religion of the Buddha in its entirety.

When, however, the Brahmans, warriors and citizens of Shravasti heard that the Buddha made a Chandala daughter a nun, they were greatly perturbed, conveyed it to the king Prasenajit and the latter immediately set out for the Master to remonstrate with him. Numerous Brahmans, warriors and citizens of Shravasti had gathered together there. Then the Buddha related the story of Trishanku, the Chandala chieftain. The latter ages ago was desirous of matching his learned son Shardulakarna to the daughter of the proud Brahman Pushkarasari. The Brahman rejected his overtures with disdain and now follows a most interesting dialogue in which Trishanku subjects to searching criticism the caste system and the Brahmanic code of morality. He demonstrates that between members of the various castes there exists no such natural difference as between diverse species of animals and plants. Moreover, there could be no caste according to the doctrines of transmigration and the theory of *karma* inasmuch as each individually is reborn in accordance with his own deeds. Finally, Pushkarasari is convinced of the erudition of Trishanku and consents to the marriage. And, concludes the Master, the Brahman's daughter was in a former birth no other than the Chandala spinster Prakriti. The Buddha himself was in that age Trishanku ; :and who else could be Shardulakarna, but Ananda.

This beautiful legend of the Buddhists was known to Richard Wagner by means of the French translation of Bournouf (Introduction p. 205 ff.) and upon it he has based his "Victors."

**Ashokavadana.** Old because already translated into Chinese in the third Christian century is also the cycle of stories called the *Ashokavadana* incorporated with the Divyavadana (XXVI-XXIX). The central figure of the tales is the great king Asoka. Historically these legends contain hardly anything, of moment. But the important exceptions are, first, the mention of the persecution of Jainism (p. 427) ; and secondly the intolerance of Buddhist monks under Pushyamitra (p. 433 f.). Rhys Davids has studied these allusions (JPTS 1896, p. 88 f.). The tales are more valuable from the literary standpoint. First of all here we have the extraordinary dramatic legend of Upagupta and Mara. It is an unusually bold idea to have Mara the Evil One, the Tempter, converted by a Buddhist monk. Still bolder it is when saint Upagupta, who longs for a vision of the Buddha, who had passed for centuries into Nirvana, implores his proselyte Mara to appear to him in the garb of the Buddha and the latter, like an experienced actor, so thoroughly personates the Buddha that the holy man sinks in obeisance before him. So dramatically conceived is the whole story that one can well believe that here simply a Buddhist drama is recapitulated. In language, style and metre the piece belongs to the art of court poetry. We are not therefore at all surprised that, as has been proved by Huber, the compiler of the *Divyavadana* has extracted in its literal entirety this magnificent section from the *Sutralankara* of Ashvaghosha.

Divyavadana pp. 356-364, translated by Windisch, *Mara and Buddha*. p. 161 ff. Huber Ashvaghosha : Sutralankara translated into French, p. 263 ff. and BEFEO 4, 1904, p. 709 ff.

A Pali version of this legend quite artless and undramatic has been discovered from the Burmese book of Lokapannattiby Duroiselle (BEFEO, 4 1904, p. 414 ff.) It is remarkable that the monastery in which Upagupta (who subsequently became the preceptor of Ashoka) lived, was founded by the brothers Nata (actor) and Bhata (soldier) and was accordingly called Natabhatika. Not inappropriately Levi calls the Ashokavadana a kind of *Mahatmya* of the Natabhatika monastery at Mathura.

**Kunala : Queen mother and step-son.**

The source of one of the most charming legends in the Ashoka cycle of tales in the *Divyavadana* remains unknown. It is the pathetic episode of Kunala. He was the son of King Ashoka, and at the instigation of his wicked step-mother was blinded of his eyes of wonderful beauty. Not for a moment did he feel indignation or hatred against her who was the cause of so much misery to himself.

**Pali parallels.**

The *Divyavadana* has many legends in common with the Pali canon. The seventh chapter is an extract from the *Mahaparinirvanasutra*. To a well-known Pali sutra or dialogue corresponds the history of Purna who goes out as an apostle to the wild and violent Shronaparantakas, determined to bear with equanimity and gentleness their invectives, assaults and attempts at murder. (Divyavadana p. 36 ff.)

Samyuttanikaya IV p. 60 ; Majjhimanikaya III, 267 ; JPTS 1887, p. 23 Pali jataka No. 4 answers to Divyavadana, p. 498 ff., the story being that of the young merchant's son who sells a dead rat and gradually acquires enormous wealth.

**Rupavati's sacrifice.**

The Rupavatiavadana, thirty-second in our collection reminds us rather of the legends in the Jatakamala. The heroine cuts off her breast to feed with her flesh and blood a starving woman who was about to eat up her child. In her, however, we see the Mahayana ideal of a Bodhisattva who when questioned as to the motive of her behaviour, replies :—

" Verily I sacrifice my breast for the sake of the child not that I may get kingdom or joys, not for heaven, not to become Indra, not to reign supreme over the world as its sole sovereign, but for no reason except that I may attain to supreme, complete, enlightenment in order that I may domesticate the untamed, liberate those that are not free, console those that are disconsolate and that I may conduct to complete Nirvana the unemancipated. As true as this resolve of mine is, may my womanly sex vanish and may I become a man." No sooner did she utter these words than she was transformed into a prince Rupavata who afterwards became king and reigned for 60 years.

In the same Kavya style as the Jatakamala there is the legend which is an artistic elaboration of the Maitrakanyaka Avadana in accordance with the tradition of the Avadanashataka of which it is the thirty-sixth story. In our *Divyavadana* it is the thirty-eighth. Extracts of this nature bring the collection of Divyavadana in harmony with the ordinary category of the Avadanamala literature.

**Kalpadruma-vadanamala.**

Poetic elaboration of avadana stories drawn partly from the Avadanashataka and partly from other sources is represented by the *Kalpadrumavadanamala* or the " Wishtree-avadana-garland," that is, a garland of avadanas which procures all desires; by the Ratnavadanamala or the " Precious stone-avadana-garland ;" and by the Asokavadanamala, or the " Avadana garland of king Asoka."

Feer p. xxiii ff.; Speyer p. xii ff., xxi ff.; Raj. Mitra, Nepalese Buddhist Literature, pp. 6 ff., 197 ff., 292 ff.; Bendall, Catalogue p. 110 ff. A legend from the Ratnavadanamala is translated by Mahendra Lal Das in the journal of the *Buddhist Text Society*, 1894, part 3.

**Unequivocal Mahayanism.**

The *Kalpadrumavadanamala* begins with an elaboration of the last story in the Avadanashataka. And just as in the latter the elder Upagupta appears carrying on a dialogue with king Asoka so all the legends in these Avadanamalas have been shaped in the form of conversations between Asoka and Upagupta. The Asokavadanamala in its first part contains legends of Asoka himself, then only follow religious instruction in the shape of historical narratives related by Upagupta to Asoka. Now all these three collections differ from the Avadanashataka not only in the circumstance that they have been cast entirely in epic *shlokas*, but especially in that they belong unequivocally to the Mahayana and in language and style remind one of the Puranas. Besides, they must belong also to the period which gave birth to the sectarian Puranas. It may be noted that as has been shown by Waddell (JASB proceedings, 1899, p. 70 ff.) Upagupta is only another name of Tissa Moggaliputta, the perceptor of Asoka. He is also a well-known celebrity in Pali literature.

Another collection which has liberally drawn upon the Avadanashataka is the *Dvavimshatyavadana* or the Avadana of the Twenty-two Sections. Here also Upagupta is represented as holding dialogues with Asoka, but they soon disappear from the stage and their place is occupied by Shakyamuni and Maitreya, the Buddha of the present period and the Buddha to come. But the legends here are related in prose and have been divided into sections in accordance with the morals inculcated by each. They deal with "acts of merit," "listening to sermons," "liberality," and so forth. The

*Bhadrakalavadana* is a collection of thirty-four legends which Upagupta relates to Asoka. Its title connects the advadanas with the age of virtue. It is similar to the Avadanamalas in that it is entirely in verse. But in plan and contents it bears a resemblance to the Mahavagga of the Pali *Vinayapitaka.*

Bendall Catalogue, p. 88 ff.; Feer xxix.; Raj. Mitra. p. 42 ff.; Speyer xxxvi.

According to S. d'Oldenburg who has translated the thirty-fourth story, which is another version of Jatakamala 31, corresponding to the Pali Jataka No. 537 (JRAS 1892, p. 331 ff.), the *Bhadra* is of a later date than Ksemendra who flourished about 1040 A.D.

**Miscellaneous Avadanas.**

Just as in the sectarian Puranas there are extensive chapters and sometimes entire independent works which are technically called Mahatmyas, of legendary import and generally invented to explain the origin of a festival or rite (vrata), so also we have a corresponding category of Buddhist texts. A collection of such legends is the *Vratavandamala* or " Garland of avandas on fasts and rites " which has nothing in common with the Avanda collection mentioned above except that it has the same framework,—dialogues between Upagupta and Asoka.

Raj. Mitra, pp. 102 ff., 22 ff., 231, 275 ff. Other texts of the same class are at pp. 229 f., 232 f., 265 ff., 269 ff., 280 ff.; L. Feer Suvarnavarana-avadanam et Vratavadanamala xii, Rome, 1899 I, p. 19 ff.

These are obviously very late Mahayana texts. A collection of a most variegated nature is the *Vicitrakarnikavadana* which has thirty-two stories, some of them derived from the Avadanashataka and others appertaining to the type of the Vratavadana. Mixed like the contents is also the language being now a barbarous Sanskrit, now Sanskrit verse, again Pali and so forth. ( Speyer, pp. xciii-c ). All these books are up to now only known in manuscript. But there are others which are accessible to us though only in their Tibetan and Chinese translations.

As regards avadana collections in Chinese, (see Feer xxx) the *Contes et Apologues Indiens* of Stanislas Julien, Paris, 1860, translated into German by Schnell, 1903, are of Chinese origin, ultimately going back to Sanskrit prime texts. But in our collections of manuscripts and in Chinese and Tibetan translations we have preserved to us not only anthologies of avadanas, but also several individual avadanas of extensive compass. For instance, the *Sumagadhavadana*, represents the legend of Sumagadha, the daughter of the famous merchant Anatha-pindada, who creates an aversion for the Jains in her husband and by a miracle converts the whole city to the religion of the Buddha. In one of her former births she was the daughter of the celebrated king Kriki, associated in legends with his wonderful dreams. These dreams have a wider significance than as affecting Sanskrit or even Buddhist literature. They belong to the literature of the world. (See Jataka No. 77 and S. d'Oldenburg in JRAS p. 509 ff., and Tsuru-Matsu Tokiwai Studies in Sumagadhavadana, Dissertation for the University of Strasburg, 1899; Raj. Mitra, p. 237.) It is remarkable that the same avadana is quoted from a Vinaya text in the *Abhidharmakosha Vyakhya* of Yashomitra. Finally, we have to make particular mention of the ponderous corpus of avadanas by the great Kashmirian Buddhist poet Kashemendra, who flourished about 1040 A.D. His work the *Avadana-Kalpalata* enjoys high reputation in Tibet.

**Avadanas in Chinese and Tibetan.**

The text with the Tibetan translation is edited in the Bibliotheca Indica series by Sarat Chandra Das and Hari Mohan Vidyabhusana. Kshemendra is a prolific writer and versifier of almost astounding fertility. We shall come across him more than once later on because he has occupied himself with various provinces of literature. However, he distinguishes himself less by his genius and taste than by his iron assiduity.

The great mass of legends into which Kshemendra works the Buddhist Avadanas in the style of the elegant poetry is more didactic than spiritual as regards the tales which he selects. The Buddhist propensity to self-sacrifice has been carried here to such refinement and to such a pitch and the doctrine of Karma has been inculcated with such extravagance and above all the moral is so thickly strewn over that it often overshoots the mark. The collection consists of 107 legends to which Somendra, the son of Kshemendra, added, besides an introduction, the one hundred and eighth tale of Jimutavahana. All these legends are mostly known to us either from other Avadana anthologies or otherwise. The Padmavati Avadana, for instance, is the story of Padmavati familiar to us in the Pali commentaries. The Ekashringa Avadana is the Rishyashringa legend so well known to us. They both occur also in the Mahavastu (NGGW, 1901 p. 26) and Luders has shown that Kshemendra has worked up this legend after the Mahavastu. The version by Kshemendra of this story has been reproduced in German verse by H. Francke.

## CHAPTER VII.

Mahayanasutras.

The entire Buddhist Sanskrit literature discussed up to now belongs to the borderland and the buffer state between the Hinayana and the Mahayana Buddhism. Now we turn to those works which stand decidedly on the Mahayana soil. There is no canon of the Mahayana, and there can be none because the Mahayana represen ts no unity of sects. We are indeed, informed of a council which is said to have been held under King Kaniska, but whether at this council any canon was established, and if so, in what language and by what sects, is left doubtful. The so-called "nine dharmas" are no canon of any sect, but a series of books which have been composed at different periods and belong to different persuasions, though all of them enjoy a high veneration in Nepal to-day. These nine works are:

Ashtasahasrika Prajnaparamita, Saddharmapundarika, Lalitavistara, Lankavatara, Suvarnaprabhasa, Gandavyuha, Tathagathaguhyaka Samadhiraja, Dashabhumishvara. All these scriptures are also designated Vaipulyasutras.

Worship of Books in Nepal.

The term dharma in the "nine dharmas" is no doubt an abbreviation for Dharmaparyaya or religious texts. A formal divine service is accorded to these nine books in Nepal, a bibliolatry which is characteristic of the Buddhism prevalent there and which is manifested in the body of the texts themselves.

Hodgson's Essays p. 13; Burnouf's Introduction p. 29 ff, 60 ff; Kern's der Buddhismus II 508 ff.

Saddharma-pundarika.

The most important and as a literary production of high value among the Mahayanasutras is the *Saddharmapundarika*, the "Lotus of the Good Law." It was translated into French as early as 1852 by Burnouf and in 1884 an English translation by Kern appeared in the Sacred Books of the East series. The Sanskrit text was edited at St. Petersburg in 1908 in the *Bibliotheca Buddica* series by the joint editors the Dutch scholar, Kern, and the Japanese professor, Bunyio Nanjio. Whoever desires to be acquainted with the Mahayana Buddhism with all its distinguishing features, with all its excellencies and shortcomings, may be recommended a study of these texts. Here very little remains of Shakyamuni as a man. The Buddha is properly speaking now higher than a god, above all the divinities, an immeasurably exalted Being, who has lived since countless æons and who will live for all eternity. "I am the father of the world," he says of himself (xv, Gatha 21), "who have sprung from myself (Svayambhu), the physician and the protector of all creatures; and only because I know how the fatuous are of perverted sense and blind that I, who have never ceased to exist, give myself out as departed." It is only because of his compassion for all creatures, his regard for the infirmities of human understanding, that he pretends to have entered Nirvana. He is comparable to the physician who had many sons and who once during their father's absence fell seriously ill. The father, on his return, treated them with medicaments, but only a few of them took the medicine, the others refusing it. In order to persuade even the latter to accept the treatment, the father goes out into a foreign country and pretends to be dead. The children, who now feel themselves orphans, take the prescribed physic and are healed. The Buddha has recourse to a similar stratagem when he apparently enters Nirvana, but again and again he emerges to proclaim his gospel. (Chapter xv, S B E 21, p. 304 ff). It is his evangel that connects him with humanity, but not like the Buddha of the Pali *sutras*, who roams about from place to place as a medicant friar to proclaim his doctrine, preaches the Buddha of the "Lotus." He takes up his stay on the Gridhrakuta peak among "a numerous assembly of monks and nuns and often still larger crowds of thousands of Buddhas and Bodhisattvas, of gods and demi-gods." And whenever he purposes "to shower down the mighty rain of religion, to sound the great drum of faith, to raise the lofty banner of faith, to kindle the illuminating torch of creed, to blow the powerful trumpet of religion, to beat the colossal kettle-drum of religion, a flash of light breaks forth from the circle of hair between his eyebrows which illuminates the eighteen thousand 'Buddha countries' with all the Buddhas and the creatures therein and reveals wondrous visions to the Bodhisattva Maitreya. For the Buddha of the "Lotus" is likewise a mighty sorcerer who loves by means of grand phantasmagoria to influence the minds of his audience. And thus diverging as is this Buddha from the one known to us in the ancient texts, so also deviates his doctrine from the Buddha of the Hinayana. True, it is his mission to conduct the creatures to "Buddha knowledge," to enlightenment. But he gives them a particular vehicle "the Buddha Vehicle," which leads them to the goal. Every living entity can become a Buddha that only listens to the sermon of the Buddha, that performs any deed of virtue, that leads a moral life. But even those who adore the relics, build *stupas*, or construct images of the Buddha of any kind whether of precious stone, marble, wooden statues or frescoes, and even children who set up stupas of sand while at play or scratch the lineaments of the Buddha on the wall, those who offer flowers or incense to the stupas or make music there,—nay, even such as have fortuitously thought of the Lord with the idea of "Veneration to the Buddha," every one of them attains to supreme illumination (chapter 2, Gathas 61 ff, 74 ff, SBE 21, p. 47 ff). The three "vehicles" are only apparent. They are all supposed to lead to Nirvana,—that of the disciple, that of the Pratyekabudhas and that of the Boddhisattvas. In reality, however, it is only the grace of the Buddha by which the one as well as the other reaches illumination and becomes Buddha. This tenet is elucidated with one of those charming parables which not seldom occur in the Saddharmapundarika.

**Parable of house on fire.**

In an old dilapidated house there lived a father with his children. Suddenly the house took fire. The father was in agony about his children. He was a strong man and could take up the younger ones in his arms and fly from the house, but the house had only one door. The children, who suspected nothing, were running about in play and took no heed of his warning. He was threatened with perishing along with his children in the surrounding fire. Now a sound idea occurred to him. Children always love toys, and he called out to them and said that he had all sorts of expensive toys, bullock-carts, tram carts, antelope carts, collected for them out of the house. No sooner did the children hear these words then they rushed out of doors and were saved. Now they asked of their father for the promised three kinds of toy carts and the father, being a wealthy man, gave them splendid and beautifully upholstered bullock-carts. The children were delighted and happy. Now who would accuse the father of falsehood in that he promised the children three kinds of ordinary play carts and gave them in reality carts of a most splendid description? Similarly the Buddha treats the children that are men, inducing them to come out by promise of the three "vehicles" from the burning and dilapidated house of this world, saves them and bestows upon them a unique vehicle, the costliest of all, the "Vehicle of the Buddha."

The Buddha is also represented in the Buddhist parable of the lost son as the good affluent father kindly disposed towards his sons, the human children :

Reclaimed son : a parable.

A rich man had an only son. He roamed about in foreign countries for fifty years, while the father was growing continually more wealthy and had become a great man. But the son lived in foreign lands impoverished and in straitened circumstances. At last he comes home as a beggar where his father was all this while longingly expecting him. The beggar son comes to the house of his father but he does not recognise his parent in the great man who, surrounded by a large retinue like a king, sits in the front of his mansion. As he sees the pomp and circumstance, he flies from the house in fear lest the beggar in tattered rags be maltreated. The father, however, immediately recognises him and sends out his servants to fetch the mendicant. Trembling and shaking with terror he is dragged along and falls down powerless. The father then gives orders to release him. The beggar stands up joyful and repairs towards the poor quarters of the city. Now the wealthy man bethinks himself of a plan to win the confidence of his son. He gets him oppressed with the meanest piece of work by the workmen in his house but takes opportunity frequently to associate with him and gradually worms himself into his confidence. Twenty years in this way pass by without the father being recognised by the son. When on the point of death he summons all his relations and announces that the beggar, who had become his confidential servant was his own son, and appoints him heir to all his estate. This wealthy man was the Buddha, the son that was lost and recovered are the human children who only very gradually draw themselves to the Buddha, the wise father, and finally acquire his fortunate legacy.

The Master is as frequently compared to a physician as to a loving father. The simile is especially expanded in which the children of the world are likened to those that are born blind and whose eyes are opened by the great physician Buddha (p. 129 ff.) That the Buddha knows no partiality but is to all equally a good father and physician is brought home by means of two charming metaphors. Just as a powerful rain cloud goes down caves and refreshes all grass, verdure and trees by its moisture and just as the latter sucked by the dryness of the earth blow into it new life, so also appears the Buddha in the world and renovates all creatures by bringing them the gift of peace. As the sun and the moon send down their rays equally on all, on the good and the wicked, on the high and the low, so the precepts of the Buddha are for the whole world (pp. 199 ff. 122 ff, 128 ff.)

**Figurative language.**

All these similes would be more beautiful if they were not carried out too extensively and extravagantly far so that the point of comparison suffers. But this hyperbole in the figurative language is quite characteristic of the book. It is an actual intoxication of words with which the reader is deadened, the thought being drowned in the inundation of verbiage. Still more immense and magnified than words are the figures. There lives, for instance, "a Buddha forty hundred thousand myriads of ten million æons, as many as there are grains of sand in the River Ganges"; and after he had attained to complete Nirvana, his true religion endured for a hundred thousand myriads of ten million ages equal to the number of ears of corns in all India; and a degenerated form of the true faith continued further for a thousand myriads of ten million ages equal to the number of the ears of corn in

**Exaggeration of phrase and figure.**

the four continents. And there arose one after another in the world "twenty hundred thousand myriads of ten million" such Buddhas (chap. xi, SBE, 21 text, pp. 376 f.355.) In the most extravagant fashion, beyond all limits of computation the Buddha is glorified, especially in the grandiose phantasmagoria of Chapter XIV in which, through the magical powers of the Buddha, the earth splits and suddenly appear from all sides many hundred thousand myriads of ten thousand Bodhisattvas each with a following as numerous as the aggregate grains of sixty Ganges streams. And while these innumerable Bodhisattvas pay homage to the Buddha fifty ages pass away during which a great silence rules but which through the supernatural power of the Lord appear only as an afternoon. To the astonished Maitreya the Buddha says that all these Bodhisattvas have been his disciples. Equally limitless and exaggerated is the adoration of the text itself. For, strangely enough, in the midst of our text there is the recurring mention of the preaching and the exposition of the book by the Buddha and its propagation by the preceptors. Thus in Chapter XI, Shakyamuni causes to appear in the air a *stupa* and from inside the stupa is heard a voice of a Buddha dead for myriads of ages;—"Excellent, excellent, exalted Shakyamuni, thou hast well uttered this sermon of the *Lotus of the good Religion*; yea, it is so, it is so, exalted, blessed Lord." Time and again the merit of the preacher of the *Lotus* and the faithful listeners of this exhortation is praised. It is cited in Chapter XXII.

**In praise of the Sutra.**

The sermon of the *Lotus* is like fire for those who are benumbed, like clothing to the naked, like a leader to the caravan, a mother to children, a boat to those who would cross the river, a taper for the dispelling of darkness. He who writes down this book or causes it to be written acquires endless merit. The female creature that hears it has lived for the last time as a female. He who listens to the sermon of the *Lotus* and declares his agreement with it shall always have a sweet breath as if issuing from a lotus and from his body will flow the fragrance of sandal.

**Persistence of Puranic influence.**

All this immoderation of language and especially the laudation of the text in the text itself are as peculiar to the Mahayana Sutras as to the Puranas. The Amitayurdhyana Sutra lays down: "When a person has committed much evil, but has not spoken ill of the great Vaipulya Sutras, and if he be a very stupid man, who neither feels reproach for his wicked deeds nor repents of them, but if he at the moment of his death encounters a good and wise preceptor who recites to him the superscription and titles of the twelve sections of the Mahayana texts, and if he has thus heard of all the Sutras. he will be absolved from the great sins which would otherwise hurl him into birth and death for thousands of ages." It is the spirit of the Puranas which is perceived in every line of the Saddharmapundarika. The few points of contact between the text of the Saddharmapundarika and that of the Shatapathabrahmana which Kern indicates by no means suffice to bring the work in line with the Vedic literature (SBE 21, p. xvi f.), and it is precisely on this count that the book cannot belong to the earliest period of Buddhism. If we did not know that it had already been translated into Chinese between 255 and 316 A.D., we should not consider it as so ancient, for the latter date must at least be its age.

**Elements of diverse epochs.**

At all events, however, the book contains elements of diverse periods. It is impossible that the Sanskrit prose and the gathas in "mixed Sanskrit" should have arisen contemporaneously, even if they did not incorporate often glaring inconsistency of contents. Frequently in the prose passages as also in the *gathas* the book is spoken of as a metrical composition. It is probable that originally the book consisted only of verse with brief prose passages interspersed by way of introduction and links between the verses. These brief prose paragraphs were subsequently expanded especially as the dialect of the verse gradually became obsolete. And, without being exactly commentary, they came to serve as an exposition. It is remarkable that just those chapters which contain no gathas prove even on other grounds to be rather accretions. These chapters, from xxi to xxvi, are more devoted to the panegyric of the Bodhisattvas while the Sadharmapundarika in the rest of the texts sings the glorification of the Buddha Shakyamuni. One of these Bodhisattvas is Bhaisajyaraja, the prince of the Physician's art who, in xxi chapter reveals magical formulæ and exorcisms (Dharanis) and in chapter xxii, after he has for twelve years fed on fragrant substance and drunk oil, covers himself in finest clothing, has an oil bath and burns himself. For twelve thousand years his body burns without cessation, and this grand sacrifice and glorious firework has the only object of showing respect to the Buddha and to the Sadharmapundarika! The xxivth chapter is devoted to the Bodhisattva Avalokiteshvara, a great redeemer. He who invokes him is free from every danger. The sword of the executioner breaks to pieces when the person condemned to death offers supplication to him. All fetters are loosened, only if his name is pronounced. He saves the shipwrecked and the caravans overtaken by robbers. A woman who desires a son or a beautiful daughter has only to invoke Avalokiteshvara and her wish is fulfilled. This chapter also contains a large gatha extract to the glorification of Avalokiteshvara, but this too is a late addition. For all the gathas are not older than the prose, many being interpolated at subsequent periods. (Kern SBE 21 p. xviii f). The ancient Chinese translation contains doubtless chapters xxi-xxvi, but in an order different from that of our Sanskrit text. This shows that the *parishishtas* or appendices were not appertaining originally to the work.

**Age of the Sutra.**

Although, however, the Sadharmapundarika represents later and earlier ingredients it displays a much greater unity of character than either the Mahavastu or the Lalitavistara. It is not possible that the older and the younger components should be separated by any extensive lapse of time. If the book had assumed its present compass between 265 and 316 A.D., when the first Chinese translation was prepared or even earlier, in its primary formation it must have well arisen about 200 A.D. Even Kern, who strives to establish that the Sadharmapundarika and the Lalitavistara have preserved materials going back to the most ancient period of Buddhism, has been able to cite instances only from the Lalitavistara. There is no ground for asserting that the older text saw the light "a few centuries earlier," as Kern assumes (p. xxii). Bendall ascribes to the fourth or fifth century a manuscript of the Sadharmapundarika discovered by him (JRAS 1901, p. 124). Fragments of the Sadharmapundarika have been discovered also in Central Asia during the explorations by Stein and others (J.R.A.S. 1911, p. 1067 ff). One fact is incontestable. The entire Sadharmapundarika, prose and gatha, presupposes a high development of the Mahayana Buddhism, especially in the direction of Buddha-bhakti, the adoration of relics, the worshipping of images and, above all, a highly flourishing epoch of Buddhist art. For, when there is such prominent mention of thousands of myriads of ten millions of stupas, which were erected for the relics of a Buddha or of the ten millions of *viharas*, which are delineated as magnificent buildings, most luxuriously furnished there must have existed at least several hundreds of stupas and viharas, *topes* and monasteries, and these were doubtless embellished with images of the Buddha in precious stones, with statues of the Buddha carved in wood or metal and with reliefs and frescoes.

See especially chapter ii, Gathas 77 ff., SBE. In Japan the Sadharma-pundarika is the sacred book of the Nichi-ren sect, Buniyu Nanjio, Short History of the Twelve Buddhist Sects, Tokyo, 1886, p. 132 ff.

**Karandavyuha: its Theistic tendency.**

To the Bodhisattva Avalokiteshvara who has been eulogised in Chapter XXIV of the Sadharma-pundarika is also dedicated an entire Mahayanasutra of great compass, the full title of which is Avalokiteshvara-gunakarandavyuha,—"The exhaustive description of the basket of the merits of the Avalokiteshvara." The title is usually mentioned in its abbreviated shape of *Rarandavyuha.* We have two versions of this book, the more ancient one being in prose and the younger in *shlokas.* The prose text was edited by Satyavrata Shamashrami in 1873. The catalogue of the India Office, library registers, an edition which seems to have appeared in 1872 at Serampore.

Burnouf, Introduction pp. 196-206; Raj. Mitra, Nep. Buddh. Lit., p. 95 ff Bendall, Catalogue p. 9 ff; La Vallee Poussin, ERE II, p. 259 f.

The metrical recension occupies theistic ground. For it is related how at the beginning of things appeared the Adibuddha or the primitive Buddha, also called Svayambhu, or Self-Being and Adinatha or the First Lord, and created the world by his meditation. Avalokiteshvara is derived from this spirit and he co-operated in the creation of the world fashioning from his eyes the moon and the sun, Maheshvara from his forehead, Brahman from his shoulders, Narayana from his heart, and from his teeth the goddess of speech Sarasvati. Precisely as this introduction is of the Puranic kind, so also are the language and style of the metrical *Karandavyuha* totally of the younger Puranas. We have no evidence that the theistic Buddhism with its Adibuddha as a creator existed in India, prior to the tenth century. Even La Vallee Poussin only demonstrates that the creed of Adibuddha was spread over India but not that it can be proved to have existed in ancient times. (ERE, I. p. 95). Further, the fact that the Tibetan translation which was made probably in 1616 A.D. and which is found in the Kanjur and is based on the prose version, which does not contain the Adibuddha section, shows that the poetic version was then unknown. (La Vallee Poussin, ERE, II, p. 259). On the other hand, the cult of Avalokiteshvara is already familiar to the Chinese pilgrim Fah-ien, about 400 A.D. He himself implores this Bodhisattva for rescue when he is overtaken by a storm on his voyage from Ceylon to China. The oldest images of Avalokiteshvara date from the fifth century. A Chinese translation of a *Karandavyuha* was made as early as 270 A.D.

L. A. Waddell, JRAS, 1894, p. 57; A. Foucher, Etude sur l'Iconographic Boudhique de l'Inde, Paris 1900, p. 97 ff., and La Vallee Poussin, ERE II. p. 256 ff.; Buniyo Nanjio, Catalogue No. 168 where the title is given as Ratnakaranda-kavyuhasutra. A second translation was made between 420 and 479.

**Potency of Avalokiteshvara.**

The basic idea is the same in both the versions of the Karandavyuha— the exaltation of the marvellous redeemer Avalokiteshvara, "the Lord looking down," that is, he who surveys with infinite compassion all the creatures. This interpretation is found in the text itself (Burnouf, Introduction, p. 201 f.), but it is possible to explain the name in other ways (La Vallee Poussin, ERE, II, p. 201 f.).

Avalokiteshvara here appears as a typical Bodhisattva but declines to enter into Buddha-hood so long as all the creatures have not been emancipated. To bring salvation to all creatures, to succour all the sorrowing, to save all from want, to exercise unbounded commiseration which does not recoil from sin, and does not stop short at the gates of hell, this is the one and the only obligation of the Avalokiteshvara. Words are placed in the mouth of Avalokiteshvara to the effect that it is better for a Bodhisattva to commit sins in the exercise of sympathy, to suffer in hell, rather than to disappoint a creature of the hopes centred by the latter in him (ERE, II, p. 257 f.). The opening chapter of the *Karandavyuha* portrays how he descends into the fireful Avici (hell) in order to set free the tormented from their pain. No sooner does he enter it, than the scorching glow turns into agreeable coolness; in place of the cauldrons in which millions of the damned are boiling like vegetable, there appears a lovely Lotus Pond. The seat of torture is transformed into a pleasance.

E. B. Cowell, Journal of Philology, vi, 1876. p. 222 ff., reprinted also in Ind Ant., viii, 249 ff. L. Scherman, the Vision Literature, p. 62 ff. Cowell compares the apocryphal gospel of Nicodemus and derives the Indian from the Christian legend.

**His peregrinations.**

From this hell Avalokiteshvara passes on to the abode of the Pretas and treats with food and drink these ghosts writhing with everlasting hunger and thirst. One of his wanderings takes him to Ceylon where he converts the cannibal female giant Rakshasi, from thence to Benares where he preaches the doctrine to the creatures who have been born as insects and worms, and thence to Magadha where he saves the inhabitants in a miraculous way from a terrible famine. In Ceylon he appears as the winged horse Balaha in order to carry away and save from perishing the ship-wrecked persons enticed by the giant sorceress.

Jataka No. 196, where the winged charger is identified with the Buddha in a previous birth. In the Karandavyuha the merchant Simhala carried off to Ceylon is the Buddha Shakyamuni in an earlier existence.

Little as is the claim of books like the Karandavyuha upon our attention, on the whole we are bound to concede that hardly anywhere else human helplessness and longing for emancipation have found a more vigorous expression than in these tracts and the idea of redemption a finer instrumentality than in the personation of Avalokiteshvara.

**Sukhavativyuha: the Land of Bliss.**

The Buddhist's longing for spiritual liberation finds a more logical outlet in the *Sukhavativyuha a* detailed description of the Land of Bliss. As the Saddharmapundarika serves to glorify the Buddha Shakyamuni, as the Karandavyuha is dedicated to the Bodhisattva Avalokiteshvara, so the Sukhavativyuha is sacred to the panegyric of the Buddha Amitabha. Among the innumerable Buddhas there is one who, by means of prayers or *pranidhana* in a former life faithfully practising the virtues of a Bodhisattva for untold ages, was born again in the world of Sukhavati in the Occident. There he produces boundless light, whence his name Amitabha; and immeasurable is the duration of his life, whence his other name, Amitayus. In this "Buddha country," the Paradise of Sukhavati, there is no hell, there is no existence as beasts, Pretas, or Asuras. This blessed land is filled with infinite fragrance. There grow trees of precious stones in many hundred thousand colours and equally marvellous lotus flowers. There are no mountains there but the land is a plain like the palm of the hand. Charming rivulets supply lovely sweet water and their splashing makes the most lovely music. The creatures that are born in Sukhavati are provided with the most fascinating qualities of body and mind and enjoy all the delights which they have only to wish for. There is no difference between men and gods. There is no such thing as day or night. There is no darkness. Amitabha is continuously praised and he who constantly thinks in reverence of him, he who bethinks himself of the growth of his good deeds, he who turns his thoughts to enlightenment, and he who devoutly prays to be born in that world, to him Amitabha appears in the hour of his death and the aspirant sees the light again in the Land of Bliss. Nay, even those who think of Amitabha with a single thought are born there. But the creatures in Sukhavati are not born of woman. They come into being seated on lotus flowers when they have firmly believed in Amitabha or as adhering to the chalice of a lotus when their faith is not sufficiently firm. Joyous and tranquil, perfectly wise and immaculate live the creatures in that world of benignity. With that extravagance of language and exaggeration of figures which are come across in Mahayanasutras is also described the grandeur of Amitabha and his paradise in the *Sukhavativyuha.*

Of this book we have two diverse recensions. The longer one which might well be the original and the shorter one which appears to be an abbreviated edition of the former with an emended introduction. Both versions have been edited by Max Muller, and Bunyiu Nanjio in the Anecdota Oxoniensia Aryan Series, Vol. I, part II, Oxford, 1883, and translated by Max Muller SBE vol. 49, part 2. A third book called the *Amitayurdhanasutra* is less occupied with the picture of the country of Sukhavati than with the exhortations to meditation or *dhyana* of Amtayus by means of which a man attains to the Blessed Land. It is translated from Chinese by J.Takakusu in SBE Vol. 49, part 2, p. 159 ff. This Sutra is unfortunately not preserved to us in the original Sanskrit, but only in a Chinese translation and is interesting in that it contains the history of Ajatashatru and Bimbisara known also in the Pali accounts. Kern, Der Buddhismus I, 243 ff, Spence Hardy, Manual of Buddhism, London, 1860, p. 317 f). A Sukhavativyuha is reported to have been translated into Chinese between 148 and 170 and there are no less than twelve versions of it dating from different centuries. In 402, Kumarajiva translated the shorter version. A translation of the Sukhavativyuha-Sutra is also credited to Hiuen-Tsiang in 1650 A.D. (Nanjio, Catalogue Nos. 23, 25, 27, 199, 200, 863). This testifies to the favour in which the text was held in China. In Japan, however, the three texts relating to Amitayus and Sukhavati form the fundaments of the doctrine of the two Buddhistic sects of Jodoshu and Shinshu. The latter has the largest number of adherents of any Buddhist sect in Japan. It is to be noted that the literary value of these texts by no means corresponds to their importance in religious history.

B. Nanjio, Twelve Japanese Buddhist Sects pp. 104 ff., 122 ff, and Anecdota Oxoniensia, Vol. I, p. xviii ff. H Hass, Amida Buddha, our Refuge, Texts for the understanding of Sukhavati-Buddhism, Leipzig 1910.

**Manjushri.**

In the cult and in the art of the Buddhist the Bodhisattva Manjushri occupies a distinguished position along with Avalokiteshvara. In the *Gandavyuha*, Manjushri is glorified as the only one who can help the aspirant to perfect enlightenment. This work is only available in manuscript. It was translated into Chinese between 317 and 420 under the title of Avatamsakasutra or Buddha-vatamsakasutra and is the cardinal text-book of the Japanese Buddhist sect Ke-gon.

Raj. Mitra Nep. Euddh. Lit., p. 90 ff; Bendall Catalogue, p. 23. According to Hodgson's Essays, p. 16 (also see p. 49) Aryasanga was the author of this book; compare also Burnouf Introduction, p. 111.

It is Professor Takakusu who informs us that the Gandavyuha is identical with the Chinese Avatamsaka for he has made a comparison of the Sanskrit with the Chinese original.

See Wassiljew, *Der Buddhismus,* p. 171 ff, and B. Nanjio, *Twelve Japanese Bundhist Sects,* p. 57 ff. The Ganavyuhasutra No. 971 in B. Nanjio' Catalogue (see No. 782) translated between 746-771 is altogether a different work.

**Karunapundarika Sutra.**

The Sutra, which has many points of contact with the Sukhavativyuha but which has also many legends of the class of Avadanas, is the *Karunapundarika*, the Lotus of Compassion. It relates to the marvellous country of Padma where the Buddha Padmottara worked and whose life was thirty world-periods. The Sutra was translated into Chinese in the sixth century.

Raj. Mitra, p. 285 ff; Bendall Catalogue, p. 73 Sylvain Levi has discovered and published a legend from the Karunapundarika in the Tokharain language (Memorial volume to Vihelm Thomsen, Leipzic, p. 155 ff.).

**Lankavatara.**

While these Mahayanasutras are devoted mainly to the cult of the Buddhas and Bodhisattvas whose wonderful qualities and mighty deeds are eulogised or legends in connection with whom are recounted, there is a series of Sutras in Buddhist Sanskrit which partake more of a philosophical or dogmatic character. Of this nature is the *Lankavatara*, or as it is also called Saddharmalankavatara. The book gives a report of the miraculous visit of the Buddha Shakyamuni to Ravana, the King of Ceylon. Ravana pays his reverence to the Buddha and presses him for a reply to a number of his enquiries touching the religion. The answers given by the Buddha which represent the doctrine of the Yogacara school go to form the main contents of the ten chapters of the Sutra. It is, moreover, interesting inasmuch as it explores the tenets of the Samkhyas. Vaishesikas, Pashupatas and other philosophical schools and religious denominations of Brahmanic origin. Remarkable is a prophetic passage in chapter 10 where the Buddha says :—

" A hundred years after my Nirvana will live Vyasa, the composer of the Mahabharata. Then will arise the Pandavas, Kauravas, Nandas and Mauryas. The Nandas, Mauryas, Guptas and Mlecchas, the most degraded of princes, will be the rulers. The domination of the barbarians will be succeeded by an upheaval which in its turn will herald the Kaliyuga."

The teaching of the Yogacara school is the same as the doctrine of Asanga and the same precepts are found in the *Mahayansahraddhotpada*.

The mention of the barbarians can only refer to the reign of the Hun princes, Toramana and Mihirakula, and consequently the book must have been composed in the beginning of the sixth century. But as again a Chinse translation of the Lankavatara had already been made in 443, the excerpt must belong to a subsequent recension or can only be an interpolation.

Burnouf Introduction, p. 458 ff; Bendall Catalogue, p. 20 fl.; S. Ch Vidyabhusana; An Analysis of the Lankavtara Sutra, JASB 1905, ff : Raj. Mitra Nep. Buddh. Lit, p. 113 f, where, however, the statement about a Chinese translation made in 168-190 is incorrect. See Bunyiu Nanjio Catalogue Nos. 175-177. Of the same species of literature is also Dasabhumis. wara Mahayanasutra in which the Buddha holds an exhortation to the gods in Indras' heaven on the ten stages, the "dashabhumi", through which an entity arrives at Budhahood. This Sutra was translated into Chinese in 400 Raj Mitra Nep. Buddh. Lit., p. 81 ff., Bendall Catalogue p. 4 f.

Samadhiraja.

Of a dogmatic nature is also the *Samadhiraja*, the *King of Meditations*. It is a dialogue between Candraprabha and the Buddha. It is shown here how the Bodhisattva by means of the diverse meditations, especially the supreme one, the sovereign meditation, can achieve transcendent knowledge of the conditions which are necessary for the preparation of the mind for the loftiest stage of thought. The conditions are veneration of the Buddhas; absolute renunciation of the world; gentleness and benevolence to all creatures; complete indifference with reference to one's own life and health; in the case of necessity, sacrifice for others; and finally the conviction of the non-reality of the world or firm faith in the universal Void or *Shunyata*. When meditating on the form of the Buddha the candidate must not think of any corporeal shape because the Buddha is composed of pure religion, he is not procreated, he is effect without cause, he is the cause of all things and without beginning, of boundless greatness and illimitable beneficence. The same ideas recur repeatedly, in between there being legends of holy men who propounded the great Samadhi.

Raj. Mitra Nep. Buddh. Lit., 297-221, Bendall Catalogue, p. 22 f.

Suvarnaprabhasa Sutra.

Based from the standpoint of negativism or Shunyatavada is likewise *Suvarnaprabhasa* or Golden Effulgence, the contents of which are partly philosophical, partly legendary and partly digress into the region of Tantra-Buddhism. The Buddha is here an eternal divine Being. A Brahman asks for a relic of the Buddha, be it no bigger than a mustard seed (chapter II). But he is instructed that it is easier to have hair grown on the back of a tortoise than to find such a relic.

For the Buddha is not really born but his true corporeal frame is the Dharmakaya or Dharmadhatu, that is, an immaterial body consisting only of religion.

According to Suzuki's Ashvaghosha's Discourse on the Awakening of the Faith, p. 62 n. Dharmakaya denotes the Absolute.

Nor did the Buddha enter Nirvana, his body being eternal. A large portion of the Sutra is occupied with the glorification of the Sutra itself. In chapter VIII appears the goddess Sarasvati, in chapter IX Mahadevi, the consort of Shiva, to belaud the Sutra. Among the legends which we find related in the *Surarnapyabhasa* we encounter that of the prince who kills himself to serve as food to a starving tigress and the father of the prince preserves his bones in a golden casket over which to erect a *stupa.* There is, however, also a recital of magical terms or Dharanis and Tantra-ritual in the book. On the whole we see a diction the most sluggish among sectarian Puranas and one would wonder how the *Golden Effulgence* had acquired such immense reputation among the Buddhists of Nepal, Tibet and Mongolia, if the people concerned were not of comparatively a low state of culture. The Sutra was translated into Chinese in the sixth century.

Burnouf Introduction, p 471 ff.; Raj. Mitra Nep. Buddh. Lit. p. 241 ff.; Bendall Catalogue, p. 12 f.; M. Anesaki, ERE IV, p. 839. According to La Vallee Poussin Bouddhisme, Etudes and Mateiiaux, p. 127, the Suvarnaprabhasa is nothing but a Mahatmya of Dharanis. A fragment of the Suvarnaprabhasa, which is also quoted in the Siksasamuccaya Bendall, p.160 ff., has been published by H, Stonner from a zylograph discovered at Idikutshari (SBA 1904 p. 1810 ff.)

**Rashtrapala Sutra.**

Partly dogmatic and partly legendary in nature is the Rashtrapalasutra, also entitled *Rashtrapalapariprucchа,* which was translated into Chinese between 589-618. The Sutra consists of two portions, the first of which is more of a dogmatic nature and contains the responses of the Buddha to Rashtrapala's questions on the qualities or Dharmas of a Bodhisattva. The second part narrates the Jataka of the prince Punyarashmi whose story has some features in common with the legend of the Buddha. But even in the first portion the Buddha briefly narrates his deeds in previous births to elucidate the Bodhisattva Dharmas and in the course of his address makes mention of fifty Jatakas. At the end of these Jatakas there is an abrupt prophesy on the future decay of the religion which is the most important section of the Sutra. For the picture sketched here so vividly and with such precision could only be a reflection of actual facts and must be a satirical portrayal of the lax morals of the Buddhist monks, since we are told, for instance :

**Prevision of degeneracy.**

" Without self-reproach and without virtue, proud, puffed up, irritable will be my monks; intoxicated with spirituous liquor. While they grasp the banner of the Buddha they will only serve men of the world, and they will have to themselves, like householders, wives, sons and daughters. They will not eschew lust so that they may not be born as beasts, spirits and denizens of hell. They will address homilies to fathers of families but will remain themselves unbridled. "

Rastrapalaparipruccha, the Sutra of the Mahayana, published by L. Finot Bib. Budd, II, St. Petersburg 1901; La Vallee Poussin "Le Museon" IV, 1903, p. 3 6 ff. With the Pali Ratthapalasutra our Sutra has nothing in common except the name Rashtrapala in Pali Ratthapala.

There must have been an entire class of such Pariprucchas or questions among the Mahayanasutras like the Puranapariprucchha and so forth ; Nanjio Catalogue, p. xiii ff. Finot, p. ix ff. 28 ff.

This vaticination of corrupt monasticism reminds us of a similar one in the Pali Theragatha. And the Chinese translation of the Rastrapalaparipruccha made between 589 and 618 shows that the circumstances depicted here must have arisen already in the sixth century. But the Sutra cannot be much older than the Chinese translation as is evidenced by the barbarous language, especially in the gathas, which is an intermingling of Prakrit and bad Sanskrit, the artificial meter and the untidy style.

The most important and the most reputed of all the "philosophic" Mahayanasutras are the *Prajnaparamitas*, sutras of perfection of wisdom. They treat of six perfections (paramitas) of a Bodhisatva, but particularly of the *Prajna* or wisdom the supreme excellence. This wisdom, however, consists in the recognition of the *Shunva vada* or negativism which declares everything as "void", denies Being as well as non-Being and has for a reply to every question a "No". It is believed to have been at first a sutra of one hundred and twenty-five thousand shlokas in which this wisdom was inculcated in the shape of dialogues in which the Buddha was the principal speaker. Subsequently this sutra was abbreviated into a hundred thousand, twenty-five thousand, ten thousand, and lastly eight thousand shlokas. According to another tradition the sutra with eight thousand shlokas was the original, it being subsequently gradually expanded. As a matter of fact, we are acquainted with Prajnaparamitas of a hundred thousand, of twenty-five thousand, of eight thousand, of two thousand five hundred and of seven hundred shlokas. In the Mahayana often as in the Hinayana there is mention of ten but more frequently of six paramitas, *viz.*, generosity performance of duty, gentleness, intrepidity, meditation and wisdom. (Dharmasamgrasa 17.)

(The Prajnaparamitas are prose works but in India it is customary to measure even texts in prose by shlokas each unit consisting of thirty-two syllables.)

(The Tibetan Sher-phyin is a literal translation of the Shatasahasrika which has been quoted as Bhagavati in the Shikshasamuccaya. It was translated into Chinese between 402 and 405 according to Anesaki (Le Museon VII, 1906). This translation contains quotations from Pali texts (Bendall C. pp. 143-148 and JRAS 1898 p. 370.)

The senseless customs of embodying constant repetitions which we find so annoying in the Pali suttas becomes in the voluminous Prajnaparamitas so limitless and excessive that it would be quite possible to strike out more than half of these collossal works like the Shatasahasrika for the same sentences and phrases recur times without number. Thus, for instance, it is not only said in the introduction that out of the whole body of the Buddha rays of light break forth and an immeasurable effulgence is spread over the entire world; but it is repeated of his teeth, bones, of each member and particle of his body that rays of light issue from them to the east, the west and so on, and in the case of each cardinal point the entire description is repeated. It is not enough for these writers to say that "everything is only name"; but this everything is detailed to exhaustion in interminable series of sentences. It is conceivable that men should entertain the philosophical view that the world is not a reality and that all is negation and that man is unable to express any verdict on any question except in the shape of a negative; but that people should from this standpoint offer universal denial and write book after book and thousands of pages might appear impossible. But this impossibility is materialised in the Prajnaparamitas. This extravagance for the sake of extravagance is explained by the supposition that the monks scribbled so much because it was with them a religious merit to transcribe as much as possible of these sacred books and to write out of them to the same extent. The same principle reiteration manifests itself in Buddhistic art. Entire vast surfaces of rocks and caves are covered with the images of the Buddha. As regards the contents of these treatises the essential doctrine in the Hundred Thousand Prajnaparamitas is the same as in the Vajracchedika Prajnaparamita. The latter resembles considerable in form the Hinayana sutra. It consists of a few pages in which the doctrine of these texts is condensed. As in the voluminous Prajnaparamitas here also it takes the form of a dialogue between the Buddha and Subhuti. The Shunyata doctrine is not explored and no attempt is made to inculcate it; but it is simply repeatedly stated. There is no pretence at argument. Starting from the ancient Buddhist dogma of the non-Ego here not only the Ego but everything else is denied,—even the doctrine of the Buddha and the Buddha himself. This we read in the Vajracchedika (Ch. 13.)

The Vajraçchedika has been edited by Max Muller and translated by him in the SBE. For Stein Fragments in Khotan see JRAS 1903. It was translated into French by Harlez (JA 1891). The same scholar printed and translated the Manchu version (WZKM 1897). It was translated into Chinese about 401. In Japan the Vajracchedika and the Prajnaparamitahrdaya are the chief texts of the Shingon sects. In the Prajnaparamitahrdaya metaphysics degenerate into magical formulæ. Fragments of the Vajracchedika in a north Aryan translation and a Adhyardhashatika Prajnaparamita in a Sanskrit recension with sections in the north Aryan have been made known to us from Central Asia by Leumann.

There are no doubt as many non-Buddhist readers who see in utterances like those of Ch. 13 profound sense as those who see nothing but nonsense in it. As a matter of fact it need not be either one or the other, but just that "middle doctrine" which proceeds in paradoxes in that it on one hand asserts nihilism in the strictest sense of the word and on the other so far recognises the phenomenal world as to admit the relative truth of things and the doctrine becomes comparatively intelligible only by the assumption of a dual nature of verity, a superior and an inferior one as has been clearly and significantly taught by Nagarjuna. It may be noted that among those who are the least enthusiastic about this phase of Buddhism is Barth who declares (RHR 1882) that "la sagesse transcendante, qui sait, qu'il n'y a ni choses existantes ni non-existantes, ni de realite qui ne soit aussi une non-realite, sagesse qu'ont proclammée et proclameront des infinites de myriades d'arhats et de bodhisatvas qui ont été et n'ont pas été, qui seront et ne seront pas; qui, grace a sa science de Buddha, a sa vue de Buddha, sont percus, apercus, connus du Buddha, lequel luimeme, n'est ni existant ni non-existant."

## CHAPTER VIII.

Nagarjuna.

The adherents of the Hinayana proclain the Prajnaparamita in a hundred thousand slokas to be the latest Mahayanasutra and attribute its authorship to Nagarjuna. The authority for this is Taranatha, the Tibetan historian (p. 71), whose work has been translated from the Tibetan by Scheifner. So far the tradition may be correct in that it is an apocryphal Sutra issuing from the school of Nagarjuna, for it consists, like all Prajnaparamitas, only of innumerable repetitions of the principles of the Madhyamika system founded by Nagarjuna. What appears in the dialogues of those Sutras as somewhat abstruse and confused is expressed systematically and with lucid clarity in the Madhyamakakarikas or Madhyamikaṣutras of Nagarjuna. This principal work of Nagarjuna, with the commentary by Chandrakirti called Prasannapada, was published by L. de La Vallee Poussin, in the St. Petersburgh Bibliotheca Buddhica, in 1903, and the twenty-fourth chapter of the commentary has been translated by the same Belgian scholar in the Mélanges Le Charles de Harlez. The Madhyamakakarika is a systematic philosophical work of the class with which we have been familiar in Brahmanic scientific literature. It is in a metrical form to help the memory. It is composed as Karikas to which the author himself usually appends his own scholia. Now the commentary composed by Nagarjuna himself to his work and the title of which we know to be *Akutobhaya* is no longer extant in Sanskrit but is known to us only in a Tibetan translation. This valuable scholia has been translated from the Tibetan by Max Walleser. Both the old commentaries of Buddhapalita and Bhavaviveka are preserved only in the Tibetan Tanjur. Candrakirti's Madhyamakavatara is also preserved no where except in the Tanjur. It is a prolegomena not only to the Madhyamika system but to the Mahayana philosophy in general. This too has been made accessible to us by La Vallee Poussin in his French version from the Tibetan (Le Museon, viii, 1907, 249 ff. ; xi, 1910, 271 ff.) The Sanskrit commentary on the Madhyamikasutra, which we possess, is the one by Candrakirti who probably lived in the first half of the seventh century. Candrakirti and Candragomi were contemporaries and rivals. Candragomi was a disciple of Sthiramati who flourished at the close of the sixth century. A contemporary of Sthiramati was Dharmapala. A disciple of the latter knew Candrakirti, while Bhavaviveka, the contemporary of Dharmapala, has been quoted by Candrakirti (N. Peri La vie de Vasubandhu, Extrait du BEFEO). According to S. Ch. Vidyabhusana (Journal of the Buddhist Text Society, v, 1897) Candrakirti, however, was a contemporary of Sankara. It is also from these philosophical Sutras that we first come to know its doctrine which, originating with the denial of the soul taught in the Theravada school, came to repudiate both Being and non-Being and is, therefore, designated the Middle Doctrine.

**Vindication of Middle doctrine.**

In this treatise the natural objection is placed in the mouth of the opponents of Negativism: If all is "void" and if there is no beginning and no end, then there could possibly be no four "noble truths," no conduct of life on the principles of recognition of these verities, no fruit of good or bad deeds, no doctrine of the Buddha (Dharma), no monastic order and, finally, no Buddha himself. Accordingly the entire system of the Buddha's religion should fall to the ground. To this Nagarjuna replies :—

"The doctrine of the Buddha is based on two verities—conventional truth, in which the profound sense is occult, and truth in the supreme sense. Whoso does not know the difference between these two truths does not understand the deep contents of the Buddha's precepts. Only as based on the truth of ordinary life can the supreme verity be inculcated and only with the help of the latter can Nirvana be attained." We see, indeed, no other possibility of reducing to sense many a passage of the Prajnaparamitas which strikes us as meaningless or preposterous except on the basis of its accommodating itself in the history of philosophy to the not unknown assumption of a two-fold truth. Vallee Poussin gives us a sound presentment of this Madhyamika doctrine in his "Buddhism" (pp. 189 ff., 290 ff. See also Anesaki, ERE, iv, p. 838.).

**Other works attributed to Nagarjuna.**

Besides Madhyamakakarikas, many other works are attributed to Nagarjuna, whether rightly or wrongly we are no longer able to decide. *Dharmasamgropha* passes for his production. It is a small dictionary of Bhuddist technical terms and the original Sanskrit text has been preserved to us. It is edited by Kenjiu Kasawara, Max Muller and H Wenzel. It is to be noted that half of the termini of this Dharmasamgraha also occur in the Dharmasarirasutra which was discovered in the sands of Central Asia by Grunwedel and which has been published by Stonner (SBA, 1904, p. 1282 ff.). On the other hand, the *Suhrllekha* or the "Friendly epistle"—a letter from Nagarjuna to a king on the basic principles of the Buddhist religion in one hundred and twenty-three verses—is known to us only in an English translation from the Tibetan version, the original Sanskrit having perished. (Wenzel in JPTS, 1886, p. 1 ff.). Unfortunately we cannot determine who this king was to whom the epistle is addressed although, according to our Chinese sources, it was Satavahana, while the Tibetans call him Udayana. It is noteworthy that the missive contains nothing which might not also appear in the Pali canon, while its several verses coincide verbally with the Pali Dhammapada and similar texts. Many slokas are in harmony with well-known Brahmanic proverbs. The Chinese pilgrim I-Tsing highly extols this work of Nagarjuna and bears witness to its being widely read and learnt by heart in India in his days (Takakusu p. 158 ff.). The first Chinese translation of the epistle dates from 431 A.D. I-Tsing himself prepared a Chinese version of the epistle of Nagarjuna which he despatched from India to a friend in China. ( Op. cit. p. 166. ).

**Nagarjuna's life.**

According to the biography of Nagarjuna translated into Chinese in 405 by Kumarajiva, this Hindu master of Chinese was born in Southern India in a Brahman family. He studied the four Vedas and acquired all the sciences. He had, however, the reputation of being likewise a great wizard. By means of his sorcery he could make himself invisible and intruded himself, followed by three companions into the royal palace, where they offended the ladies of the harem. They were discovered, the three colleagues of Nagarjuna were executed and he himself escaped by just previously having vowed to become a monk. He redeemed the pledge, in ninety days studied all the three *Pitakas* and mastered their meaning but was not satisfied with the same and commenced to search for other Sutras till finally he received the Mahayanasutra from a venerable hermit in the Himalayas. With the assistance of Nagaraja, the sovereign Serpent, he also came by a commentary on the Sutra. He energetically propagated Buddhism in Southern India. His biographer would have us believe that he was at the head of the religious propaganda for over three hundred years (Wassiljew, p. 232 ff.). The Tibetans, however, are still more extravagant, and make him six hundred years old when he died. Of these legends themselves much can be true ; Nagarjuna, just like the somewhat earlier Ashvagosha, came of a Brahmin origin. Very probably Nagarjuna lived at the close of the second Christian century. Our authorities are Rajatarangini (/ – 173), Kern ( Manual of Buddhism, 122 ff. ). and Jacobi (JAOS, 31, 1911, p. 1 ff.). His work betrays familiarity with Brahmanic knowledge. At any rate he must have, as founder of a principal branch of the Mahayana-Buddhism, enjoyed great respect so that centuries after him in his case was represented the phenomenon familiar among literatures of the world. To him were ascribed several works which were intended to secure high reputation. Throughout Northern India, Nagarjuna is also the Buddha " without the characteristic marks," and his productions are quoted along with " Sutras from the Buddha's own mouth." ( B. Nanjio *Twelve Japanese Buddhist Sects*, p. 48 ff.). In the Chinese Tripitaka, Nagarjuna is the reputed author of twenty-four books. (S. Beal Ind. Ant. 16, 1887, p. 169 ff.). We expect the translation of Nagarjuna's *Catustava* or four hymns from the collaboration of Vallee Poussin and Thomas. Nevertheless, Nagarjuna was as little as Ashvaghosha, the real founder of the Mahayana. The Mahayana doctrine of the text inculcating it must have appeared already in the first Christian century, for we find translations of Mahayana manuals in Chinese in the second century. Besides the Gandhara sculptural art, which is the peculiar art of the Mahayana Buddhism of India, had its development in the period between the rise of Christianity and the four subsequent centuries. The most ancient Chinese translation of a Buddhist text is the "*Sutra of the forty-two Articles*," which is reported to have been prepared in 67 A.D. by Kassapa Matanga from Indian, that is, Sanskrit originals ( B. Nanjio Catalogue-No. 678 ). But we do not know whether these were Mahayana texts. The earliest Chinese translations of the Mahayana texts are those of the

*Sukhavativyuha*, between 148 and 170 A.D., of the *Dasasahasrika Prajnaparamita*, between 75 and 220 A.D. (B. Nanjio Catalogue No. 235 and No. 5). Other Mahayana texts were rendered into Chinese between the third and the fifth century. (Grunwedel Buddhist Art in India, pp. 81, 150 ff., 167).

**Aryadeva.**

Along with the biographies of Ashvaghosha and Nagarjuna translated into Chinese by Kumarajiva about 405 A.D., we come across a life of Deva or Aryadeva who also is mentioned as a great master of the Mahayana "in antiquity" by I-tsing and Hiuen-tsang. But his "biography" is entirely legendary and of his works all that is surviving in Sanskrit is a fragment of a dogmatic poem which has the uncommon interest of being a polemic directed against the Brahmanic ritual. It inveighs, for instance, against the doctrine which assigns the power of purifying sins by a bath in the Ganges. But the verses do not contain anything specifically Mahayanistic (Haraprasad Shastri, JASB Vol. 67, 1898, p. 175 ff.) Otherwise all that we know of Aryadeva is from quotations in Sanskrit and from Tibetan and Chinese Buddhist literature. Candrakirti cites *Shataka-Catushataka* and *Shataka-Shastra* of Aryadeva and also *Aryadevap..diya* in his Madhyamakavritti. (La Valee Poussin, pp. 16, 173, 552 and 393; also La Vallee Poussin, Le Museon, p. 236 ff., on the confusion of the name of Aryadeva with Candrakriti and the epithet of Nilanetra and Kanadeva as attached to Aryadeva, *see* N. Peri, Apropos de la date de Vasubandhu, p. 27 ff. Extract from BEFEO, xi, 1911).

**Asanga.**

Asanga or Aryasanga was to the Yogacara school of Mahayana Buddhism what Nagarjuna was to the Madhyamika sect. The Yogacara branch teaches Vijnanavada, which is a doctrine that nothing exists outside our consciousness which consequently repudiates *Sunyavada* or the doctrine of the *void* equally with the reality of the phenomenal world. But at the same time it admits in a certain sense the Being contained in thought and consciousness. The subtle Bodhi can be attained only by the Yogacara, that is, he who practices Yoga; and that, too, only gradually after the aspirant has completed his career as a Bodhisattva in all the ten stages *(dasabhumi)*. The practice of Yoga or mysticism which was already not quite foreign to Hinayana Buddhism was reduced by Asanga to a systematic connection with the Mahayana Buddhism. The principal text of this doctrine is the *Yogacarabhumisastra*, of which only one part, the *Bodhisattvabhumi*, is conserved in Sanskrit. The whole work was regarded by the Yogacaras as a revelation by Maitreya. It is a scholastic philosophical book of the class of Abhidharma texts.

(On the doctrines of the Yogacara school see Vallee Poussin, p. 200 ff; Outlines of Mahayana Buddhism, London, p. 125 ff. and Levi in the Introduction to his Translation of Mahayana Sutralamkara. On the Yogacara literature in Tibetan sources see Zerbatskoi, Le Museon VI, 1905, p. 144 ff. The Bodhisattvabhumi, the old text-book of the Yogacara school in English, by S. Bendall and Vallee Poussin, Le Museon, VI, 1905, p. 38 VII, 213.)

**More philosopher than poet.**

As revealed also by Maitreya, or the future Buddha, is also regarded the Mahayana *Sutralamkara*; but the scholar Sylvain Levi who discovered the work fixes its authorship on Asanga. And indeed, the entire text consisting as it does of memorial verses or *karikas* and commentary or *Tika* is a production of Asanga. Without being an important poet, Asanga knew how to employ with ingenuity the Buddhist

Sanskrit idiom and often to make use of artistic meter, *sloks* and Arya strophies. But he was decidedly more a philosopher than a poet. Even though in the last two chapters he glorifies the perfection of the Buddha and concludes with a hymn (verse v); he displays in his scholastic enumeration of all the excellencies of the Buddha, more erudition than inspired veneration. Only in the ninth chapter in which Asanga concentrates all his mental powers in a clear exposition of the concepts of Bodhi and Buddhahood, does he relieve with vividness and a lively imaginative diction the insipid monotony. Thus, for instance, *Bodhi*, by means of which the illuminates the world, is compared in a series of metaphors with the sun.

**Asanga.**

Asanga, more properly Vasubandhu Asanga, is the eldest of three brothers who were born in Purusapura, modern Peshawar, in the extreme north of India, as the sons of a Brahman of the Kaushika family. They probably lived in the fourth century and were all three adherents of the Sarvastivada school. Takakusu places Vasubandhu between 420 and 500 (JRAS, 1905, p. 1 ff.). Wogihara assigns Vasubandhu a date between 390 and 470 and Asanga somewhere between 375 and 450 (op. cit. p. 16). Sylvain Levi decides for the first half of the fifth century as regards the activity of Asanga. But N. Peri has made it probable that Vasubandhu was born about 350 A.D. (Apropos de la date de Vasubandhu BEFEO XI, 1911, Nos. 3-4.). The youngest son Vasubandhu Virincivatsa is not important in literature. All the more distinguished was the middle of the three brothers, Vasubandhu, one of the most remarkable figures in the history of the Buddhist letters. I-tsing reckons Asanga and Vasubandhu among the celebrated men of middle ages, that is, the period between the time of Ashvaghosha, Nagarjuna and

Aryadeva on the one hand and his own times on the other Takakusu, p. 181.). A biography of Vasubandhu in which that of his brother Asanga is also embodied was composed by the Indian monk Paramartha (499-569) which was translated from Chinese by Takakusu in the learned French journal *T'oung Pao* (V., 1904, pp. 1 ff.). It was published as an extract by Wassiljew in his most interesting *Buddhism* which has been translated into French, German but still awaits an English translator (German translation, p. 235 ff.). Still more of a legendary nature than the Chinese is the Tibetan biography incorporated with Taranatha's *History of Buddhism* (107 ff.). Paramartha imported from Magadha to China the works of Asanga and Vasubandhu in the year 539. With an astonishing erudition Vasubandhu combined a great independence of thought. His *maggnum opus*, the Abhidharmakosha, is unfortunately not preserved in the original Sanskrit. We only know the *Abhidharmakoshavyakhya*, which is a commentary on the work by Yashomitra and the Chinese and Tibetan versions of the text. The oldest Chinese translation is that by Paramartha, made between 563 and 567. A second rendering prepared between 651 and 654 originated with the celebrated Hiuen-Tsiang himself. The *Abhidharmakosha* was a work treating of ethics, psychology, metaphysics composed in Sutras and Karikas after the fashion of Brahmanic philosophical manuals. The book presupposes the *Vibhashas* or the texts of the school of the Vaibhashikas. The Vibhashas are reputed to have been compiled by Katyayaniputra and cast into a literary mould by Ashvaghosha. Despite the fact that the Kosha is a work of the Sarvastivada School, which appertains to the Hinayana, it is considered as an authority by other sects. The treatise has been used by the Chinese and Japanese Mahayanists as a text book and it has given rise to a voluminous commentary literature.

For other authorities, consult Raj. Mitra, Nep, Buddh Lit., p. 3 ff.; Bendall Catalogue, p. 25 ff.; Burnouf. Introduction, p 502 ff.; Sylvain Levi ERE. 1, p. 20 and La Vallee Poussion in ERE IV, p. 129 ff.

Standing entirely on the soil of the Hinayana is the *Gathusamgrapha* of Vasubandhu with which we are acquainted in its Tibetan version. It is a collection of maxims with an intelligent commentary, excerpts from which have been cited by A. Schiefner. These 24 Gathas are apophthegms conceived wholly in the spirit of the *Dhammapada.* The commentary shows us the philosopher Vasubandhu also as a humorous evangelist and the book is otherwise justly attributed to him. Here is an illustration:

**Buddhist humour.**

"A jackal used to follow a lion because it yearned for the remnants of flesh devoured by him. Once upon a time the lion was hungry, and having killed a large bear, called upon the jackal to carry it. Now as the jackal was too feeble to bear the load and at the same time was afraid lest the lion in his anger should put it to death, could not make up its mind to agree to the demand. But it knew that the lion was proud and said: "In order to carry this burden two things are necessary, to groan and to bear the load. I cannot do both at the same time. You must take up one of the two." As the lion was proud and was not willing to groan, he asked the jackal to groan and agreed to carry the load himself. Accordingly the lion bore the burden and the jackal followed groaning after the lion. Just in the same way I bear the burden of the preaching of the doctrine, but you are only in the position of assenting and say, That is so."

Schiefner op. cit. p. 582; for Vasubandhu's Gathasamgrapha, Mélanges Asiatiques, VII (Bulletin XXIV, St, Petersburg, 1878) p. 559 ff.

As a philosopher Vasubandhu also wrote a discourse to combat the Samkhya philosophy. It is called the *Paramartha Saptati* or Seventy verses of Supreme Verity. The Sanskrit original has perished, but it would appear to be a refutation of the *Samkhyasaptati* of Ishvarakrishna. Paramartha mentions a heretic named Vindhyavasha as the author of the Samkhya book against which Vasubandhu's polemic was directed. It is remarkable, however, that to the Chinese also Vasubandhu is the reputed critic of Ishvarakrishna's work.

**Opponent of Samkhya philosophy.**

(Takakusu, T'oung Pau, 1904, p. 15 ff.; BEFEO, Vol. IV 1904, p. 1 ff.; JRAS, 1905, p. 16 ff. According to Takakusu Vindhyavasa is identical with Ishvarakrishna.)

It was not till late in life that Vasubandhu was converted to the Mahayana by his brother. Now he repented, his biography relates his earlier depreciation of the Mahayana so much that he was prepared to cut off his tongue, but his brother suggested to him that it would be a superior penance to employ henceforward his tongue with as conspicuous success for the elucidation of the Mahayana principles as he had done to combat its doctrine previously. Vasubandhu acted up to the counsel and wrote after the death of Asanga a large number of commentaries on the *Sadharmapundarika* the *Prajnaparamita* and other Mahayana Sutras together with other learned works, as to whose existence we know only from their renderings in Chinese and Tibetan. Paramartha praises the charm and the convincing power of his works and winds up with these words:

"Accordingly, all who study the Mahayana and the Hinayana in India use the productions of Vasubandhu as their text-books. There is nowhere a promulgator of the doctrine of Buddism belonging to another school or in a heretical sect who is not seized with fear and perturbation as soon as he hears his name. He died in Ayodhya at the age of eighty. Although he led a secular life his true character was hard to understand."

(For other authorities, consult Raj. Mitra Nep. Buddh Lit., p. 3 ff.; Bendall Catalogue p. 25 ff.; Burnouf Introduction, p. 502 ff.; Sylvain Levi, ERE 1, p. 20, and La Vallee Poussin in ERE, IV, p. 129 ff.)

A treatise on the doctrine of the *Vijnanavadis* in twenty memorial verses with a commentary called *Vimshakakarika Prakarana* is translated from the Tibetan by La Vallee Poussin (*Museon*, 1912, p. 53 ff.) Takakusu, T'oung Pao, 1904, p. 27.

**Candragomi.**

To the School of Asanga belongs Candragomi who as a grammarian, philosopher and poet, enjoyed high renown in the Buddhist literary world. He was a contemporary of Candrakirti whose doctrine he assailed and was alive at the time of I-tsing's visit to India in 673. According to Taranatha who has got a considerable deal of legendary nature to report about him, he composed innumerable hymns and learned works. Of the literary productions we own only a religious poem in the form of an epistle to his disciple, the *Shishya Lekha Dharma Kavya.* In this the Buddhist doctrine is propounded in the elegant style of Kavya.

Minayeff, JRAS, 1899, p. 1133 ff., assigns him the close of the fourth and beginning of the fifth century. B. Liebich, WZKM 13, 1999, 308 ff., places him between 465 and 544. But for Sylvain Levi's views, BEFEO, 1903, p. 38 ff. see above.

**Shantideva.**

The most conspicuous amongst the later apostles of Mahayana Buddhism, who also distinguished himself as a poet, is Shantideva who lived probably in the seventh century. If we credit Taranatha he was born in Saurashtra or modern Gujarat, as the son of a king; was impelled by the goddess Tara herself to renounce the throne, the Bodhisattva Manjushri himself in the guise of a Yogi initiating him into the sciences; became a prime minister to the king Pancasimha and ended by taking to monastic life. Taranatha ascribes to him the three works, *Shikshasamuccaya*, *Sutrasamuccaya* and *Bodhicaryavatara.*

Taranath, op. cit. 162 ff., although we know of a Sutrasamuccaya only by Nagarjuna, see Winternitz WZKM, 1912, p. 246 ff.

Taranath, op. cit. 162 ff., although we know of a Sutrasamuccaya only by Nagarjuna, see Winternitz WZKM, 1912, p. 246 ff.

The Shikshasamuccaya or the Compendium of Doctrine is a manual of Mahayana Buddhism which consists of 27 *Karikas* or memorial verses and a large commentary compiled by the author at the same time with the *Karikas.* We purposely say that the commentary by Shantideva is "compiled" because it is composed almost entirely of quotations and extracts from the sacred texts which he has grouped together round his *Karika's* and arranged in chapters.

The work accordingly displays an extraordinary erudition and vast reading but little originality. However, it is most perfectly adapted to be an introduction especially to the technical study of the Mahayana on account of the numerous and often large citations from texts, which have perished, of great value. This is more especially so because Shantideva proves himself in such cases, as we can check very exact and reliable in his quotations.

**Core of doctrine.**

The basic thought of the work and in fact the core of the Mahayana ethics is given expression to in the first two *Karikas.* They are;—

"When to myself just as well as to others fear and pain are disagreeable, then what difference is there between myself and others that I should preserve this self and not others? He who would make an end of sorrow, would attain to the farther end of joy, must fortify the roots of faith and set his heart determined on enlightenment."

The Siksasamuccaya has been edited by the English scholar C. Bendall in the *Biblotheca Buddhica* Series of St. Petersberg with a lucid masterly introduction and a conspectus of the contents. The edition is based on a unique manuscript but the editor has brought to his task his rare knowledge of the Tibetan into which the original Sanskrit was translated, between 816 and 838, the Sanskrit being written most probably in the middle of the seventh century.

**Importance of the book.**

By means of numerous extracts from the Mahayana-sutras Santideva proves the salutariness of Bodhicittaṁ, or the heart set upon enlightenment, the determination to enter upon the path of a Bodhisattva with a view thereafter to become a Buddha. But he who has made this high resolve must exercise self-denial and practice self-sacrifice for the sake of others to the uttermost limit of possibility. He must be prepared to give up for the sake of others not only his worldly possessions but his personal salvation hereafter. He must not shrink from appropriating to himself the sins and sorrows of other creatures in hell. The Bodhisattva must say:

"I take upon myself the sorrows of all beings. I have resolved to undertake them, I bear them, I do not turn away from them, I do not fly from them, I do not tremble, I do not quake, I fear not, I re-trace not my steps backwards, I do not despair. And why so? It is imperative that I assume the burden of all beings. I have no inclination for pleasures for I have made a vow to save all creatures. Liberate I must all creatures from the primeval forest of birth, from the primeval forest of old age, from the primeval forest of sickness, from the forest of heresy, from the forest of all good deeds, from the primeval forest born of ignorance. I have not thought merely of my own emancipation, for I must save all creatures by means of the ferry, of the resolve for omniscience, from the flood of Samsara. I have made up my mind to abide for interminable myriads of æons on the spots of torture. And why so? Because it is better that I alone should suffer than that all these creatures should sink into the state of torment. I deliver myself up as a pledge."

**Other virtues.**

The above is an extract from the *Vajradhvajasutra* ( La Vallee Poussin, *Boudhisme*, p. 322 f. 337 f). Next after compassion rank all other perfections ( Paramitas ) necessary to the pure conduct of a Bodhisattva,—meditation standing at the head of the list. It leads to supreme sagacity which is an insight into the " Void " or Sunyata, to the understanding of the Nil and the faith which has its expression in the adoration of the Buddha in the building of *stupas* and the like. And yet all this, notwithstanding, his mind must ever be directed to the salvation of other creatures " May I bring all creatures into the conditions of Nirvana ! " This has to be his constant thought. Santideva here quotes from the *Ratnameghasutra* ( op. cit. 348 ).

**Quotations from previous works.**

Bendall gives a catalogue of the numerous texts which are strung together in *Siksasamuccaya* especially those which are represented by a large number of citations or by copious extracts. Thus the Akasagarbhasutra is drawn upon to dilate upon various kinds of sin, including the five criminal transgressions of a king, the eight offences of a Adikarmika-Bodhisattva and so on ( p. 59 ff.). On sins and penances two passages, a short one and a longer are reproduced from the Upalipariprucoha (pp. 147 f, 168 ff.). Tolerably numerous are the extracts from theUgrapariprucoha or Ugradatapariprucoha, for instance, on the obligations of married life (p. 78) and on the life of the ascetic in the forest. The latter subject is also treated of in an extract (p. 193 ff.) from the Candrapradipasutra as the Samadhiraja is here called and which is frequently laid under contribution. Of frequent occurrence is the Ganda-vyuha on the noble friend (p. 34), and on the virtues of him who is resolved upon Bodhi (p. 101 ff.). From the Vimala-kirtinirdesha, which is several times depended upon, we get at a large piece on the virtues of a Bodhisattva (p. 324 ff.). Santi-deva quotes as an independent text the Avalokanusutra which is embedded in the Mahavastu. A long passage from the Ratnolkadharani on the merits of a Bodhisattva furnishes us a " Dharani " which is no mere incantation and which can hardly be differentiated from a Sutra. This citation is also interesting as indicating the avocations and names of the ascetic orders (p. 331 ff.). The more important of the other works quoted in the Siksasamuccaya by Santideva are the Tathagataguhyasutra, Dasabhumikasutra, Dharmasamgi-tisutra, several recensions of the Prajnaparamita, Karuna-pundarika, Ratnakutasutra, Ratnamegha, Lankavatara, Lalitavistara, Salistambasutra, Saddharmapundarika, Suvarna-prabhasa, etc.

The Ranakutasutra is said to have been translated into Chinese before 170 A.D. As to its contents as given in the Chinese rendering see Wassiljew. Buddhismus, p. 167 ff.

**Moral ideal.**

Although the Siksasamuccaya is the production of a scholar of little originality and the Bodhicaryavatara is the creation of an eminent poet, there is no question but that we owe both to the same author. Apart from external grounds the two books so fundamentally different in their character take the same standpoint as regards the doctrine. In both the texts the moral ideal is the Bodhisattva who has resolved to attain to enlightenment, who strives to obtain his object in the first place by means of inexhaustible compassion for all creatures, and secondly, by means of adoration of the Buddha and who perceives supreme wisdom in the recognition of " Vanity " or Shunyata.

The text of the *Bodhicaryavatara* was edited by the Russian scholar I. P. Minayeff in the *Zapiski*, and it has also been reprinted in the Journal of the Bhuddhist Text Society. La Vallee Poussin published for the Bibliotheca Indica Prajnakaramati's commentary on the Bodhicaryavatara and also a translation of it.

Some of the passages occurring in the Shiksasamuccaya have been taken over by Shantideva in his Bodhicaryavatara, *e.g.*, Shiksasamuccaya, p. 155 ff. Bodhicaryavatara, vi 120 ff. Note that in the Bodhicaryavatara (v. 105) Shantideva recognises the necessity of a study of his Shiksasamuccaya.

Barth (RHR 42, 1900, p. 55) characterises Shiksasamuccaya as "la scholastique verbeuse et delayee usque ad nauseam" whilst he (RHR, 1893. p. 259 ff.) greatly appreciates the Bodhicaryavatara as a counterfoil to the "Imitatio Christi" of Thomas á Kempis. The Bodhicaryavatara teaches by no means how to imitate the Buddha but how to become a Buddha. Compare Poucher RHR, 1908, vol. 57 p. 241 ff.

**Books contrasted.**

The *Shiksasamuccaya* expands itself in learned garrulity into a flood of quotations. The *Bodhicaryavatara* which means admission to the Bodhi life, or the conduct of life leading to enlightenment, not seldom rises to the loftiest strains of religious poetry. Shantideva himself disclaims any literary object for his production. He observes that he composed it "for his own satisfaction" or with the view that it may be of use to any one so inclined. But he gives expression to his religious sentiments with such warmth and inspiration that he becomes a poet almost in spite of himself.

The work begins with the glorification of the *Bodhicitta*, meditations on enlightenment and the resolve to become a Buddha for the sake of the salvation of all creatures. Thus the poet says (i. 8):

"When you overcome the many hundreds of birth sorrows, when you free all beings from their misery, when you enjoy many hundreds of pleasures, then do not, ever on any account, relax your thought of the "Bodhi."

The poet pours out in inspired words his sentiments, after having thus directed his attention to enlightenment. He voices his inner joy at the good deeds of all creatures regarding their emancipation. He prays to all the Buddhas of all the quarters of the world that they may kindle the lamp of religion for all the ignorant. He implores all the Bodhisattvas to delay their own *Nirvana*. He supplicates for the liberation of all creatures and finally offers himself up to all the creatures:

"By virtue of the merit which I have acquired through good deeds, may I bring mitigation to the sorrows of all creatures. May I be medicine to the sick. May I be their physician and their nurse so long as their malady endures. May I be a protection unto those that need it, a guide to such as have lost their path in the desert and a ship and a ford and a bridge to those who seek the farther shore. And may I be a lamp unto those that need light, a bed of repose to those that want rest; a servitor to all the creatures requiring service." (III, 6; 7; 17; 18).

The obligations that the Bodhisattva lays upon himself (chapters iv to viii) include the pledge to strive after Bodhi. He is responsible for the weal of all beings. He must exert himself for all perfections (Paramitas). Before all he must be prepared for self-sacrifice. He must likewise observe all the regulations of the religion and all the precepts of good conduct as prescribed in the holy scriptures which he must accordingly study with energy. And here certain texts are particularly recommended to the aspirant (v. 103, ff.). The worst of our enemies are anger, hatred and passion. We have to fight them. It is they who do us evil, not our foes. The latter we must love like all other creatures. For when we love the creatures we rejoice the Buddhas; in injuring them we injure the Buddhas. "When some one does me an evil turn, that is only the fruit of some previous act or *karma*. Why should I be wrath with him?" We should not hate even those who destroy the images of the Buddha, the *stupas*, nay even the good religion itself.

**The aspirant's obligations.**

To the Buddhas and Bodhisattvas who have so often ruined their bodies for the sake of other creatures and even have repaired to the inferno, to them he is beneficent who is kind to other creatures. Therefore must one show only kindness even to those who have done him an evil turn (see VI; 33; 68; 120; 124; 126). The Bodhisattva from the first diligently strives to avoid any difference between his Ego and others; and to identify himself wholly and entirely with others. This is a function which the Bodhisattva has particularly to practice.

**Self and others: the difference.**

"I must destroy the sorrow of the stranger because it pains like one's own grief; I must therefore do good to others because they are beings like myself." Just as a man loves his hands and feet because they are his members, so also all living beings have the right of affection inasmuch as they are all members of the same world of animate creation. It is only mere usage which makes us look upon this our body, which in fact does not exist, as our Ego. Exactly similarly by habit we can bring ourselves to see our Ego in others (VIII 90 ff.).

**Psychic identity.**

With admirable eloquence, which can only spring mroe reverential conviction, Shantideva manages to advance almost as an obvious proposition that to the pious disciple of the Bodhi there is complete "equality between others and one's self," technically called *paratmasamata* and he finally reduces it to "transformation of the neighbour into oneself," known as *partatmaparivartana* (La Vallee Poussin, ERE 11, 749, 752 f.).

**Philosophical doubt.**

The ninth Chapter is of a less philosophically ambitious nature and its contents are pure learning. In it the philosophical doctrine of the *void* or nihilism is developed according to the Madhyamika system. This chapter has been edited with the commentary by La Vallee Poussin in his *Bouddhisme*. However irreconcilable the negativism of this system may appear to us with the renunciation and self-sacrifice with reference to other creatures taught in the first chapters, nevertheless with Shantideva also the familiar doctrine of the difference between the two varieties of Truth is the means by which to bridge the apparent contradiction. In the end everything in the world is vacuity and nullity. But it is only the delusion as regards the Ego, the *Atmamoha*, which is pernitious. The delusion as regards duties, *Karva moha*, is beneficent (La Vallee Poussin Bouddhisme, p. 109 ff.).

Still it is sufficiently strange that after all the teaching of active compassion the poet comes to the conclusion: (ix, 152 f.).

" Since all being is so vacuous and null, what can, what shall be, acquired? Who can be honoured, who can be reproached? How can there be joy and sorrow, the loved and the hateful, avarice and non-avarice? Wherever you search for them you find them not."

**Reaction.**

It seems to be the curse of Indian mentality that whenever it soares too high it lands itself in absurdity. Thus the legends of sacrifice often turn into ludicrous tales and so does the whole fabric of the philosophy of Mahayana end in— Nothing. On the other hand, with some justification we can look upon as a later accretion the tenth chapter which with its invocations to Vajrapani and Manjushri and its panegyric of acts show a spirit totally counter to that of the other chapters. Already Taranatha reports that there was some suspicion regarding the genuineness of this chapter. (La Vallee Poussin, *Bodhicaryavatara* tr. p. 143 f.).

## CHAPTER IX.

**Stotras, Dharanis, Tantras.**

We have already pointed out the great similarity between Mahayanasutras and Puranas. And just as we know that numerous Mahatmyas and Stotras are joined on to the Puranic literature so we find many analogous texts in the literature of the Mahayana. The Buddhist Svayambhu-purana, the Mahatmya of Nepal, and like productions are well known. Svayambhu, or the Adibuddha, or the primeval Buddha, is here the Buddha turned into God in a monotheistic sense; and the Purana recounts entirely in the style of the Vaishnavite and Shaivaite Mahatmyas legends of the origin of the country of Nepal, the shrine of Svayambhu and numerous places of pilgrimage or *tirthas* capable of performing cures and miracles and protected by snake deities or Nagas.

See also R. Mitra Nepalese Buddhist Literature, p. 248 ff; Hodgson p. 115, ff.; Sylvain Levi, Le Nepaul, 1915, 1, p. 208 ff.

**Hymns: Buddhist and Hindu.**

Besides, the Buddhist stotras or hymns are in no way differentiated from those which are devoted to the veneration of Vishnu or Shiva. Such stray stotras have found admittance into older texts like the Mahavastu and others. But we have a complete collection of such hymns, some of which are in the Kavya style and in metrical form. An example is the *Kalyanapancavimshatik*, the Twenty-five-blessings hymn in twenty-five Sragdhara verses, by a poet called Amritananda, and the *Lokesvarashutaka*, a hymn to the Lord of the world in a hundred verses by another poet called Vajradatta. A selection of forty-nine litanies relating to Shakyamuni and other Buddhas and Bodhisattvas is the *Suprabhatastava*. A hymn of the kind which from of old has been so common in India consisting of a succession of names or honorific epithets to the god is the *Paramarthanamasamgiti*.

An untold number of Nepalese deities are invoked for the sake of their blessings. See H. H. Wilson, Works II., p. II. ff.

Raj. Mitra, Nep. Budh. Lit., pp. 99, 112, 239, 175.

Stotras which are still only in manuscripts are *Samantabhadrapranidhana*, *Mrgushatakastuti*, *Saptabuddhastotra* and so forth.

Catalogue of Sanskrit Manuscripts in the Bodheian Library, Vol. II, by M. Winternitz and A. B. Keith, Oxford, 1905, p. 255 ff. The Saptabuddhastotra has been translated by Wilson, Works Vol. II, p. 5 ff.

**Tara and her poet devotees.**

A large number of Stotras are sacred to the Buddhist goddess Tara, the saviour, the female counterpart of Avalokiteshvara. A panegyric composed entirely in Kavya style by the Kasmirian poet Sarvajnamitra on Tara is the ***Sragdhara-stotra***, otherwise called the ***Aryatarasragdharastotra***, which is in thirty-seven strophes. Sraghadhara or the bearer of garland is at once an epithet of Tara and the name of a meter in which the poem is composed. The poet lived in the first half of the eighth century. According to the legend he was a personage distinguished for his liberality and according to Taranatha a son-in-law of the king of Kashmir. After he had given away in charity all his treasures he is reported finally to have had recourse to the life of an itinerant monk. Once he happened to encounter a Brahman on the way who appealed to him in his poverty and besought him for money for the marriage of his daughter. In order to furnish money to the man Sarvajnamitra sold himself to a king who had just instituted a great human sacrifice for which he was in need of a hundred men. But when the poet heard the laments of his brothers in sorrow with whom he was about to be sacrificed he sung his hymn to Tara and the goddess descended and rescued the hundred victims condemned to death. Whilst the Sragdharastotra has poetic value the ***Aryatara-namashatottarashatakastotra*** or the eulogy in one hundred and eight names of the noble Tara is only a litany of names and epithets of the goddess. The *Ekavimshatistotra*, the song of praise in thirty-one or twenty-one strophes is but a loose string of invocations to the goddess Tara.

According to L. A. Waddell, JRAS, p. 63 ff, the cult of Tara was introduced about 600 A.D.

History of Buddhism, p. 168 ff.

These three stotras have been edited and translated by O. de Blonay, Materiaux pour servir a l'histoire de la deesse Buddhique Tara (Bibl. de l'ecole des hautes etudes, fasc. 107). The Sragdharastotra with a commentary and two Tibetan versions have also been edited by Satis Chandra Vidyabhusana. In the introduction the editor enumerates no less than ninety-six texts relating to Tara. Of these only sixty-two are preserved in Tibetan translation. A great adorer of this goddess Tara was also Candragomi whom we mentioned above and to whom a *Tarasadhan shataka* has been attributed. (Blonay, p. 17 f.)

**Dharanis or Necromantic formulae.**

A great and essential element of the Mahayanistic literature is constituted by Dharanis or magical formulæ. The necessity for formulæ for exorcisms, and charms for blessing and witchcraft which was taken into account in the earliest ages in the Vedic Mantras, especially those of the Atharvaveda, was too vigorously working in the Indian popular mind for Buddhism to be altogether devoid of it. We already know how the Buddhists of Ceylon employ some of their most charming *suttas* as Parittas or Pirits. In a similar fashion the Mahayanistic Buddhists in India transforms to some extent the sacred texts themselves into necromantic charms. To these we have to add innumerable invocations to the numerous deities in the Mahayana of a Buddhistic or Hindu origin and—last but not least—the favourite mysterious words and syllables already occurring in the sacrificial mysteries of the Yajurveda. An instance of a Sutra composed for magical objective is the *Meghasutra.* It commences, as do other Mahayanasutras, with the words :

"So have I heard, once upon a time the Master was dwelling in the palace of the snake princes Nanda and Upanda." It proceeds to recount how the serpent deities made worship to the Buddha and the Bodhisattvas upon which one of the serpentine kings thus interrogated the Exalted One :

"How, Lord, may all the sorrows of all the snakes be assuaged and how may the snakes so rejoice and be happy that they may shower down rain over India at the proper time and thereby help the growth of grass, scrubs, vegetation and trees, cause to sprout all seeds and cause all sap to well up in trees, thus blessing the people in India with prosperity ?" Rejoicing over the enquiry the Buddha replies :—

"By means of a religious exercise, Dharma, Oh King of Snakes, all the sorrows of all the snakes may be instantly assuaged and they may be blessed with prosperity." "Which religious exercise is this ?" "It is Benevolence, *Maitri.* The gods and men, Oh Prince of Serpents, who live in such benevolence will not be burnt by fire, wounded by sword, drowned in water, killed by poison, overpowered by a hostile army. They sleep in peace ; they wake in tranquillity ; protected they are by their own virtue. Therefore, Oh Prince of Serpents, thou must be actuated with benevolence as regards thy body, with benevolence as regards thy speech, with benevolence with regard to thy thought. But further, Oh Prince of Snakes, thou must put into practice the Dharani called *Sarvasukhandada*, the Giver-of-all-happiness. This assuages all the pain of all the serpents, lends all sanity, brings down upon this India rain showers at the right season and helps the growth of all grass, scrubs, vegetables and trees, causes all seeds to sprout and all sap to well up." "And how does this Dharani run?"

And here follow the Dharanis proper. They consist of numerous invocations to female deities like the Preserver, the Conserver and others to Buddhas and Bodhisattvas, with interlarded apostrophes like "Clear away the wicked, purify the way," and adjurations to snakes like "Come ye great snakes, rain it down over India"; and finally isolated and unintelligible syllables such as "Sara sire sire suru suru naganam java java jivi jivi juvu juvu, etc." At the end comes again a description of the wizards' rites which are performed with these Dharanis, and the assurance that in times of a draught there is no better means of calling down a shower of rain than the use of these Sutras.

A much simpler form of an adjuration to snakes, which, however, is supposed to act as an antidote to snake poison is to be found in the Vinayapitaka, Cullavagga V, 6, where the snakes are tranquillized by the Buddhistic benevolence called Metta in Pali and Maitri in Sanskrit. (See also Jataka 293 and Digha Nikaya, 32.) A Sutra similar to the Meghasutra is the *Dishasvastikasutra* which is preserved in a fragment discovered at Turfan in Chinese Turkistan in the Uigurian language, (Tishastvustik by W. Radloff and Baron A. von Steail-Holstein Bibl. Buddhica, XII, St. Petersburg, 1910).

The Dharanis often appear as parts of a Sutra in which the circumstances are reported under which they were revealed. But there are also numerous Dharanis which are preserved in individual manuscripts, and, on the other hand, entire large collections of Dharanis. In these we find formulae of exorcisms against the influence of evil spirits, poison, snakes and demons ; charms for healing the sick and for longevity ; magical utterances which bring success in war and others which bring it about that a man is reborn in the paradise of Sukhavati, that a man comes to no evil birth, that a man is freed from sins. There are also Dharanis by means of which one can charm a Bodhisattva or protect oneself from infidelity. Not only can wind and water be influenced by Dharanis but they can effect, according to wish, the birth of a son or daughter. An unusual favourite in Nepal is the *Pancaraksha* or the Five-fold Protection which is a collection of five Dharanis : (1) Mahapratisara, a protection against sin, malady and other evils ; (2) Mahasahasrapramardini, against the evil spirts ; (3) Mahamayuri, against snake poison; (4) Mahashitavati against hostile planets, wild animals and venomous insects and (5) Maharaksha, against diseases. Such Dharanis as serve against all manner of evil powers are frequently employed also as amulets.

Dharani literary means " a means to hold fast " especially a spirit or a secret power. It does not signify "a formula possessing great efficacy" as interpreted by Burnouf and Wilson. Burnouf deals in detail with Dharanis; Introduction, pp. 466, 482 ff.; Wassiljew Der Buddhismus, p. 153 ff., 193 ff., 217 ; La Vallee Poussin Bouddhisme, Etudes et Materiaux, p. 199 ff.: C. Bendall JRAS 1880, p. 286 ff. A Mahameghasutra was translated into Chinese between 397 and 439 and other translations were made between 589 and 618 and 746-771. B. Nanjio Catalogue Nos. 186-188, 244, 970.

For instances of Dharanimantra, Raj. Mitra Nep. Buddh. Lit., p. 80 f., and Dharani Collections, pp. 93 f. 174, 176, 267 f., 283, 291 f. Numerous MSS. are also registered in Bendall's Catalogue. La Vallee Poussin conjectures (JRAS, 1895, p. 433 ff.) that the Dharani called Vidyadharapitaka which is quoted in the Adikarmapradipa is the same as the Dharanipitaka. A like Dharanipitaka is said to have been included in the canon of the Mahasanghikas according to Hiuen-Tsiang (Kern Manual, p. 4).

(Raj. Mitra. Nep. Buddh. Lit., pp. 164 ff., 173 f. Winternitz and Keith, Catalogue of Sanskirit Manuscripts in the Bodleian Library, Vol. II, p. 257 ff.)

In the Nepalese law courts the Buddhist people are sworn on the *Pancaraksha* (Hodgson Essays, p. 18).

**Sanskrit Dharanis in Japan.**

Many Dharanis are only a kind of philosophical Sutras, the doctrines of which they are intended to present in a nutshell, but in the process it becomes less a question of the substance of the doctrine than words which are mysterious and unintelligible. Of this variety are the two *Prajnaparamitahridayasutras*, the Sanskrit texts of which are enshrined in the palm leaves in the ancient cloister of Horiuzi in Japan since 609 A.D. These Sutras inculcate the *hrdaya* or the heart of the Prajnaparamita which is a *mantra* to assuage all pains, which embodies the perfection of all wisdom and which runs thus: "Oh Lord, thou that hast gone, gone, gone to the further shore, gone entirely to the further shore, hail." This is by the way nothing but an erroneous ethymology of the term *Paramita.* Even this apostrophe which may be said in a certain measure to represent the essence of the negative doctrine of Prajnaparamitasutras stands on no more elevated spiritual level than the *Ushnishavijayadharani* which is likewise bequeathed to us by the palm leaves of Horiuzi and consists merely in a series of unintelligible invocations.

The ancient palm leaves containing the Prajnaparamitahridayasutra and the Ushnishavjayadharani, edited by Max Muller and B. Najio (Anecdota Oxoniensia, Aryan Series, Vol. I, part III), Oxford, 1884, SBE, vol. 49, part II, p. 145 ff.

The Ganapatihridayadharani (Raj. Mitra Nep. Budh Lit., p. 89 f.) is addressed to the Shaivit god Ganapati, although it is "revealed by the Buddha."

**Antiquity of Dharanis.**

These Dharanis have found wide and deep admission into, the ancient Mayahanasutras. We find them in chapters 21 and 26 of the *Saddharmapundarika* which are later interpolations and in the last two sections of the *Lankavatara*, one in the oldest Chinese rendering made in 443 A.D. Accordingly we cannot consider the Dharanis to be altogether younger products. We meet with them in the Chinese translations dating from the fourth century. It may be conjectured, however, that originally they were unintelligible Sutras which dispensed with the Buddhistic doctrine just as do the Parittas of the Pali literature. But gradually the unintelligible mysterious syllables acquired prime importance and became the core, the *bija*, which lay concealed in the magical potency of the formula. And finally under the influence of Shaivit Tantras they became powerful thaumaturgic, and the essential elements in Buddhistic Tantras which originally they were not.

The Tantras, however, are a branch of Buddhistic literature which is worth consideration as a testimony to the complete mental decadence in Buddhism. They treat partly of rites, Kriyatantra, and ordinances, Caryatantra, and partly of the secret doctrine, Yogatantra, intended for the Yogi. The best of these works belong to the former class in which the ancient Brahmanic ritual is revived. Of this category is the Adikarmapradipa, a book which describes in the style of the Brahmanic manuals of ritual (Grhyasutras, Karmapradipas) the ceremonies and religious functions, which have to be performed by the Adikarmaka-Bodhisattva, that is, the adherent of the Mahayana, an aspirant after spiritual illumination.

**The Adikarma-pradipa.**

The *Adikarmapradipa* is made up of the Sutra text technically known as the *mulasutra* with a running commentary incorporating prescriptions regarding the initiatory ceremony for the disciple who may be a layman or a monk, sprinkling with water, ablutions and prayers, and further rules on gargling the mouth, brushing the teeth, morning and evening prayers, offering of water to the souls of the departed (Pretas), the giving of charity dinners, worshipping of the Buddha and other sacred creatures, the reading of the Prajnaparamita, meditations and the rest, which are to be practised by the candidate or the neophite as contradistinguished from the full Yogi.

**Varieties of Tantras; Yogi's training.**

To the *Kriyatantra* texts also belongs the *Ashtamivratavidhana* which contains the ritual to be observed on the eighth day of each fortnight. The rite entails the drawing of mystic diagrams and movements of the hand, oblations and prayers with mysterious syllables which are addressed not only to the Buddha and the Bodhisattva, but also to the Shaivit deities.

Wilson, Works II, p. 31 ff.

But a majority of the Tantras belong to the second category, that of the Yogatantra. These treatises are derived indeed from the mysticism of the Madhyamika and Yogacara schools. What the Yogi endeavours to arrive at is the supreme knowledge of the Nullity or Shunyata. But it is worthy of attention that he exerts himself to attain this object not only by means of ascetism and meditation, but also with the help of necromantic exercises and adjurations, hypnotism and physical excitements. To the latter contribute the use of meat and intoxicants as well as sexual excesses. Accordingly in these Tantras we encounter an agglomeration of mysticism, witchcraft and erotics with revolting orgies They comprise the practice of the five M's, *mamsa* or flesh. *matsya* or fish, *madya* or spiritous liquors, *mudra* or mysterious movements and finally and primarily *maithuna* or sexual intercourse. Of real Buddhism in these texts there is left next to nothing. On the other hand they are most intimately allied to the Shaivit Tantras from which they are differentiated only by the external frame and by the verbal statement that they are " enunciated by the Buddha." The prominence assigned to female goddesses, Yoginis, Dakinis and others is characteristic. It were idle to seek to meet with sense or rationality in these books. Their authors were in all probability wizards who pursued the study practically and for the most part in search of impure objects.

**Degrading instructions**

Nevertheless many of these books enjoy great reputation. For instance the *Tathagataguhyaka* or *Guhyasamaja* belongs to the nine Dharmas of the Nepalese Buddhists. The book indeed begins with instructions on the various classes of meditation, but presently deviates into exposition of all manner of secret figures and formulæ which are necessary for the *latria* of the Buddha and it is not satisfied with the hocus-pocus of the magical words and rites, but enjoins as a means to the most elevated perfectoin the eating of elephant, horse and dog flesh and daily intercourse with young Chandala maidens. The *Mahakalatantra* is next the model of a colloquy between Shakyamuni and a goddess and it is claimed to have been "announced by the Buddha." It, however, contains instruction on the mystical significance of the letters of the alphabet, composing the name Mahakala or Shiva, on the means of discovering hidden treasures, acquiring kingship, getting a desired woman and even Mantras and magical rites to deprive men of reason and to subjugate or slay them. The *Samvarodayatantra* is again, despite its form of a conversation between the Buddha and Vajrapani, more of a Shaivit than a Buddhistic text. In it the Linga cult and the worship of the Shaivit gods is expressly recommended. In the *Kalacakra* which is said to have been revealed by the Adibuddha we have already the mention of Mecca of Islam. In the *Manjushrimulatantra* Shakyamuni proclaims *inter alia* that four hundred years after him Nagarjuna will appear.

(Raj. Mitra. Nep. Buddh. Lit., p. 261 ff.; Burnouf Introduction, p. 480; Raj. Mitra. Nep. Buddh. Lit., p. 172 f.; Burnouf Introduction, p. 479 f.)

**Supreme Yogiship.**

There is no room for doubt that all these books were written long after the times of Nagarjuna and the Mahayanasutras and the possibility is precluded that Nagarjuna, the founder of the Madhyamika school, could have composed also the Tantras. Nevertheless he is the reputed author of five of the six sections of the *Panckrakrama.* At all events this book deals more with Yoga than with Tantric usages properly so called. As its title signifies the Panckakrama is an exposition of the "five steps," the last of which is the final position of the supreme Yogi. The preliminary steps consist in the purification of the body, speech and mind so that they acquire the "diamond" nature of the body, the speech and the mind of the Buddha. But the medium through which the five stages are reached comprises magical circles, magical formulæ mysterious syllables and the worship of Mahayanistic and Tantric goddesses. In this manner the Yogi acquires the loftiest step where all else ceases and there is absolutely no duality at all.

Edited with an introduction by La Vallee Poussin Etudes et Texte, Tantriques (Recueil deTravaux publies par la faculte de philosophie et letters, Universite de Grand, fasc. 16), Grand et Louvain, 1896. Burnouf Introductions p. 497 ff. Vajra "The Diamond" plays a chief part in the mystics of the Tantras.

Of such a Yogi it is said :

" As towards himself so is he towards his enemy. Like his wife is his mother to him ; like his mother is the courtezan to him ; like a Dombi (a wandering minstrel of the lowest caste) is to him a Brahman woman ; his skin to him is like the garment ; straw is like a precious stone ; wine and food like excreta ; an abuse like a song of praise ; Indra like Rudra ; day as night ; the phenomena as dreams ; the extant as the perished ; pain as enjoyment ; son as a vicious creature ; heaven as hell,—and so to him the bad and the good are one."

**The authorship.**

If in reality a Nagarjuna was the author of this section it must be another person of the same name than the founder of the Madhyamika system. But as the author of the third sections is given out to be Shakyamitra, he is probably the same as the person mentioned by Taranatha as a contemporary of Devapala of Bengal, about 850 A.D. and this period may well belong to the entire book. When Taranatha says that during the period of the Pala dynasty in Bengal, that is from the seventh to the ninth century, Yoga and magic preponderated in Buddhism we may well credit him and the rest of the Tantras may have arisen rather in this than in an earlier age. Taranatha in his history of Buddhism in India gives us an adequate conception of Tantric Buddhism. Here indeed we have the mention of Mahayana and Tripitaka of Buddhistic science and Buddhistic self-sacrifice, but a much more prominent part is played by *Siddhi* or the supernatural power acquired through Tantras and Mantras.

In the Catalogue of Buddhist Sanskrit MSS. in the Royal Asiatic Society by E. B. Cowell and J. Eggeling ( JRAS, 1876, reprint p.28) we find the mention of *Pancakramopadesha* by Srighanta. The tantra literature has no popular origin, but is "learned" in its way. La Vallee Poussin (JRAS, 1899, p. 141 f.) is inclined to regard Tantra and Tantra-Buddhism as ancient. But no proofs have been adduced in support of this theory. (See Rapson, JRAS, 1898, p. 909 ff.,) Haraprasad Shastri (JASB, Proceedings 1900, p. 100 ff.) assigns the Tantra literature to the fifth or the sixth century. Taranatha was born in 1573 and completed his history in 1608 which was written with Indian and Tibetan materials. He reports even in his time at page 189 ff. actual practising wizards. Barbarous like the contents of the Tantras, is as a rule also the Sanskrit in which it is written, and one would rather pass over this literature in silence were it not for the fact that it has been so widely spread in Northern India, Tibet and latterly in China that to it is attached great culture—historic importance.

**Printed Tantra literature.**

An anthology called *Subhushitasamgraha* published by Bendall (Le Museon, 1903, p. 275 ff.) contains extracts from the Madhyamaka and the Tantra texts. Purely magical texts are the *Sadhanas* published by F. W. Thomas (*ibid* p. 1 ff). The manuscript catalogues give an idea of the great compass of Tantra literature in India. In Tibet the Tantras were the best means of amalgamating Buddhism with the analogous creed of wizards. The Tantras were imported into China in 1200. Some of the Sanskrit tantric MSS. discovered by A. O. Franke, are dealt with by F. Kielhorn, (JRAS, 1894, 835 ff). In Japan the Shin-gon sect is based on Tantra texts. (B. Nanjio, *Short History of the Twelve Japanese Buddhist Sects.*) On Tantras and the Tantra Buddhism in general, see Burnouf Introduction p. 465 ff, 578 f; Wassiljew *Der Buddhismus*, p. 201 ff., but especially La Vallee Poussin *Bouddhism Etudes et Materiaux*, pp. 72 ff., 130 ff., and *Bouddhisme*, pp. 343 ff., 368 ff.

# CHAPTER X.

## CHRISTIANITY AND BUDDHISM

### Resemblances and Differences.

So far as Buddhism has been a world-religion a great part of the Buddhist literature belongs to the world-literature. We have seen in several places that Buddhistic fables, anecdotes, stories and legends have not only immigrated along with Buddhism into East Asia but have their manifold parallels in European literatures,—a circumstance, however, which does not establish that Buddhistic stories have wandered into Europe but that frequently the reverse has been the case. We have also seen that the legend of the Buddha himself has many features in common with the Christian religion and that individual dicta and similies in the *suttas* or dialogues in the Buddhist "Tipitaka" and in the Mahayana *sutras* remind us more or less strikingly of passages in the Chiristian Gospel.

**Are similarities accidental?**

The question, however, to what extent such resemblances between the Buddhist and Christian literatures actually exist and what importance is to be attached to them is of such a moment that we must once again examine it as a whole. Is it a question here of a few more or less accidental similarities and harmonies which are to be explained by the fact that the legends, similarities, and expressions in question have sprung from the same situation and religious spirit; or is it a matter of actual dependence of one literature upon the other? Does the Christian Gospel stand under the influence of the Buddhist holy writ derived from the pre-Christian times? Or have the later Buddhist texts like the *Lalitavistara* and *Saddharma-pundarika* been influenced by the Christian Gospel? These problems have repeatedly been the subject of research and have found various answers.

**Seydel's hypothesis.**

It was especially Rudolf Seydel who believed that he had proved numerous instances of harmony between the life of Jesus, according to the Gospel, and the legend of the Buddha, so that he set up the hypothesis that the evangelists employed, along with a *primitive* Matthew and a *primitive* Mark, also an ancient Christian poetic Gospel which was influenced by Buddhism, and that from the latter were borrowed all those legends, similitudes, and expressions which have answering parallels in the Buddhist texts. He considered this hypothesis to be necessary, because the similarities according to his view appear not solitary but in abundance and to constitute regular groups, in fact, a connected whole. A single stick, he believed, can be easily broken but with much more difficulty a bundle of them or rather a bundle of bundles. Quite true. If, however, the stick is no stick but a phantom of a stick, it is no use, nor is a bundle of them nor a bundle of bundles either. As a matter of fact it is not difficult to show, and has been shown repeatedly, that the majority of similarities adduced by Seydel cannot bear a more precise test.

**"Loans" from Buddhism.**

More cautious than that of Seydel is the attitude of the Dutch scholar G. A. van den Bergh van Eysinga towards the problem of Indian influence on the Christian scriptures. From the start he set aside all which can be easily explained on the ground of similarity of circumstances under which the texts arose, on the ground of the similarity of religious development, and lastly on the ground of general human nature. Still according to him there are real similarities which can be accounted for only as loans, but we have not to assume a literary dependence but that only by verbal communication in the times of the Roman Caesars Indian material, motives, and ideas reached the West and that a few of these features were borrowed in the structure of the legends of the *earliest Christianity*. Of the fifty-one parallels which Seydel believed were discovered, Bergh van Eysinga holds only nine to be worth discussing and six only out of these to be more or less to the point.

**American scholar's researches.**

What Seydel undertook to give with the help of insufficient material—in his time Buddhist literature was very incompletely known—namely, harmonies between the Buddhist and Christian scriptures, has been once again attempted on the basis of much more exact knowledge of Pali and Sanskrit texts by the American scholar, Albert J. Edmunds. It is not his object, as he expressly states, to demonstrate the dependence of the Christian scriptures upon the Buddhist but only to place the two religions in juxtaposition so that their comparison may enable us to understand them better. Nevertheless, he is inclined to the view that Christianity as the more eclectic religion of the two borrowed from Buddhism, and that it was especially Luke who knew the Buddhist epic. But the comprehensive contexts of the passages brought forward by Edmunds, and which are comparable only half-ways in both the literary circles, most clearly prove that there is no instance in which a loan on the part of the four evangelists *must* be assumed; that in most cases there is only similarity of thought which does not presume a literary connection; that in the best of examples we can admit only a *possibility* of a mutual influence, and that this possibility is heightened to probability in altogether very few cases. And frequently enough the passages placed in parallels by Edmunds demonstrate how much greater are the divergencies than the similarities.

Let us read for instance the parallel texts in Edmunds regarding the miraculous conception and birth of Christ and of the Buddha and the dissimilarities immediately arrest our attention. No doubt in both cases we have miracles. But there they are, as we learn from the history of religions as well as mythology and folk-lore, at the birth of great men everywhere. To the Virgin birth the Greek mythology offers a much closer parallel than the Buddhist legend. But the Buddha was not conceived and given birth to by a maid but by a wedded queen. Besides the texts touching the temptation of the Buddha by Mara, and Christ by Satan, show more divergencies than similarities and the temptation of Zoroaster by Ahriman indicates that here we have not to do with simple textual loans but at the most with the historico-religious connections of much earlier times. Likewise in the legend of the transfiguration of Jesus as compared with the report of the phospherescent body of the Buddha in the *Mahaparinibbanasutta*, I can only see a striking and highly interesting historico-religious parallel but no borrowing from the Buddhist literature.

**Parallel texts.**

Much greater is the similarity between the legends of Asita and of Simeon in Luke. In spite of several divergencies, which even here are undeniable, I consider it to a certain extent probable that the Buddhist legend was known to the author of the Christian narrative. Possible also is a connection between the legend of the Buddha, who as a boy separated himself from his companions and was found in deep meditation, and the narrative of the twelve-year old Jesus who instead of returning with his parents to Nazareth stopped behind in the temple of Jerusalem and engaged in a conversation with the teachers. I hold likewise possible a connection between the benediction on the Lord's Mother by the woman in Luke (XI. 27f) and in the *Nidanakatha*. And even if it is not surprising that a saint

**Legends.**

is served by an angel, still it is noteworthy that angels received the *fasting* Jesus and the *fasting* Buddha; hence here also a connection is possible.

**Miracles.**

To the miracles of Christ two parallels have been found in the *Jataka* book. As Jesus fed with five loaves and two fishes five thousand men, so in a Jataka five hundred men are feasted by means of a cake which multiplies itself. And just as Peter walks over the water and is about to sink underneath as soon as his faith wavers, so in another Jataka a believing layman walks across a river so long as he thinks of the Buddha with cheerful mind and begins to sink as soon as the inspiring Buddha thoughts are discarded at the sight of the waves. But both these accounts occur only in the "stories of the present" in the Jataka commentary and from their late time of origin it is not precluded that they originally belonged to Christianity. From post-Christian times is also derived the narrative of the poor maiden who bestows upon the monks her all, two copper pieces, which she had found in a heap of sweepings and is commended on that account by the Buddha according to whom her gift must be as highly prized as that of a wealthy person who gives away all his goods and treasures. She has not to wait long for the reward of her good deed. Soon after, she is found by a passing king who falls in love with her and carries her home his queen. It is not to be doubted that the Buddhist narrative in the form in which we know it in the Chinese translation of Ashvaghosha's *Sutralankara* stands, as regards time, far behind the Gospel story, so wonderfully beautiful in all its simplicity, of the two pennies of the widow. Here too it is not impossible that the Buddhists may have learnt it from Christian missionaries. It is also not inconceivable that an older and better shape of the Buddhist legend has been lost to us. The concord in respect of such a minor detail as the "two pennies" makes it in the highest degree probable that the Buddhist and Christian stories have not arisen independently of each other.

Less probable it is that the parable of the "lost son" in the *Saddharmapundarika* is connected with that in Luke. Even Seydel says, "the simile of the *Lotus* has in truth nothing to do with Christianity except that a son returns in poverty, and above all the motive of comparison in each of the parallels is wholly and entirely different." The similarity between the legend of Jesus and the Samaritan woman in John, and that of Ananda and the Pariah maiden in the *Divyavadana* is not very great. In both the cases, moreover, we have to deal with the Buddhist texts of post-Christian times.

**Resurrection and Nirvana.**

The death of Christ has also been compared with the entry of the Buddha into *nirvana*. Seydel has indicated that the events are accompanied by an earthquake; while Edmunds points out that Jesus as well as the Buddha die in the open air. And yet the differences in both the religious texts are nowhere so great. What a dissonance between the *Mahaparinibbanasutta* and the XXVIIth Chapter of Matthew! Here is the moving tragedy of a martyr and a victim of fanaticism, there the tranquil passing of a sage—a glorious euthanasia. In the gospel of Matthew there is an earthquake and graves open in horror of the misdeed; in the *Mahaparinibbanasutta* the earthquake is to announce its approbation of the beautiful consummation of the complete *nirvana* of the Lord Less probable still in respect of the legends is the connection between the isolated expressions and similes employed by Jesus and the Buddha. It is mostly only a matter of such general similarity or such generality of thought that the same might as well occur, and in fact does occur, in the sacred books of all the religious; as, for instance, in the *Majjhimanikaya* 110 where there is a mention of the seed and the harvest of good works which is comparable to the similitude of the sower in Matthew (XII 18 f); or in the *sutta* of the "true treasure" where similar thought is expressed as in Matthew VI 19. "Lay not up for yourselves treasures upon the earth, where moth and rust doth consume, &c."

**Results of comparison.**

And when we put together the results of comparison of the four gospels with the Buddhistic texts we see that the discordances are much greater than the harmonies. In the entire character itself of the legends which bear comparison there is a vast divergence. While in Buddhism all the miracles are explained by *Karma*, by the act continuing to operate through re-birth, the Christian miracles are only a manifestation of God's grace and omnipotence. Very pertinently remarks Edv. Lehmann: "For the taste of the Indians the occurrences in the Christian narratives have always an insufficient motive, and to us Christians, the Indian narratives —even from pure aesthetical standpoint—strike as almost unsupportably well-motived." Accordingly it is out of the question that the Buddhist literature should have exercised *direct* influence on the Gospel. On the other hand it is certain that since the period of Alexander the Great and especially in the times of the Roman Caesars there were both numerous commercial links and spiritual relationship between India and the West, so that a superficial acquaintance with the Buddhistic ideas and solitary Buddhist legends was quite possible, even probable, in the circles in which the Gospels originated. Positive proof of the knowledge of Buddhism in the West, however, we possess only from the second or third century after Christ. And this is also the period of the rise of apocryphal Gospels in which we are able to demonstrate quite a series of undoubted loans from Buddhistic literature.

Equally certain it is that one of the favourite books of Christianity in the Middle Ages, the romance of *Barlam and Josaphat*, was composed by a pious Christian on the basis of the Buddhist legend with which he was acquainted, may be, through the *Lalitavistara.* For the framework of this romance, in other respects wholly and entirely breathing a Christian spirit, is Buddhistic and the main features of the Buddhistic legend in it are reproduced, for instance, the three occasions on which the Bodhisattva went out and made his acquaintance with age, disease and death. A few of the interpolated parables are well known in Indian literature, like the "man in the well," and in the story itself there are references to India. In Eastern Iran or in Central Asia, where as we now learn from the discoveries at Khotan and Turfan by Stein, Grunwedel and Le Coq, for centuries Zoroastrians, Buddhists, Christians and Manichians lived in close contact with each other, a Christian monk might easily have learnt the Buddhistic legend and been inspired thereby to a poem for the propagation of the Christian doctrine. This poem was, as we conjecture, composed in the sixth or seventh century in the Pahlavi language and later translated into Arabic and Syriac. Georgian and Greek translations must have been based on the Syriac text. From the Greek text are derived the several recensions in Arabic, Hebrew, Ethiopian, Armenian, Slav and Ruminian. The numerous European translations and redactions—Lope de Vaga has treated the material dramatically—can be traced to a Latin text translated from the Greek. There have been adaptations of the romance in German since 1220. In course of centuries the actors in this poem became so familiar to the Christian peoples that they were regarded as pious Christian folk who had actually lived and taught, so that finally the Catholic Church made saints of the two heroes of the narrative, Barlaam and Josaphat. Josaphat, however, is no other than the Bodhisattva.

**Vitality of Buddhism.**

And as in the Middle Ages so also down to our days the Indian Buddha legend has shown vitality and has inspired poet after poet to epic and even dramatic presentments. Thus the "Light of Asia" by the English poet Edwin Arnold could even in the nineteenth century arouse such enthusiasm that it went through sixty editions in England and one hundred in America and thoroughly established the poet's fame.

We have already seen that a Buddhist legend survives in Richard Wagner's poetry. In the last days of his life the personality of the Buddha occupied him and it is not to be wondered at that after Wagner's death the rumour was afloat, no doubt without warrant, that the poet had worked upon a musical drama called "Buddha."

The neo-Buddhistic movement of our day has shown itself less fruitful in respect of literary creations. Apart from translations it has hardly gone much beyond anthologies, catechisms, and shallow propagandistic writings. But if we see in this neo-Buddhism spreading in Europe and America only one of the many paths of error in which the struggle for a new philosophy has conducted us, nevertheless we must admire the vitality of Buddhism and the Buddhist literary works which have inspired again and again the minds of thinkers and poets of all nations and still continue to so inspire. And I hope to have shown in this chapter that there is still a good deal hidden in Buddhist literature which is worthy of being transferred to the literature of Europe and to be made the common property of the world-literature.

## CHAPTER XI.

### ANCIENT INDIAN NATIONAL LITERATURE.

**Importance and extent of Indian literature.**

The history of Indian literature is the history of the mental work of at least three thousand years expressed in speech and script. And the theatre of this mental operation of hundreds of years almost uninterrupted continuance is the country which stretches from the Hindukush to Cape Comorin and covers a surface of a million and a half square miles, that is to say, comprises an area equivalent to the whole of Europe minus Russia,—a country which extends from the eighth to the thirty-fifth degree of north latitude, in other words, from the hottest regions of the equator deep into the temperate zone. The influence which this literature exercised already in ancient days on the mental life of other nations reaches far beyond the frontiers of India down to Farther India, Tibet, China, Japan, Korea and in the south over Ceylon and the Malaya Archipelago and the group of islands in the Indian and the Pacific Oceans, while in the west traces of Indian mental culture are observable deep into Central Asia, and east to Turkestan where buried in sandy deserts Indian manuscripts have recently been discovered. (See Appendix IV.)

In its contents the Indian literature comprises all that the word-literature includes in its wider connotation,—religious and profane, epic and lyric, dramatic and didactic, poetry as well as story-literature and scientific treatises in prose.

In the foreground stands religious literature. Not only the Brahmans in the Veda and the Buddhists in the Tripitaka but also many others of the numerous religious sects which have appeared in India own an enormous mass of literary product,—hymns, sacrificial litanies, magic charms, myths and legends and sermons, theological treatises, polemical writings, manuals of ritual and religious ordinance. In this literature there are accumulated for a history of religions inestimable material which no investigator of the religious phenomenon can afford to inattentively pass by. Alongside of this activity in the region of religious writings going back to thousands of years and perpetuated down to this day there have appeared in India, since earliest times, heroic poems which in the course of centuries have been composed into two great national epics,—the *Mahabharata* and the *Ramayana*. From the material of these two epics for centuries Indian poets of the Middle ages shaped their creations and there arose epic poems which are, in contrast with the national poems, designated artistic epics. If, however, this artistic ministrelsy owing to its excessive artificiality hardly answer to our taste the Indian poets have bequeathed to us lyrical and dramatic compositions which in their tenderness and insight, partly also in their dramatic portrayal, challenge comparison with the finest products of modern European literature. And in one branch of fine letters, that of poetic maxims, the Indians acquired a supremacy unattained as yet by any other nation. India is also the land of stories and fables. The Indian collections of tales, anecdotes and prose narratives, have played no insignificant role in the history of the literature of the world. In fact, the researches into the story literature, the fascinating study of folklore and the pursuit of their motifs and migrations from nation to nation, have become a science in itself as a continuance of the fundamental work of Benfey on *Panchatantra*, the Indian collection of fables.

**Peculiar traits of Indian genius.**

It is a peculiarity of Indian genius that it never drew a rigid line of demarcation between the purely artificial products and methodical creations so that a differentiation between polite literature and scientific writing is, properly speaking, not possible in India. What appears to us as a collection of stories and fables passes for the Indian as a manual of politics or ethics. On the other hand, history and biography in India are nothing less than themes to be treated by bards as a variety of epic poetry. Besides, properly speaking, a difference between the forms of poetry and prose does not exist in India. Every subject can be handled in verse or in prose equally well. We find romances which are distinguished from epics only in this that they are devoid of metrical mould. A particular predilection is evinced since the most ancient days for an admixture of prose and verse. And for what we call strictly scientific literature India uses only partly the prose form, verse being employed in a much larger volume. This applies to works of philosophy and jurisprudence just as well as mathematics, astronomy, architecture and so forth. The Indians, indeed, have composed their grammars and dictionaries in verse, and nothing more perhaps is characteristic of the Indian genius than that a voluminous epic of the artificial kind in twenty-two cantos has been devoted to the express object of illustrating and emphasising rules of grammar. From early times philosophy has been at home in India. At first it appeared conjointly with religious literature. Later on it became independent of the latter, and it has always been a theme of literary labour. Similarly already in remote antiquity law and custom,—likewise in connection with religion—have been made the subject of legal literature composed partly in prose and partly in verse. The importance of these legal writings for comparative jurisprudence and sociology is to-day fully appreciated by eminent jurists and leaders of social science. Centuries before the birth of Christ, in India was studied grammar, a science in which the Indians surpassed all nations of antiquity. Lexicography also goes back to high antiquity. The artificial poets of India of later days sang not what was bestowed upon them by the gods, but they studied the rules of grammar and searched into dictionaries for rare and effective poetic expressions. They composed poetry according to the canon laid down in scientific treatises on metre and prosody. From the first the Indian mind had a particular penchant for devising schemes and for pedantically scientific treatment of all possible subects. We find accordingly in India not only a rigid and partly ancient literature on mathematics, astrology, arithmetic and geography but also music, singing, dancing, theatricals, soothsaying, sorcery, nay, even erotics reduced to a system and treated in special manuals. Each individual branch of literature here enumerated in the course of centuries accumulated a mass of uncontrollably immense productions. Not the least contributions came from commentators who displayed a diligent activity on almost every province of religious literature as well as poetry and science. Thus it comes about that some of the most momentous and at the same time ponderous works on grammar, philosophy and law represent merely commentaries on more ancient books. On these scholia were composed further supercommentaries. In India, indeed, it is not seldom that an author supplies annotations to his own works. It is no wonder therefore that the entire body of Indian literature is well nigh of overpowering extent, and in spite of the catalogues of Indian manuscripts which are to be found in Indian and European libraries and which contain several thousands of titles of books and names of authors, numberless works of Indian literature have perished and many names of ancient authors have either been known only by means of quotations in later writers or have been totally lost to us.

**Aryan unity of speech.**

All these facts,—the age, the wide geographical expanse, the volume and the wealth, the æsthetic and still more the cultural value of Indian literature,—would completely suffice to justify our interest in its vast, peculiar and ancient literature. And there is something more which lends special interest to the national books of India. The Indo-Aryan languages together with the Iranian tongues composed the eastern branch of the great family of languages to which belongs the English speech and the idioms of most countries of Europe and which is denominated the Indo-Aryan group. It was just this Indian literature the investigation of which led to the discovery of the science of languages,—a discovery which was truly epoch-making in that it throws such surprising new light on prehistoric international relations. For, from the affinity of the languages we are led to linguistic unity in ancient times, and from these latter again we deduce an intimate connection between the peoples employing these Indo-Aryan tongues. No doubt serious errors are common relating to the affinities of the Indo-Aryan peoples even to this day. People talk of an "Indo-Aryan Race" which simply does not exist and has never existed. Again we sometimes hear that the Indians, Persians, Greeks, Romans, Germans and Slavs are of one and the same blood,—the descendants of the self-same Indo-Aryan "primitive people." All these are unwarranted and hasty anticipations. If, however, it is more than doubtful whether the people who spoke the Indo-Aryan languages were derived from the same aboriginal septs, it is beyond question that the unity of language, the important instrument of all mental activity, pre-supposes a spiritual affinity and a unity of culture. If the Indian is not the flesh of our flesh and the blood of our blood we can discover in the Indian world of thought our own mentality. For recognition, however, of the "Indo-Aryan spirit," that is, to attain to what is claimed as peculiar in the Indo-Aryan thought and mind and poetry of these people, it is imperatively necessary that our insular acquaintance with Indo-Aryan essentials such as we have acquired by a study of European literatures should be supplemented by a knowledge of the Indo-Aryan spirit such as has been developed in the Far East. Therefore Indian literature constitutes a necessary complement to the classics of ancient Greece and Rome for every person who would eschew a one-sided consideration of Indo-Aryan essentials. True, Indian literature in its artistic value cannot be compared with that of Greece. It is certain that the thought-world of India has not in the remotest degree exercised such influence on European spiritual life as Greek and Roman culture has done. But should we desire to learn the origins of our own culture and should we wish to understand the most ancient Indo-Aryan civilization we must go to India where are preserved for us the most ancient writings of the Indo-Aryan people. For in whichever way the problem of the antiquity of Indian literature is decided, this stands firmly established that the remotest literary monuments of India are at the same time the oldest Indo-Aryan written records in our possession. But even the intermediate influence which the literature of India has exercised on European thought is not altogether trivial. We shall see in the course of our further investigations that the story literature of Europe is by no means insignificantly indebted to India. And as regards the literature of the Germans and their philosophy both of them from the beginning of the nineteenth century have been affected by Indian thought and it is highly probable that its influence will tend to intensify and develop in the course of future centuries.

**Impact of Indian genius on German thought.**

For a mental relationship, which is deducible from the Indo-Aryan speech unity, is still clearly discernible and is no where more so as between the Indian and the Teutonic races. The surprising points of contact between the two have often been indicated, for instance, by G. Brandes and Leopold von Schroeder. Critics have before now called attention to the common predeliction of both for abstract speculation and a tendency to pantheism but in many other respects also the two approach each other in a remarkable degree. Some of the European poets have sung of the "sorrows of the world." And the "sorrows of existence" is the basic idea on which is constructed the doctrine of the Buddha. More than one poet have bewailed the tribulations and misery of the world, the transitoriness and nullity of all that is terrestrial in words which forcibly remind the reader of the melancholy verses of Nikolus Lenau. When Heine says :—

> Sweet is sleep, death is better
> It were best of all not to have been born,

he gives expression just to those sentiments beloved of the Indian philosophers who know of no effort more passionate than for a death which knows of no re-birth. Even the sentimentality and the feeling for nature have identical peculiarities for the two peoples while to both the Hebrew and the Greek poesy sounds foreign. The Germans love delineation of nature just as well as the Indians and both love to bring into close relationship the joys and sorrows of man with his natural surroundings. In a totally different province the similarity between German and Indian fables asserts itself. We have already spoken of the tendency of the Indians towards the devising of scientific schemes and we can assert with justification that the Indians were the learned nation of antiquity. Just as the Indians in the gray dawn of the remotest past philologically analysed their oldest sacred scriptures and reduced linguistic phonomena to a systematic science and advanced in grammar so far that modern science of languages to this day leans on their early achievements, just in the same way the Germans of to-day are incontestably leaders in the domains of philology and science of languages. In the region of Indian philology and in the investigations of Indian literature the Germans have been pioneers. We owe it to the British that as the rulers of India they were compelled by practical necessity to the study of Indian languages and literature. Much has been done for the literature and culture of old India by eminent Frenchmen, Italians, Dutch, Danes, Americans, Russians and—let it not be forgotten—indigenous Indian scholars. The Germans have participated in the publication of texts, commentaries, exegesis, in the editing of dictionaries and grammars. This leads us to a brief survey of the history of beginnings of European researches into Indian linguistic archæology.

## CHAPTER XII.

### BEGINNINGS OF INDIAN STUDIES IN EUROPE.

The immense mass of Indian literary works which could scracely be now controlled by a single scholar has been made accessible for research purposes in the course of a little more than a century.

In the 17th and still more in the 18th century individual travellers and missionaries acquired a certain knowledge of Indian languages and made themselves familiar with some one or another book pertaining to Indian literature. Their efforts, however, were not sown in a fertile soil. In the year 1651 Abraham Roger, a Dutch, who had lived as a missionary in Policat, north of Madras, reported on the Indian Brahmanic literature of India and published a few of the sayings of Bhartrihari translated into Portuguese for him by a Brahman, a collection upon which later on Herder drew for his "Voices of Nations in Song". In the year 1699 the Jesuit father, Johann Ernst Hanxleden, went to India and worked there for over thirty years in the Malabar mission. He himself used Indian vernaculars and his "Grammatica" was the first Sanskrit grammar written by a European. It has never been printed but was used by Fra Polino de St. Bartholomeo. This Fra Polino,—an Austrian Carmelite, whose real name was J. Ph. Wessdin,—is undoubtedly among the most eminent evangelists who were the pioneers in the field of Indian literature. He was a missionary to the Coast of Malabar from 1776-1789 and died in Rome in 1805. He wrote two Sanskrit grammars and several learned treatises and books. His "Systema Brahmanicum" published in Rome in 1792 and his "Travels in the East Indies" displayed an extensive knowledge of India and Brahmanic literature and at the same time a deep study of Indian tongues and particularly the essentials of the Indian religion. Even his works have left few traces behind.

**Great Britain and Brahmanic learning.**

About this time, however, the British commenced to be interested in the languages and literature of India. It was no less a personage than Warren Hastings, the real founder of British domination in India, who gave the first fruitful impetus to a study of Indian literature which has since continued without interruption. He recognised (this the British since have never forgotten) that the British rule in India could not be consolidated unless the rulers agreed to conciliate, as far as possible, the social and religious tenets of the indigenous people. At his suggestion, therefore, it was decided in the council responsible for the Government of India that native scholars should co-operate with judicial officials to enable British judges to take cognizance of the ordinances of Indian jurisprudence in their decisions. When Warren Hastings was appointed Governor-General of Bengal and was entrusted with supreme powers relating to the entire British possessions in India he had, with the help of a number of Brahmans learned in ancient Hindu law, composed a work based on old Sanskrit sources in which under the title of "*Vivadarnavasetu*," or the "Bridge across the Ocean of Disputations," were incorporated all the important elements of Indian law on inheritance, succession and the like. But when the work was accomplished there was found no one in a position to transalate directly its Sanskrit text into English. Recourse was therefore had to the prevailing imperial tongue of the time. The Sanskrit work was first rendered into Persian and from the latter an English version was prepared by Nathaniel Brassey Halhed. This translation was published at the expense of the East India Company under the name of "A Code of Genteoo Law" in 1776 (Gentoo is the Portuguese for Hindu). A German translation of this law book appeared at Hamburg in 1778.

The first Englishman to acquire a knowledge of Sanskrit was Charles Wilkins, who was encouraged by Warren Hastings to study with the Pandits at Benares, the principal seat of Indian learning. As the first fruit of his Sanskrit studies he published in 1785 an English translation of the philosophical poem of *Bhagavadgita* which was thus the first Sanskrit book to be directly translated into a European language. Two years later followed a translation of the Fables of *Hitopadesha* and in 1795 a translation of the *Shakuntala* episode from the *Mahabharata*. For his Sanskrit grammar which appeared in 1808 for the first time Sanskrit types were cast in Europe. These were cut and prepared by himself personally. This Englishman, Charles Wilkins, was also the first who laboured on Indian inscriptions and translated some of them into English.

**Early English scholars.**

Still more important for the development of European efforts in the vast domain of Indian literature was the activity of the celebrated Orientalist William Jones (1746-1794) who started for India in 1783 to take up the situation of a superior writer in Fort William. Jones had already in his younger years busied himself with Oriental poetry and rendered into English, Arabic and Persian poems. No wonder therefore that arrived in India, he turned with enthusiasm to the study of Sanskrit and Indian literature. Exactly a year after his arrival he became the founder of the Asiatic Society of Bengal, which developed an extraordinarily valuable career by the publication of periodicals and especially the printing of numerous Indian texts. In 1789 he published his English translation of the celebrated drama of *Shakuntala* by Kalidasa. This English translation was turned into German in 1791 by Forster and kindled to the highest degree the enthusiasm of celebrities like Herder and

**Jones and Colebrooke.**

Goethe. Another work of the same poet Kalidasa, the lyric of *Ritusamhara*, was brought out in Calcutta in 1792 by Jones and this was the first Sanskrit text to be published in print. Of still greater moment was it that Jones translated into English the most celebrated law book of Manu which commands the supreme position in Indian legal literature. The translation appeared in Calcutta in 1794 and was called " Institutes of Hindu Law or the Ordinances of Manu." A German translation of this book appeared in 1797 at Wiemar. Again, William Jones was the first to aver with certainty the genealogical connection of Sanskrit with Greek and Latin and to surmise it for the German, Celtic and Persian languages. He also called attention to the analogy between ancient Indian and the Græco-Roman mythology.

While the enthusiastic Jones, owing to the spirit which he brought to bear upon the treasures of Indian literature, and bringing them to light, provided a powerful stimulant, the more sober Thomas Colebrooke who continued the labours of Jones was the actual founder of Indian philology and antiquity. Colebrooke had entered upon an official career as a lad of sixteen in Calcutta in 1782 without troubling himself about Sanskrit and its literature for the first eleven years of his stay in India. But when Jones died in 1784 Colebrooke had already picked up Sanskrit and undertook to translate from Sanskrit into English a digest of Indian law prepared from Sanskrit text-books on inheritance and contract under the direction of Jones. This translation saw the light in 1797-98 and its exact title was " A digest of Hindu Law of Contracts and Successions." It covered four folio volumes. Henceforward he devoted himself with indefatigable zeal to the investigation of Indian literature and he was interested—in contrast to Jones—not so much in poetry as in the scientific works in Sanskrit. We owe him accordingly not only more works on Indian law but also pioneer dissertations on the philosophy of religion, grammar, and ancient mathematics of the Hindus. It was he who in 1805 in his celebrated essays on the Vedas supplied for the first time precise and reliable information on the ancient sacred books of the Indians. For the so-called translation of the *Yajurveda* which appeared under the title of *Ezour Vedam*, in 1778 in French, and in 1779 in German, was only a literary fabrication, a pious fraud, which originated probably with the missionary Robert de Nobilibus. The French poet Voltaire received from the hands of an official returned from Pondicherry this supposititious translation and presented it to the Royal Library of Paris. The poet considered the book to be an ancient commentary on the Vedas, which was translated into French by a venerable Brahman hundred years old and he frequently relied upon this *Ezour Vedam* as a source of Indian antiquity. As early, however, as 1782 Sonnerat proved the work to be spurious. Colebrooke was also the editor of the *Amarakosha* and other Indian lexicons, the celebrated grammar of Panini, the Fables of *Hitopadesha* and the artistic poem of *Kiratarjuniya*. He was also the author of a Sanskrit grammar and studied and translated a number of inscriptions. Finally he had treasured an extraordinarily rich collection of Indian MSS. which is reported to have cost him £10,000 and which on his return to England he presented to the East India Company. This valuable mass of manuscripts is among the most precious treasures of the India Office Library in London. Among the Englishmen, who like Jones and Colebrooke, studied Sanskrit at the close of the 18th century in India was Alexander Hamilton. He returned to Europe in 1802 and travelling through France sojourned at Paris for a brief while. There an accident occurred disagreeable to himself, but unusually favourable to the cause of science. For the hostilities interrupted only for a short period by the Peace of Amiens broke out afresh between England and France and Napoleon issued an order that all the British who were staying at the outbreak of the war in France should be prohibited to return to their home and detained in Paris. Alexander Hamilton was among these English detenus. Now, in 1802 the German poet Friedrich Schlegel also happened to go to Paris to stay there with a few interruptions down to the year 1807, – just the period covered by the involuntary sojourn of Hamilton. In Germany interest had already been awakened in the work of the English. A sensation was created, especially by the English translation of *Shakuntala* by Jones which was immediately done into German in 1791. Between 1795 and 1797 the productions of Jones were translated into German; so also was Jones' "Digest of Hindu Law" in 1797. Nor were the works of Fra Polino de St. Bartholomeo unknown in Germany. It was above all the romantic school at the head of which stood the brothers Schlegel on which the literature of India exercised especial fascination. It was indeed the time when people were growing enthusiastic over foreign literatures. Herder had already with his "Voices of Nations in Songs" and his "Ideas on the History of Mankind" (1784-1791) called attention to the Orient. The Romantists threw themselves heart and soul into everything connected with foreign and distant lands and were particularly partial to India. As Fr. Schlegel said, from India was expected nothing less than a key to the hitherto obscure history of the primitive world, and the friends of poetry hoped, since the publication of *Shakuntala* for many similar charming idylls of the Asiatic soul, instinct like it, with animation and love. Small wonder therefore, that Fr. Schlegel, when he became acquainted in Paris with Alexander Hamilton, immediately seized the occasion to study Sanskrit with him. During 1803 and 1804 he had the benefit of his instruction and the further years of his stay in Paris he employed in study in the library there, which even then possessed about two hundred Indian manuscripts. A catalogue of this was published by Haton in Paris in 1807. In collaboration with Langles he translated Hamilton's Notes from English into French. Fr. Schlegel's great work came out in 1808, "On the language and the wisdom of the Indians; a contribution to the foundation of the knowledge of antiquity." This book was written with enthusiasm and was calculated to be an inspiration. Besides, it contained renderings of extracts from the *Ramayana*, Manu's law book, the *Bhagavadgita*, and episode from the *Mahabharata* bearing on *Shakuntkla*. These were the first direct translations from Sanskrit into German. All that had appeared in Germany prior to this on Indian literature was borrowed from English publications.

**Sanskrit learning and Germany.**

But while Friedrich Schlegel gave an impetus to Sanskrit studies it was his brother August W. Schlegel who was the first to develop extensive activity in Germany by means of the publication of the editions of texts, translations and similar philological works. He was, moreover, the first professor of Sanskrit in Germany and as such was appointed to the chair founded at the university of Bonn in 1818. Like his brother in Paris who commenced his studies in 1814, he started his investigations in Paris. His teacher was the French savant A. L. Chezy, the first French scholar who learnt and taught Sanskrit. He was also the first professor of Sanskrit at the College de France and had rendered service to Oriental literature as an editor and translator of Indian books. In the year 1823 appeared the first volume of the periodical "The Indian Library" founded and mostly written by August Schlegel. It contains numerous essays on Indian philology. In the same year he published also a good edition of the *Bhagavadgita* with a Latin translation, while in the year 1829 came out the first part of the most important work of Schlegel, his edition of the *Ramayana* which has remained incomplete.

A contemporary of August Schlegel was Franz Bopp. Born in 1791, he proceeded to Paris in 1812 to occupy himself with Oriental languages and there sat along with Schlegel at the feet of the French scholar Chezy and acquired Sanskrit. But while the brothers Schlegel enthused over India as romantic poets and regarded the study of Indian literature as a kind of "adventure," Bopp entered upon the subject throughout as a prosaic investigator and it was he who by means of his essays on the "Conjugation system of the Sanskrit language in comparison with that of Greek, Latin, Persian and German languages," which appeared in 1816, became the founder of a new science, the science of comparative philology which had such a great future before it. But even to researches in Indian literature Bopp made unusual contributions. In his "Conjugation system" he gave as an appendix several episodes from the *Ramayana* and the *Mahabharata* in metrical rendering from the original text and a few extracts from the Veda taken over from the English translation of Colebrooke. With rare fortune he seized upon the marvellous history of king Nala and his faithful consort Damayanti out of the colossal epic of the *Mahabharata* and made it generally accessible by means of a critical edition accompanied by a Latin translation. It was just the one out of the numerous episodes in the *Mahabharata* which approaches nearest to a complete whole and does not merely belong to the finest pieces in the great epic but as one of the most fascinating efforts of Indian poetic genius is specially calculated to arouse vivid interest for Indian letters and a fondness for Sanskrit study. It has since then grown into quite a tradition at all the universities where Sanskrit is taught to select the Nala episode as the first reading text-book for the students, for whom it is eminently suitable owing to its simplicity of style. Bopp for the first time edited and translated into German quite a series of legends from the *Mahabharata*. His Sanskrit grammars which saw light of day in 1837, 1832, 1834 and his "glossarium Sanscritum" have powerfully advanced the study of Sanskrit on the continent.

It was a piece of good fortune for the young science and for the study of Sanskrit which long thereafter was connected with it that the gifted, many-sided and influential W. Humboldt became enamoured of it. He started to learn Sanskrit in 1821 since, as he wrote in a letter to August Schlegel, he had seen "that without sound grounding in the study of Sanskrit not the least progress could be made either in the knowledge of languages nor in that class of history which is connected with it." When Schlegel in the year 1828 indulged in a retrospect of his Indian studies, he gave prominence as a special piece of luck for the new science, to the fact that it had found in Humboldt a warm friend and patron. Schlegel's edition of the *Bhagavadgita* had called Humboldt's attention to this theosophical poem. He dedicated to him some treatises and wrote about it at the time, 1827, to Gentz, "it is the most profound and loftiest yet seen by the world." And when later on in 1828 he sent to his friend his study on the *Bhagavadgita* which had meanwhile been criticised by Hegel, he declared that the greater the apathy betrayed in Hegel's judgment, the greater was the value he attached to the philosophical poem of India. "When I read the Indian poem," he wrote, "for the first time and ever since then my sentiment was one of perpetual gratitude for my luck, which had kept me still alive to be able to be acquainted with this book."

Another great name in German literature connected with India was, to the good fortune of our science, a poet inspired with the romance of India. This was Friedrich Ruckert, the incomparable master of the art of translation. It was he who made some of the choicest portions of Indian epical and lyrical treasures the common property of the German people.

Up to 1839 it was almost exclusively the so-called classical Sanskrit literature which attracted the attention of the European scholar. The drama of *Shakuntala*, the philosophical poem of *Bhagavadgita*, the law book of Manu, maxims by Bhartrhari, the fables of *Hitopadesha* and stray passages from the great epics; this was nearly the sum total of the principal works with which scholars were occupied and which was regarded as the stock-in-trade of Indian literature. The great and all-important region of the Indian literature, that of the Vedas, was next to unknown and people were not yet aware of the existence of the entire great Buddhist literature.

**Dara Shukoh's Persian Upanishad.**

The little that up to 1830 was known of the Vedas was confined to the miserable and inaccurate data furnished by the early writers on India. Colebrooke gave the first reliable information in the essays we noticed above on the Vedas in 1805. It took several years before a German translation of the English rendering was prepared in 1847. Comparatively the most that people became acquainted with was in the province of the *Upanishads*, the philosophical treatises belonging to the Vedas. These *Upanishads* were translated from their original Sanskrit into Persian early in the seventh century by the ill-starred brother of Aurangzeb, Prince Mohammed Dara Shukoh, the son of the great Moghul Shah Jehan. From the Persian it was rendered into Latin under the title of *Upnekhat* in the beginning of the nineteenth century by the French scholar Anquetil Duperron, the founder of the revival of Parsi learning in India. Imperfect and strewn with errors as the latter was, it was important for the history of science in that the German philosopher Schelling, and more particularly Schopenhauer, were inspired by Indian philosophy on its basis. It was not the *Upanishads* which we understand and elucidate to-day with all the material and our exact knowledge of the philosophical system of India at our disposal but the *Upnekhat*, the altogether faulty rendering of Anquetil Duperron which Schopenhauer declared to be "the issue of supreme human wisdom." And about the same time when in Germany Schopenhauer was delving into the *Upanishads* of the Indians for his own philosophical speculations, there was living in India one of the sanest and noblest of men ever produced by this country, Ram Mohan Roy, the founder of Brahmo Samaj, a new sect which sought to amalgamate the best in the religions of Europe with the faith of the Hindus. This Indian construed the same *Upanishads* so as to read in them purest belief in God and endeavoured to instruct his people that the idolatry of modern Indian religions was to be rejected but that in its stead Indians need not necessarily adopt Christianity but that in their own holy writ, in the ancient Vedas, if they could only understand the latter, was to be found a pure doctrine of monotheism. With a view to proclaim this new tenet which was, however, contained in the old scriptures and propagate it by means of the sect which he had founded, the sect of Brahmo Samaj or the Church of God, and at the same time in order to prove to the Christian theologians, and missionaries whom he highly esteemed that the finest of what they believed in was already embodied in the *Upanishuda*, in the years 1816 to 1819 he rendered into English a large number of *Upanishads* and issued editions of a few of them in the original texts.

**Beginnings of Vedic studies.**

But the real philological investigation of the Vedas commenced only in 1838 after the appearance of the edition in Calcutta of the first section of the *Rigveda* by Friedrich Rosen who was prevented from the completion of his task by premature death. And it was above all the great Frenchman of learning, Eugene Burnouf, who at the commencement of the forties was professor at theCollege de France, who gathered round him a circle of pupils, the future eminent Vedic scholars. Burnouf laid the foundation of Vedic studies in Europe. One of his pupils was Rudolph Roth who, with his *Essay on the literature and history of the Vedas* in 1846 inaugurated the study of the Vedas in Germany. Roth himself and a number of his disciples devoted themselves in the following years and decades with passionate zeal to the exploration of the diverse ramifications of the most ancient literature of India. F. Max Muller was the most celebrated pupil of Burnouf familiar to us. He was initiated into the study of the Vedas by the French master at the same time with Roth. Urged by Burnouf, Max Muller conceived the plan of editing the hymns of the *Rigveda* with the voluminous commentary of Sayana. This edition, which is indispensable for any further research, appeared in 1849-1875. A second and an enlarged edition appeared in 1890-1892. But before this was completed, Thoomas Aufrecht, with his handy print of the complete texts of the hymns of the *Rigveda* rendered signal service to this branch of Indian research.

**Leader of re-search in three great religions.**

The same Eugene Burnouf, who rocked the cradle of the Vedic studies, laid the foundation stone of Pali reasearch and investigation of Bhuddhist literature with his "*Essai sur le Pali*," published in collaboration with Chr. Lassen in 1826 and his "*Introduction a l'histoire de Bouddhisme indien*," still a mine of information, in 1844. The

Parsis too owe the savant pioneer labour in Avesta exegesis. He was the teacher of K. R. Kama, father of Parsi antiquarian studies.

With the invasion of the immense province of Vedic literature and with the introduction into the writings of the Bhuddists the gospel of infancy of Indian philology came to its termination. It has grown into a great science, the devotees of which increase from year to year. One after another now saw the light of day critical editions of the most important texts and the learned of all the countries vied with each other in their attempts at interpreting them. The achievements of the last sixty years in the province of Indian literature have been described in detail in several special chapters. Here we have only to survey the principal landmarks along the path of Indology, and the most important events in its history.

**Christian Lassen.**

Before all mention has to be made of a pupil of Aug. Schlegel, Christian Lassen, who in his broad-based German "*Indian Antiquary*," which began to appear in 1843 and comprised four thick volumes, the last appearing in 1862, strove to encompass the entire knowledge of his day about ancient India. That this work has now become antiquated is no reproach to the author but only a brilliant testimony to the immense progress which our science has made in the second half of the nineteenth century.

**The great Dictionary.**

Perhaps the greatest impetus to this advancement and probably a capital event in the history of Sanskrit research was the appearance of the Sanskrit lexicon by Otto Bohtlingk and Rudolph Roth. It was published by the Academy of Science of St. Petersburg. The first part came out in

1852 and in 1875 the entire work in seven folio volumes was given to the world.

**Histories of literature.**

And in the same year 1852 in which the great St. Petersburg dictionary started to appear, A. Weber made the first attempt to write a complete history of Indian literature. The second edition of the work appeared in 1876. It does not merely represent a landmark in the history of Indology but to this day, despite its shortcomings in style, which renders the book indigestible to the layman, it remains the most reliable and the most complete handbook of Indian literature possessed by us.

**Catalogues of *Mss.***

If, however, we desire to have an idea of the almost amazing progress which research in Indian literature has made in the comparatively brief period of its existence we should read the essay of Aug. Schlegel, written in 1819, "on the present condition of Indian philology," in which little more than a hundred Sanskrit works are enumerated as known to the world in editions or translations. Let us then cast a glance at the "Literature of the Sanskrit Language," published in 1839 at St. Petersburg by Friedrich Adelung, in which not less than three hundred and fifty diverse Sanskrit works are registered. Next let us compare with the latter Weber's "History of Indian Literature" which in 1852 discussed and appraised well nigh five hundred books of Indian Sanskrit. Furthermore, let us examine the "*Catalogus Catalogorum*", brought out in parts in 1891, 1896, and 1903 by Theodore Aufrecht, which contains an alphabetical list of all the Sanskrit books and others based on the examination of all the existing catalogues of manuscripts. This is truly a monumental work. Aufrecht laboured for forty years over it. He studied the catalogues of Sanskrit manuscripts in all the great libraries of India and Europe. And the number of the Sanskrit manuscripts noticed in this catalogue amounts to several thousands. Yet this catalogue includes neither the immense Bhuddist literature nor the literary productions embodied in Indian languages other than Sanskrit. Research into Bhuddist literature has powerfully advanced since the great English scholar T. W. Rhys Davids established in 1882 the Pali Test Society. A. Weber again, with his great treatise on the sacred scriptures of the Jains in 1883 and 1885, annexed to science the new branch of texts which is not lower in antiquity to the writings of the Bhuddists.

**Encyclopaedia Sanskrit knowledge**

Such is the enormous mass that has gradually accumulated of Indian literature that now-a-days it is hardly possible for a single scholar to control the whole province. It is now some years since it was found necessary to publish in a comprehensive work a general survey of all that has been achieved in the individual branches of Indology. The plan of the work which began to appear since 1897 under the title of "Grundriss" of Indo-Arian philology and antiquity, was devised by George Buhler, the most eminent Sanskrit scholar of the last decades. Thirty scholars from Germany, England, Holland, America and, last but not least, India have set to work in co-operation under Buhler, and since his death under Kielhorn, to prepare the individual volumes of this work. The appearance of this Grundriss is at once the latest and the most delightful event in the development of the history of Indology. When we survey the knowledge on ancient India and its literature brought together here in a series which is not yet completed we can only compare it with what Lassen, only a few decades ago, was in a position to give in his great work on *Indian Antiquity* and regard with justifiable pride the progress which the science has made in a relativeley brief period.

## CHAPTER XIII.

## THE CHRONOLOGY OF INDIAN LITERATURE.

Considerable as has been the advancement in the study of Indian literature its history proper remains yet in many ways obscure and unexplored. In the first place the chronology of Indian literature is shrouded in almost painful obscurity and there are yet remaining unsolved most of the connected problems for the investigator. It would be convenient and desirable to group Indian literature into three or four great periods confined within stated number of years and to reduce the various literary events to one or another of these definite epochs. But every attempt of this kind must prove abortive in the present condition of our knowledge and the suggestion of hypothetical number of years would only be a blind venture which would do more harm than good. It is much better to be perfectly clear regarding the fact that we have no exact chronological data whatever as regards the most ancient period of Indian literary history and only a few definite ones for the later ages. It was years ago that the famous American Orientalist W. D. Whitney declared what has since been repeatedly stated : "All the data given in the literary history of India are like nine pins to be set up again." And for the most part the dictum is true to this day. Even now the views of the most eminent scholars on the age of the most important Indian literary works diverge from one another, not by years or decades but, by centuries if not by one or two thousand years. What can be established with some certainty is at the most a species of tentative chronology. We can often say, "This or that work, this or that class of literature, is older than a given other"; but on the actual age of it we can only make surmises. The most reliable criterion for this relative chronology is still the language. Less trustworthy are peculiarities of style; because in India it is a matter of frequent occurrence that younger books imitate the diction of an older category of literature in order to assume an appearance of antiquity. But frequently even this relative chronology is vitiated by the circumstance that many works on Indian literature, and just those which are most popular and which are accordingly of the greatest moment to us, have undergone a multiplicity of redactions and have reached our hands through many transformations. If we find, for instance, in a book which is tolerably "datable" extracts from the *Ramayana* or the *Mahabharata*, the first question that arises is whether this citation refers to the particular epic as we possess it or to an older shape of it. Uncertainty is intensified by the fact that for the great majority of the books of the ancient literature the names of the authors are next to unknown. They have been transmitted to us as the works of principal families, or schools, or monastic orders, or the production is attributed to a legendary personage of prehistoric times. When finally we come to the age where we have to deal with books of authors of ascertained individuality, the latter as a rule are quoted only by their family names, which help the literary historian of India just as much as if an investigator of English literature were to have to struggle with names like Smith, Jones or William. If, for instance, an author appears under the name of Kalidasa, or if the name of Kalidasa is mentioned anywhere, it is by no means certain that the great poet of that name is necessarily meant. It might as well be some other Kalidasa.

**A few dated events.**

In this sea of uncertainty there are only a few fixed points which may be stated here in order not to frighten away the student from the research as utterly hopeless.

Now here in the first place there is the evidence of language which shows that the hymns and the litanies, the prayers and the magical formulæ in the Veda are incontestably the most ancient portion of our possession of Indian literature. Certain also it is that about 500 B.C., Buddhism arose in India and that it pre-supposes the entire Vedic literature as completed and closed in its main lines, so that we may affirm that the Vedic literature is, excepting for its latest ramifications, on the whole pre-Buddhistic ; in other words, that it was closed prior to 500 B.C. To be more accurate, the death of the Buddha is assigned with tolerable certainty to the year 477 B.C. Besides the chronology of the Buddhistic and the Jain literature is happily not so vague as the Brahmanic. The traditions of the Buddhists and the Jains relating to the origin and the conclusion of their canonical works have been proved sufficiently reliable. And the inscriptions preserved in the ruins of the temples and topes of these faiths supply us with considerable clue to the history of their literature.

**Extra-Indian helps.**

But the most definite data in Indian history are those which we have issued not from the Indians themselves. Thus the invasion of Alexander the Great of India in 326 B.C. is a positive landmark which is of importance also for the Indian literary history, especially when it is a question to decide whether in a given Indian literary production Greek influence is to be assumed. Further, we learn also from the Greeks that about 315 B. C. Chandragupta, the Sandrakottos of the Greek writers, successfully led a revolt against the satraps of Alexander, took possession of the throne and became the founder of the Maurya dynasty in Pataliputra, the Palibothra of the Greeks and the Patna of to-day. About the same time or a few years later it was that the Greek Megasthenes was deputed as Ambassador to the court of Chandragupta by Seleucus. The fragments which we own of his description of India, which he called the *Indica*, give us a picture of the standard of the Indian civilisation of those days and afford us a clue to the chronological cassification of many Indian literary works. A grandson of Chandragupta was the celebrated king Asoka, who in 259 B.C. was crowned king and from him are derived the most ancient datable Indian inscriptions yet discovered. These inscriptions chiselled partly into rocks and partly on columns are at the same time the most ancient testimony to Indian writing at our command. They show the mighty king as a patron and protector of Buddhism who utilised his sovereignty, extending from the northernmost border to the southernmost limit of India, to spread the doctrine of the Buddha over the country and who in his edicts on rocks and pillars recounts not, like other rulers, his victories and deeds of glory but exhorts his people to virtuous conduct, warns them of the perils of sin, and preaches love of neighbour and tolerance. These unique edicts of king Asoka are themselves valuable literary monuments hewn in stone, but they are of moment also, being suggestive of a literary history on account of their script, their idiom, and their religious historical connections. In the year 178 B.C., one hundred and thirty-seven years after the coronation of Chandragupta, the last scion of the Maurya dynasty was hurled from the throne by King Pushyamitra. The mention of this Pushyamitra for instance in a drama of Kalidasa is an important indication for the determination of the age of several works in Indian literature. The same remark holds good of the Græco-Baktrian king Menander who reigned about 144 B.C. He appears under the name of Milinda in the celebrated Buddhist book *Milindapanha*. Next to the Greeks it is the Chinese to whom we owe some of the most important time-data in Indian literature. Beginning with the first century of Christianity we hear of Buddhist missionaries going to China and translating Buddhist books into Chinese and of Indian embassies to China as well as Chinese pilgrims who visited India to pay homage to the sacred places of

Buddhism. Books belonging to Indian, that Is Sanskrit, literature were translated into Chinese and the Chinese supply us precise dates as to when these renderings were achieved. It is espicially three Chinese pilgrims, whose itineraries are preserved, that give us much instructive information on Indian antiquity, and literary productions. They are Fa-hian who came to India in 399, Hiuen-Tsiang who made his great journey to India in 630—635 and Itsing who sojourned in India during 671-695. The chronological data of the Chinese contrast with those of the Indian being remarkably precise and trustworthy. As regards the Indians, the remark is only too true which was made by the Arab traveller Alberuni, who in 1039 wrote a very valuable work on India, namely, "The Indians unfortunately do not pay much attention to the historical sequence of events; they are very negligent in the enumeration of the chronological succession of their Kings and when we press them for explanation they do not know what to say and are ever ready to relate fables."

**Indian's sense of history.**

Nevertheless we need not believe what is so often asserted that the Indians have been entirely deficient in the historical sense. In India too there was a historical literature and at all events we come across numerous inscriptions with exact dates which would hardly have been the case if the Indians lacked all appreciation of history. It is true that in their writing of history the Indians have never learnt to distinguish between poetry and historical veracity, that to them the events were always more important than the chronological sequence, and that in literary matters they laid no stress on the difference between the earlier and the later. What appears to the Indian as sound, true and correct he thrusts back to the remotest antiquity; and when he wishes to invest with particular sanctity a given doctrine or when he desires the widest circulation and repute for his book, he disguises his name in a modest incognito and gives out some ancient sage as the author of his book. This process is noticed in modern times and it was not otherwise in bygone centuries. Thus it comes about that so many entirely modern books pass under the respectable ancient names of Upanishads and Puranas. They are so much sour wine in old bottles. The intention, however, of a deliberate fraud is as a rule not general. Only as regards literary property utmost indifference is prevalent. It is only in later centuries that authors give their names with greater accuracy, with the names of their parents, grandparents, teachers and patrons and adding necessary biographical information about themselves. The authors of astronomical works are wont to give the exact date of the day on which their book was completed. From the fifteenth century, finally, the inscriptions give us the key to the age of many authors. And Indian epigraphy which has made great progress in decipherment in the last twenty years with their "Corpus Inscriptionum Indicarum" and the periodical "*Epigraphia Indica*" are witnesses to exact dates of Indian records supplying suggestive contributions to the solution of the chronological problems.

# APPENDIX I.

## CONSTITUTION OF THE BUDDHIST CANON

BY

SYLVAIN LEVI.

All the organized religions are compelled at a certain stage of their development to constitute a Canon, that is to say, a definite collection of texts which are enjoined upon the faithful as the rule of orthodoxy and which is adduced against the adversary as indisputable authority. Judaism has the Law and the Prophets. Christianity has the Gospel and Epistles. Islaam has its Quran. The Brahmans have the Veda. Buddhism has its Three Baskets, called the Tripitaka, which comprise in their entirety "the Word of the Buddha." Let us rapidly survey these Three Baskets, that of the *Sutras*, the *Vinaya*, the *Abhidharma*. The choice of the texts admitted into the canon instructs us about the spirit of the religion which expresses itself in them.

The Basket of Vinaya is the rules of the monastic life, for the use of the monks as well as the nuns. From this circumstance the Vinaya is double, *Ubhato.* Each rubric in it appears twice, one for men and one for women. The sections are five in number:—*Fatimokkha*, *Mahavagga* *Cullavagga*, *Suttavibhanga*, *Parivara.* The Patimokkha, intended to be publicly read on recurring stated days of confession, is hardly anything else but a catalogue of sins and the regulations pertaining to them. The Mahavagga and the Cullavagga give the detailed code of duties, daily or otherwise. Each of these prescriptions is introduced by the narrative of the events which gave rise to justify it, giving in fact the *raison d'être* of each rule. The narrative moves sluggishly. The Mahavagga opens with a piece of biography of the Buddha. The Cullavagga comprises the history of the councils summoned after the death of the Buddha. The

Suttavibhanga is an actual commentary on the *Putimokkha* of which it describes the origin, interprets the sense and discusses the application. The Parivara is a kind of Deuteronomy, recapitulation and catechism at the same time.

The Basket of Sutras comprises an enormous mass of sermons and instructive anecdotes introduced with the stereotyped formula: "This have I heard. One day the Master was residing at . . . . " It is divided into four sections: The long collection of *Digha Nikaya*, composed of the longest texts, thirty-four in number; the *Medium Collection* or Majjhima Nikaya which embodies texts of medium size, one hundred and fifty-two in number; the Miscellaneous Collection or *Ṣamyutta Nikaya*, a kind of potpourri in which are thrown collections of all kinds, seven thousand five hundred and sixty-two in number; the Numerical Collection or *Anguttara Nikaya* in which the texts relating to the numerical rubrics are gathered together and classified in ascending order from one to eleven, totalling in all nine thousand five hundred fifty-seven texts.

To these four collections we have to add a fifth, admittedly artificial, including all that which has not been thrown into any of the previous groups. It is called the Minor collection or the *Khuddaka Nikaya.* The works nominally attributed to the disciples of the Buddha have even come here to be incorporated, without giving offence, into the body of texts reverenced as "the Word of the Buddha." The components of the Minor Collection are :—

*Khuddaka-patha*, a small group of texts partly incorporated also in other sections;

*Dhammapada*, a treasure of utterances of the Buddha in verse;

*Udana*, a series of brief edifying stories each concluding with an apophthegm;

*Itivuttaka*, small sermons introduced by a set of formula (*Vuttamhetam*);

Sutta Nipata, an admirable body of certainly ancient pieces and already previously grouped into sub-sections;

*Vimana Vatthu* and *Peta Vatthu*, narratives in verse of the acts of the good and evil beings respectively, which have earned for their authors heaven or hell.

*Theragatha* and *Therigatha*, poems composed by ascetics and nuns of eminent merit;

Jataka, 547 tales of the anterior existences of the Buddha;

*Niddesa*, commentary on the 33 pieces of the Sutta Nipata, and attributed to Shariputa;

*Patisambhidamagga*, a series of scholastic notes on the path of sacred knowledge;

*Apadana*, biographies in verse of saints, male and female;

The *Buddhavamsa*, a history of the succession of the Buddhas;

The *Cariya Pitaka*, a versified narrative of the previous births of the Buddha.

The third Basket is that of the *Abhidharma*. Classed as the equal of the two other Baskets, in reality it occupies an inferior rank. It consists of seven books of metaphysics *Dhammasamgani, Vibhanga, Kathavatthu, Puggalapannatti Dhatukatha, Yamaka, Patthana.*

Such is the whole canon. Now we shall see how it was constituted. Immediately after the death of the Buddha one of the principal disciples, Kashyapa, called a council of 500 monks, all of them saints, at Rajagraha. Ananda the cousin and favourite disciple of the Master, recited the Sutras. Upali who was before initiation a barber, and who was known as the most competent authority in the matter of discipline, recited the Vinaya. Mark that there is no mention of *Abhidharma* yet. It remained the exclusive property of gods to whom the Buddha preached it. It was only at a later period that it was brought down to the earth. A century after the Nirvana a second council was assembled at Vaishali, to settle ten questions of monastic discipline which were exercising the church. The assembly proceeded to recite once again the canon. One more century elapsed. Now was reigning the powerful king Ashoka at Pataliputra and the whole of India confessed his authority. The Buddhist community was rent by schisms. A new council, this time official and convoked by imperial authority; fresh recitation of texts under the presidency of Tissa Moggaliputta, who communicated to the council the last text embodied in the *Abhidharma* Basket. It is called the *Kathavatthu*. Now missions were sent out to carry the word of the Buddha to the extreme limits of the empire and even beyond. Mahendra, the son of Ashoka converted Ceylon and carried there the Three Baskets about 250 B.C. For two centuries old tradition preserved them with scrupulous fidelity, but political troubles at last appeared to threaten their preservation. About 50 B. C. Vatta Gamani, the king of Ceylon, convoked a Singhalese council which fixed the sacred books in writing. Since then copies piously prepared in monasteries assured the perpetuity of the texts.

We have upto now spoken the language of the most faithful adepts of the Pali canon. The monks or laymen of

Ceylon, Siam, Burma and Cambodia could subscribe without reservation to the history of the canon as traced by us so far. But let us change the territory and the dogma also gets modified.

In India itself Buddhism has disappeared. Only extreme north, Nepal, sees it vegetating, decrepit and moribund. The Gurkhas, the masters of the country, have adopted Brahmanism and the Nevars, subjugated and impoverished, look with indifference at the crumbling ruins of centuries. The degenerated convents no longer preserve anything except fragments of the Buddhist literature. The ancient canon has vanished. The church has substituted for it the nine dharmas or Laws: The *Prajna-paramita* in 8,000 lines, the *Gandavyuha*, the *Dashabhumishvara*, the *Samadhiraja*, the *Lankavatara*, the *Saddharmapundarika* "the Lotus of the Good Law," the *Tathagata Guhyaka*, the *Lalitavistara* and the *Suvarnaprabhasa.* To these sacred books we have to add others which are certainly ancient, the *Mahavastu*, the *Divyavadana* &c. All these texts are written either in Sanskrit or in a language which is a neighbour of Sanskrit but different from Pali. The want of arrangement and the gaps in the Nepali collection, however rich otherwise, has injured it in the opinion of scholars who are seduced by the orderly beauty of the Pali canon. For a long time these texts were represented to us as later recensions of the original Pali, ill-understood by incompetent translators. As a radical blemish in Sanskrit Buddhism we are pointed to the absence of the Vinaya in this collection. But the *Mahavastu* represents this Vinaya, as a part of the Vinaya of the Lokottaravadis, comprised in the school of the Mahasanghikas. Besides the *Divyavadana* has recently been recognised as composed to a great extent of fragments of the Vinaya of the Mulasarvastivadis. An impartial examination has also discovered in other Nepalese texts independent recensions of texts admitted otherwise in the Pali canon.

Tibet converted to Buddhism at the commencement of the seventh century, has an immense sacred literature, falling into two groups: the Kanjur, originally written Bka-gyur and the Tanjur, originally written Bstangyur. The Kanjur is the canon in the narrowest sense of the word. It is the word of the Buddha. The Tanjur contains the Fathers of the church, exegetic literature and the technical manuals. The Kanjur is divided into seven sections: Dulva, Sherphyin, Phat-chen, Dkon-brtsegs, Mdo, Myan-das and Rgyud.

The Dulva, that is to say the Vinaya, is an enormous compilation in 13 volumes. In fact it is the Vinaya of the School of the Mulasarvastivadis, which was drawn up in Sanskrit and of which Nepal has preserved to us long extracts. This colossal Vinaya, written with art, overflows with miscellaneous matter of all kinds. The rules often have the appearance of being mere pretexts for relating long histories, heroic, comic, fabulous and romantic. The Tibetan Vinaya is a complete canon in itself.

The five succeeding sections are collections of Sutras: The Sher-phyn in 28 volumes contains all the numerous recensions of the Perfection of Wisdom (*Pragmaparamita*); the most expanded equals in extent a hundred thousand verses, The Phal-chen (*Avatamsaka*) in 6 volumes, the Dkon-brtsegs (*Ratnakuta*) in 6 volumes, the Myan-das (*Nirvana*) in two volumes are collections of Sutras grouped by the analogy of the doctrine or the subject treated. The fifth section, the Mdo (*Sutra*), in 30 volumes has absorbed all the Sutras which have not found admittance into the three other groups. Finally the Rgyud (*Tantra*) in 22 volumes is the magical literature, held in such high esteem in Tibet.

Excepting thirty Sutras, incorporated as an appendix to the last volume of the section on Mdo and which are themselves represented as translation from Pali, the texts of the Kanjur have no exact correspondence with the canon of the Pali church. The Pali church claims to be the inheritor of the Elders, the Sthaviras, called in Pali Theras. Its doctrine is called Theravada. It only aims at arresting the wheel of transmigration and anchoring men at the port of Nirvana. The saved are the Arhats. The Tibetan collection like the Nepalese has attached itself to another doctrine which calls itself the Great Vehicle, Mahayana. The Great Vehicle takes hold of the saint in his position of Nirvana, just as the Little Vehicle, Hinayana, terminates his endless birth. It leads him, purified and rendered sublime, to a life of activity to achieve the salvation of the entire universe.

China made docile by the Buddhist apostles, since the first century of the Christian era has not ceased to absorb during more than 10 centuries with a serene impartiality, all the texts imported into it by missionaries, adventurers, pilgrims. They came from India, Ceylon, Burma, from the world of the Iranian and the Turk. The Three Baskets of China have nothing of the canon except the name. All the doctrines have found place in them. From 518 to 1737 the canon of the Buddhist books has been drawn up in China not less than 12 times. Further we have to refer to the collection of Korea which with original texts borrowed from China, was constituted in 1010 and which is transmitted to us in a unique copy preserved in Japan.

The cadre of the Chinese canon indicates its spirit. It preserves the traditional division of the Three Baskets. But under each rubric it opens two sections: Mahayana and Hinayana, the Mahayana being at the head. The Basket of the Sutras of the Mahayana reproduces in part some classics of the Tibetan Kanjur: *Prajna-paramita Ratnakuta, Avatamsaka, Nirvana.* It adds also the *Mahasamnipata* and finally opens a special series of Sutras remaining outside of these groups. It distributes them into two sections according as they have been translated once or more than once.

The Chinese Basket of the Sutras of the Hinayana essentially consists of four collections or Agamas which are denominated the Long, the Medium, the Mixed, the One-and-More. Under these designations we recognise the counterpart of the four Pali Nikayas. The resemblance is really striking but it does not amount to identity. For the most part it is the same texts which are found in the two diverse spheres but the arrangement and the details differ. The development of the same Sutra shows notable divergences. The transcription of proper names leads us to a Sanskrit original or at least a quasi Sanskrit. Did there then exist in one of the sacred languages proper a redaction of these four collections, independent of the Pali, preserved by an indigenous tradition ?

The Basket of Vinaya includes in the class of the Mahayana a series of manuals on the discipline of the Bodhisattva. Thus there are as many monastic rules as there are monastaries and philosophical and moral dissertations removed far from the Vinaya and having no connection with it. But the class of Hinayana contains no less than five Vinayas related more or less intimately to the Pali. Here we come across in its entirety the monastic code of the Dharmaguptas, the Mahishakas, the Mahasanghikas, the Sarvastivadis and finally that of the Mulasarvastivadis of which the Tibetan Kanjur also possesses a version and of which the Nepalese compilation has preserved fragments in the original Sanskrit language. Other unconnected texts give us information on the Vinaya of still other schools, that of the Kashyapiyas, and the Sammatiyas. We have here quite obviously to do, in all these Vinayas, with independent redactions based on a common tradition connecting the somewhat insipid Pali Vinaya with the almost epic Vinaya of the Mulasarvastivadis.

The Basket of *Abhidharma* in its two sections offers a contrast by its richness to the dry sobriety of the Pali Abhidhamma. Here we meet, in a faithful though somewhat incomplete image, with the active intensity of philosophic thought and controversy in the diverse schools of Buddhism. Among the seven treatises of the canonical Hinayanist Abhidharma at least two remind us by their title of the answering Pali ones, the Prajnapti-shastra and the Dhatukaya. corresponding to the *Puggala-pannati* and *Dhatukatha.*

In continuation of the Three Baskets the Chinese have admitted one more category analogous to the Tibetan Tanjur. It comprises the Fathers of the church, Indian and Chinese.

For the last twenty years the inventory of the Buddhist canon has been enriched by an important accession and which continues to enlarge it. The researches and the excavations in Central India have brought to light the original texts which were believed to have irrevocably perished and rather unexpected translations. The discovery by Dutremil de Rhins and by Petrovsky, of the two halves of a Dhammapada written in a very ancient alphabet and composed in a Sanskrit dialect has opened a series of sensational finds. Stein, Grunwedel, Von Lecoq, Pelliot have one after another brought materials which remain yet for the most part undeciphered. But from now we possess authentic fragments of that Sanskrit *Samyukta Agama* which the Chinese translations led us to surmise and upto now we have three Sanskrit redactions of the Dhammapada which the Pali canon used to be proud alone to have possessed. We see announced quite a Buddhistic literature in Turki translations and also renderings in Tokhari, a language entirely unknown till yesterday and which has just been added to the family of Indo-European tongues.

From now on we stand no longer in the presence of a unique canon and a privileged one such as the Pali canon has too often been represented to us. We now know of other canons equally rich, equally comprehensive, equally well arranged with the Pali canon, either in original texts or in translations in very diverse tongues. How to make now our choice between the rival claimants? To which must be assigned the palm of authenticity claimed by each with equal confidence?

Pali, to believe its literature, is the language of the Buddha. But Pali is only an incorrect designation. Its true name is Maghadhi, the language of Maghadha. And the Buddha lived in Maghadha and preached to the people of it. He addressed himself to all without distinction of caste. He would have nothing to do with Sanskrit, the sacred language of the Brahmans. He must have spoken the current vernacular, the Maghadhi. But the Maghadhi is known to us from epigraphical records from grammars, and from literary texts. It has two fundamental and salient characteristics. It invariably substitutes "l" for "r." Raja in Maghadhi is Laja. Secondly, the nominative singular of masculine of words ending in "a" which in other Sanskrit dialects is found to end in "o," terminates in Magadhi with an "e." Instead of *devo*, God, in Maghadhi we have *deve*. Now Pali keeps the letter "r" and also the flection in "o." Therefore it is foreign to Maghadha. The cradle of Pali is yet to be discovered. Ujjayini, Gujarat, Orissa have all been suggested. But Maghada is outside this. If the Buddha spoke Maghadhi, the Pali canon could in no case represent his direct teaching.

The Pali canon vaunts that it was "sung" for the third time during the reign of Ashoka at the special invitation of the king. Ashoka then must have had to employ Pali texts and we possess a rescript of Ashoka to the clergy of Maghadha engraved in rock. In it the king selects seven texts the study of which he recommends to the monk and the layman. They are *Vinaya samukase*, *Aliyavasani*, *Anagatabhayani*, *Munigathȧ*, *Moneyasute*, *Upatissapasine*, *Laghulo-vade musavadam adhigicya Bhagavata Budhena bhasite.* Of these seven titles only the last is found in the Pali collection. It is No. 61 in the *Majjhimanikaya.* The Sanskrit canon also has it since we meet with it in the Chinese translation of the corresponding collection, which is No. 14 of the Madhyma Agama. But the linguistic peculiarities of the words which occur in this simple title suffice to prove that the Sutra in question was not composed in Pali,—nor in Sanskrit, nor in any of the epigraphical dialects of Ashoka. For the titles of the other works we have suggestions of ingenious identifications with other texts in the Pali canon, but none of the proposed identifications is satisfactory. Besides the Buddhistic monuments grouped round the reign of Ashoka,—at Bharhut and Sanchi—bear inscriptions votive or explanatory which are drawn up in dialects none of which is Pali.

The guarantee of the three councils is not more serious. The first council is a pious invention which will deceive no one. The second council remains suspended in the air without any historic connection and is supposed to be accounted for by a petty controversy about monkish discipline. Moreover all the Buddhistic schools appropriate the same story, even the Mahasanghikas against whom the second council was convened, if we credit the Pali tradition. The legend does not come to history till the time of Ashoka. But the saint again who presides over the third council is entirely unknown outside of this episode. The meagre legend formed around the personality of this strange leader is too much reminiscent of the legend of another saint named Upagupta, who is delineated in the other accounts as the spiritual preceptor of king Ashoka. The first positive date starts with the first century before Christ. For the council which then fixed the sacred texts by reducing them to writing was a local convocation which, at the most, concerned certain monasteries of Ceylon. But the tradition of the Sarvastivadi school places in the same period a council summoned for the same object and of considerable importance. The king Kanishka, whose Scythian hordes subjugated Northern India, wanted, moved either by politics or by devotion, to fix the dogma. A council held in Kashmir settled the Sanskrit canon and prepared a commentary on the Three Baskets. A writer of genius, Ashvaghosha, lent the resources of a brilliant style to the lucubratious of the theologian. Whilst the Pali canon remained yet for a long time confined to the island of Ceylon, where its powerful enemies, the Mahishasakas, held it in check, the Sanskrit canon of the Sarvastivadis propagated itself along the trade routes to Turkestan and China, and the ships of Hindu colonists carried it to Indo-China and Indian archipelago. Other schools, less prosperous, but still living, elaborated also about the same epoch their canon in the neo-Sanskrit dialects,—Prakrit and Apabhramsha.

To sum up: the constitution of the canon is a late event which probably occurred in the various schools at about the same time a little before the Christian era. Without doubt its causes are to be saught in the political and economical history. The sudden diffusion of writing and specially the materials of writing gave rise to an upheaval comparable to that of the discovery of printing. But if the formation of the canon is a late event, that is not to say that certain at least of its elements are not of an ancient date.

No one can yet write an exact history of the canon but we are in a position to figure to ourselves with tolerable approximation the successive stages of its elaboration.

The tradition, too complacently accepted, assumes the primitive unity of the church and expresses it by the first council. The facts however protest against the supposition. The head of an important group arriving just at the close of the session of this council and called upon to recognise the canon fixed by it replies: "The law and the discipline have been well chanted. Nevertheless, I would preserve them as I have heard them myself and collected them from the mouth of the Master himself." It could not well be otherwise. The personal prestige of the Buddha, ambition, and interest had brought into the community of the brethren men from all classes. Ascetics, barbers, sweepers, jostled with princess merchants, philosophers. Reduced by the death of the Master to their original inclinations, each endeavoured with perfect sincerity to suit himself to the doctrine that had been received. Against these menaces of disorder and anarchy the church had but one safeguard. Every fortnight the monks whether travelling or sojourning in a place have to gather together by groups and hear the recitation of the fundamental rules of the order (*Pratimoksha*) and confess the transgressions they have committed. The institution of each of the rules was connected, or it was alleged that it was connected, with an actual occurrence during the Buddha's life time. The recital of these episodes and the biography of the persons concerned gave as many themes to the exercise of imagination and style. Add to this that the life in the monastery, which was constantly developing, was also always giving rise to practical problems which had to be solved in the name of the Founder of the Order. The monasteries, which were the richest and the most frequented, thus came to make collections which were perpetuated and which were growing. The wandering anchorites, who were always on the move visiting cloister after cloister, maintained a constant communication which tended to level too sharp divergences. Reduced by process of pruning to their common elements the Vinayas of all the schools conformed without effort to a kind of archtype, which did not represent any primitive Vinaya, but which was the average of all the Vinayas.

Outside the monastic prescriptions, the literary invention of the monks was exercised on their recollections, real or imaginary, and on the biography of the Buddha. Carried about by the same medium of intercourse, the best of the literary pieces did not take long to assume concrete form, hardly altered by accidents of travelling or by local taste or local idiom. In proportion as the number of these biographies multiplied the necessity was felt of classifying them. The Sanskrit and Pali texts have perpetuated the memory of one of these ancient classifications divided into 9 (Pali) or 10 (Sanskrit) rubrics: Sutra, Geya, Vyakarana, Gatha, Udana, Ityukta, Jataka, Adbhuta dharma, Vaipulya (Pali Vedella) and further, only in Sanskrit, Nidana, Avadana, Upadesha. The classical usage has preserved several of these denominations. The others have no doubt disappeared at the time of the constitution of the canon so that their sense had been condemned to perpetual obscurity. The canon itself has preserved to us one of the collections which had preceded it, the admirable *Suttanipata*, the whole of which is to be found in Pali and evidences of which are not wanting in Sanskrit. But in its turn the *Suttanipata* is only a group of sub-collections which in Sanskrit preserve their individual existence like the *Arthavarga*, *Parayana*, etc. Several of the texts recommended by Ashoka in his edicts of Bhabra seem to belong to this *Suttanipata*. As is manifestly evidenced by all the canons poetry, or at least the metrical form, remained at first the indispensable apparel of the literary compositions intended to be transmitted. Later on, when the invading prose found in the art and material for writing a useful auxiliary, it became necessary to create fresh cadres.

---

# APPENDIX II.

## SUTRALANKARA.

---

### A Romance of Literature.

---

**Prefatory.** Truth is often stranger than fiction. The following romantic story is entirely based on facts. It is common knowledge that some time about the fourth Christian century Buddhism was introduced from India into China. A number of sacred Hindu books, mostly Buddhistic but some of them containing most interesting fragments of Brahmanic literature by way of refutation, were translated into Chinese. One of these books is the *Sutralamkara.* It comprises a series of Buddhistic sermons in the guise of anecdotes and stories terminating with a moral inculcated by Buddhism. The original was in Sanskrit Along with a vast number of Sanskrit books that perished in India this book also was considered lost. To the credit of French philological science the Chinese translation of it, which is extant, was identified by the late lamented scholar, Eduard Huber, who died a premature death in French Cochin, China, about a couple of years ago. The author of the Sanskrit book of sermons was Ashvaghosha. Being a Buddhist he was more or less completely ignored by Brahmanic writers, except a few who mentioned only to combat his compositions. Thanks to the late professor Cowel of Cambridge, it is now established that Ashvaghosha was not only a great poet and a master of style, whose brilliant diction popularised Buddhism, but was also a model and a pattern which the better known Kalidasa was not loth to imitate.

---

From Sylvain Levi in J. A., July August.1908.

**The outraged Pandit.**

Only twenty years ago Ashavaghosha figured as no more than a memory in the history of Sanskrit literature. The progress of our studies has suddenly brought him to the front in the premier rank among the masters of Hindu style and thought. Hodgson, who discovered in Nepal the remnants of a Sanskrit Buddhist literature, was acquainted since 1829 with the work of Ashvaghosha called the *Vajrasuci* or the Diamond Needle. He prepared an English translation of it with the help of an educated Indian which he published in 1831. It appeared in the Transactions of the Royal Asiatic Society under the title of *Disputation respecting Caste* by a Buddhist. Hodgson had vainly searched for information on the age and the country of the author. All that people knew about him in Nepal was that he was a Mahapandit and that he wrote, besides this little tract, two Buddhist works of greater compass, the *Buddha-carita Kavaya* and the *Nandi-Mukhasughosa Avadana*, both highly reputed, and other works. In 1839, Lancelor Wilkinson, the British Agent at Bhopal, printed the Sanskrit text of the *Vajrasuci* enriched at the same time with an amusing addition. It was called the *Wujra Soochi* or Refutation of the Argument upon which the Brahmanic institution of caste is founded by the learned Boodhist Ashwa Ghosha; also the *Tunku*, by Soobaji Bapoo, being a reply to the *Wujra Soochi* in 1839. Indignant at the attacks by Ashvaghosa against the system of castes, the Brahman Soobaji Bapoo in the service of Wilkinson could not bring himself to consent to attend to the Buddhist text except on condition of adding a refutation of it. Ashvaghosha might well be proud of it. The point of the Diamond Needle which he flattered himself he had prepared was by no means dulled by the attack of the offended Brahman. Thus the violent Buddhist polemist who had so frequently and so cruelly humiliated the pride of the Brahman once more enters the scene after centuries of silence in the shock of religious controversy.

**Buddhist and Brahmanic controversy.**

Burnouf, to whom Hodgson had generously handed over along with other manuscripts the copy of *Vajra-suci* and the *Buddha-carita* indicated in his Introduction to the History of Indian Buddhism the interest of these two works. He proposed himself to revert to the question of the identity of the author "later on." The Chinese Buddhistic documents analysed by Remusat had meanwhile taught that one of the patriarchs of the Buddhist Church, the twelfth since the death of Shakyamuni, had borne the name of Ashvaghosha. With his strong commonsense Burnouf declined to see in one single personage the patriarch and the author on the faith of a resemblance of names. He was inclined rather to consider the two productions as the work of an ascetic or religious writer of more modern times. Next to Burnouf, the *Vajrasuci* had the good fortune to interest another Indianist of equal erudition, Albrecht Weber. In a memoir submitted to the Berlin Academy in 1859, Weber pointed to a Brahmanic recension of the *Vajasuci*. It was classed in the respectable category of *Upanishads* and attributed to the most fortunate and most fierce adversary of the moribund Buddhism of those days, the great Shankara Acharya. Weber believed himself justified in affirming the priority of the Brahmanic recension; Ashvaghosha had carried the war into the territory chosen by the advocates of the Brahmanic institution of castes. In an appendix to his memoir Weber grouped together valuable information on the patriarch Ashvaghosha, extracted from Tibetan and Chinese sources which had been communicated to him by the learned Schiefner. The figure of Ashvaghosha began to appear in more precise lineaments. He now emerges as a doctor, musician, stylist and an ingenious controversialist. Above all Ashvaghosha seemed to range himself among the entourage of another no less enigmatical celebrity, the great king Kanishka, the barbarous ruler who subjugated India about the beginning of the Christian era and who so profoundly affected the historic destinies of the country.

**Chinese aid.**

In 1860 an anonymous German translation, which was in reality made by Benfey, rendered accessible to Indianists the admirable work of the Russian scholar Wassilieff on Buddhism. As familiar with the doctrines as with the languages of China and Tibet, Wassilieff was able to write vigorously on the influence of Ashvaghosha on Buddhist philosophy. In 1869 the *History of Buddhism in India* by the Tibetan Pandit Taranath, translated from the Tibetan by Schiefner, enriched the biography of Ashvaghosha with details which were, however, of a legendary character. But it confirmed the literary importance of the celebrated doctor. The Tibetan tradition, faithful heir to the Hindu tradition, recognised in Ashvaghosha an exceptional personage endowed with such varied gifts that the European critic preferred to divide him into several persons bearing the same name. It is to the English scholar Beal that belongs the honour of resuscitating the literary glory of Ashvaghosha. Beal himself has suffered real injustice. Pioneer in bringing to light the immense collection which is incorrectly called the Chinese Tripitaka, he succeeded in extracting from it a mass of facts, documents, abstracts, and legends by which have profited the science of archæology, history and Indian literature and the whole of which has not been to this day arranged sufficiently systematically to attract the attention it deserves. The Chinese experts have ignored the labours of Beal because he laboured with reference to Indian antiquities. The Indianists, on the other hand, have looked upon him with suspicion because he looked for authentication at the hands of Sinologists alone. People have pointed out his mistakes and blunders. But those only who have tackled Buddhist Chinese know the difficulties which the best of scholars have to encounter. They were rather amazed, let it be said, to Beal's honour, to see that without the knowledge of Sanskrit and without the help of another Indianist he had committed so few faults. Above all they admire the surety of his grasp which directed his choice in the Chinese chaos. He was only officially called upon to classify the collection of Chinese Buddhism in the India Office and he was struck by the interest of the book *Sutralankara* and its author Ashvaghosha. He singled out its merits and even translated several of its stories in a brief series of lectures delivered at the London University in 1882. A little later he published in the Sacred Books of the East (volume XIX) a translation from the Chinese version of the Sanskrit *Buddha-carita.* Burnouf at the very beginning of the studies which he founded was mistaken, as regards the value of the Sanskrit original. But as soon as new theories on the development of Sanskrit literature and the formation of the Buddhist legends were elaborated, the epic of Ashvaghosha on the life of the Buddha did not take long in attracting attention. Fresh indexes came in a little later, to corroborate the attribution of the work to the great Ashvaghosha which had remained so doubtful in Burnouf's judgment.

**Japanese co-operation.**

A Japanese scholar whom Sylvain Levi considers it an honour to count among his pupils, Rayauon Fujishima, translated in the *Journal Asiatique* 1888 two chapters, dealing with hymns and the state of Buddhism in India from the memoir of Yi-tsing.

The Chinese pilgrim Yi-tsing had passed twenty-five years in western countries from 671 to 695, passionately occupied in study, especially the religious discipline of the school of Buddhism to which he belonged, *viz.*, the Mula-Sarvastivadis. His testimony deserves our confidence. Yi-tsing knows only one Ashvaghosha whom he classes, as does also Hiuan-tsang, another renowned Chinese traveller, among the Suns of the World alone with Nagarjuna and Deva. This Ashvaghosha is the author of "numerous hymns, the *Sutalankara*, and of the poem on the life of the Buddha."... Yi-tsing even gives a summarised analysis of this poem and records that it is studied everywhere in the Five Indias as well as in the Southern Seas (Indo-Asia), because to read Ashvaghosha is to be at once educated, instructed and delighted. Now how was a Western scholar to resist such a tempting promise? Here was a unique opportunity for research, Sylvain Levi knew it was the eve of a momentous literary discovery.

The National Library of Paris possesses a manuscript of the *Buddha-carita*. Sylvain Levi copied it and prepared an able edition and translation of it, publishing as a specimen the first canto in the *Journal Asiatique*. Subsequently he learned that an English scholar of repute, Cowell, professor at the University of Gambridge, had commenced to print in the *Anecdota Oxoniensia* a complete edition of the same text. With rare chivalry Sylvain Levi effaced himself before the English scholar. The entire text appeared in England in 1893, soon followed by an English translation. Cowell familiar alike with the classics of India had no hesitation in recognising in Ashvaghosha a precursor and even a model of Kalidas. He suggested striking similarities to prove that the Ennius of India, as he called him, had more than once lent his treasures to the Vigil. He further established that the authentic work of Ashvaghosha stopped with the fourteenth canto and that a later compilator has clumsily fabricated the last three songs with a view to giving a kind of integrity to the mutilated poem. Like the *Vajrasuci*, the *Budha-carita* became soon the object of close study on the part of the most eminent Indianists, Buhler, Kielhorn, Boehtlingk, Leumann, Lueders, who exercised their ingenuity on the restoration of the corrupted text.

**In search of the treasure.**

The fundamental problem of Hindu chronology led the great French scholar, Sylvain Levi, a little later, to the *Sutralancara*. In his quest of documents on the Indo-Scythian king Kanishka he came upon in the Chinese version two stories which extolled the orthodoxy and the piety of this great king. (Journal Asiatique, 1896-97.) Mastered by the beauty of the work in the Chinese rendering, Levi did not despair to recover the original Sanskrit in Nepal and he set out on a long and costly voyage from Paris in search of this lost treasure of India. His great efforts, however, ended only in the discovery, in the Himalayan Valley, of another work bearing the same name, of a much later date and of an altogether different nature. Next the indefatigable scholar proceeded to Japan. Here he found no *Sutralankara* in Sanskrit but was surprised to see a fresh work of Ashvaghosha which was till then unknown in Europe, namely, the *Mahayana Shraddhotpada*, widely read in the schools and monasteries of Japan where it passed for the historic basis of the doctrine of the Great Vehicle. Under the guidance of eminent Buddhist priests of Japan, Sylvain Levi studied it, comparing with the two Chinese versions and he prepared a French translation of the whole which he brought to Europe. There he had no opportunity of printing it yet. Meanwhile a Japanese scholar, Teitara Suzuki, of the Seminary of Kyoto, drawn to America by the movement of neo-Buddhism, published in 1900 at Chicago, under the patronage of Dr. Paul Karus, a faithful translation of this Japanese rendering of the Shraddhotpada. In this tract the polemist of the *Vajrasuci*, the story-teller of the *Sutralankara*, and the poet of the *Budha-carita*, reveals himself to us in a fresh capacity. Ashvaghosha here is a profound metaphysician, the bold originator of a doctrine called into being for the regeneration of Buddhism.

Such a great man could not possibly traverse the stage of this world without leaving in the memory of man unforgettable traces. Shorn of fantastic ornamentation and reduced to its essential lineaments the traditional biography of Ashvaghosha may be summed up thus.

**Life of Ashavaghosha.**

Ashvaghosha appeared a hundred years after the Nirvana of the Buddha according to one Chinese authority; three hundred years after it, according to another; and five or six hundred years after it, according to two other Chinese sources. One source makes it as late as eight hundred even. His birthplace seems to have been Gangetic India, the ancient district of Saketa or Ayodhya in the Kingdom of Sharavasti. According to the colophon to the Tibetan version of the *Buddha-carita* his birthplace was Pataliputra or Benares. As regards his lineage he was born in a Brahman family, acquiring all the specific education of his caste as well as instruction in general literary arts. According to Hiuen-tsang his knowledge comprised all that was known. As a musician he invented melodies which were so moving that they had to be proscribed by the government of the day. As a dialectician he triumphed over all his adversaries. A zealous devotee of the Brahmanic gods, especially Maheshvara, he was converted to Buddhism by Parshva who especially came down from Northern India to win him over to the Buddhist faith. According to others it was Purna, otherwise known as

Punyashas. A third source ascribes the honour of his conversion to Aryadeva. Now his fame extended to the limits of India. The King Kanishka pushed his arms as far as Saketa to carry away with him the matchless doctor. Ashvaghosha thus became his spiritual adviser and the physician of his soul. If we follow the later version he refused to repair to the court of the Indo-Scythian himself sending him one of his disciples instead.

The literary remains of Ashvaghosha are preserved partly in original Sanskrit, partly in Chinese and partly in Tibetan translation. In Sanskrit we have *Buddha-carita* which was translated into Chinese between 414 and 421 by Dharmaraksha. We have also the *Vajrasuci* which was translated into Chinese between 973 and 981 by Fahien. In passing, the Chinese translation describes the *Vajrasuci* as a work of Dharmakirti. The ascription is not improbable, Dharmakirti, like Ashvaghosha, had received first his Brahmanic education. The Tibetan translation has a special interest for Indians in that it has preserved the memory of the important religious controversy against Shankaracharya. The *Upanishad* placed under the name of Shankara marks a phase in this religious struggle. It is possible that Dharmakirti published a new edition, revised and completed, of the treatise originally composed by Ashvaghosha. The problem is highly important for the literary history of India, because *Vajrasuci* cites passages from Manu and the *Mahabharata.* We can imagine the important consequences of discovering, if we can, the authentic text of Ashvaghosha in the original Sanskrit.

**Chinese reverence for Sanskrit texts.**

The works of Ashvaghosha, which remain to us both in Chinese and Tibetan translations, are the Gurupancashatika, the Dashakushalakarmapatanirdesha and lastly the exceedingly curious Ghantistotra, which owing most probably to its secret character was not translated but *phonetically transcribed in Chinese characters.* The complete Tibetan title of the Gurupancashatika indicates the Tantric character of this work which is evident from its introductory stanzas. Besides, the whole work is replete with references to the mystical symbols and doctrines of Tantra, the *Vajra Mandala*, and *Abhisheka.* The Chinese version is presented to us as a simple small compilation by the Bodhisattva Ashvaghosha. In fact, in the age of Hiuen-tsang the reputation of Ashvaghosha as a magician was established. The Tibetan Tanjur in addition to this contains two tracts which obviously form two halves of a single work, the Sanskrit title of which must have been *Samvatibodnicittabhavrnanopadeshasamgraha* and the *Shokavinodanaashtakshanakata.* The Chinese have preserved several other works of Ashvaghosha translated by Paramartha. Among these the *Mahayanashraddhortadashastra*, translated first by Paramartha in 553 and then again by Shikshanada between 695 and 700, deserves mention. Finally we have in Chinese the celebrated *Sutralankarashastra* translated from Sanskrit by Kumarajiva about 405. Besides these we have other productions of Ashvaghosha of minor import and doubtful authenticity. Such are the hymns in 150 verses called *Shatatapancashatika-Namastotra*, which is attributed by the Tibetan collection of Tanjur to Ashvaghosha, but which Yi-tsing, the author of the Chinese translation, expressly ascribes to Matriceta. In his memoirs Yi-tsing mentions Ashvaghosha and Matriceta as two entirely different personages. The celebrated hymn was translated by him from Sanskrit into Chinese at Nalanda, the centre of Buddhistic learning. The *Nandimukhashvaghosha Avadana*, imputed by Hodgson to the poet Ashvaghosha, has nothing in common with him, except the name of one of the personages, a devotee of the goddes Vasundhara.

**Was he a king?**

The variety of the classes of literature cultivated by Ashvaghosha is perfectly in keeping with the tradition, which makes of this author a contemporary of the king Kanishka. As regards the question of the relation between the times of Ashvaghosha and Kanishka it is not without interest to show that the excavations at Sarnath have brought to light two documents, issued by a king Ashvaghosha. One of these is engraved just on the pillar which bears the edict of Ashoka and is placed immediately after the edict. The other is a simple fragment of a stele. Vogel, who has published the two inscriptions, infers from the paleographic and linguistic characters that this Ashvaghosha Raja is a contemporary of Huvishka who succeeded Kanishka. We cannot think of an identity, but the name was current in the Indo-Scythian period and the form of the name furnishes a chronological index too often neglected in India. Cunningham found at Kosam, the site of the ancient Kaushambi, a coin of Ashvaghosha, and Vincent Smith has described another in the collection of the Asiatic Society of Bengal, on the reverse of which the name of the king is inscribed in the ancient Brahmi characters, and on the obverse occurs the bull.

Ashvaghosha, therefore, must have appeared at one of those critical periods when there occur political, economical, and social transformation and upheaval in the ideas currently received, and men receive new aspirations, new formalities and new tests. The invasion of Alexander confined to the basin of the Indus sufficed to create by a counter-stroke an imperial India under the sceptre of Mauryas on the ruins of the ancient principalities. The invasion of the Scythian hordes, the intrusion of Chinese, Greek and Parthian adventurers carried to the heart of Brahmanic India unknown cults, rites and usages. Buddhism operated upon by contrary forces must have been cleaved intc two halves. One section, faithful to the ideal, common to Hindu asceticism, took refuge in the pursuit of personal salvation. The other attracted by the promises of an apostolate, which might extend to the limits of the world, desired an open, active, instructed, and so to say, secular church. The title itself of the *Sutralankara* of Ashvaghosha sounds as a programme and the programme of a revolution. Would not the old patriarchs of the past have shuddered at the idea of *embellishing* a Sutra, of remodelling the work of the Master who "has well said all that he has said"? Ashoka proclaims and perpetuates this belief in the perfection of the Buddha's speech in the Bhabra edict. Centuries after Ashvaghosha, Asanga had still more an excuse to adopt the bold expression in his Mahayana *Sùtralankara* and in his *Yogacaryabhumi-shastra.* There is no question here of equivocation. Alankara denotes the flowers of rhetoric which India has cultivated with scientific thoroughness and which it has catalogued with the passion of an amateur devoted to the tulips. The *Sutralankara* is the Sutras or Buddhist doctrinal discourses placed in a literary form. It is, as we should say, the Bible for the ordinary people. In this attempt, which was bound to have scandalized the simple souls of the monks, Ashvaghosha acquired such reputation that the church ended by soliciting his assistance. The biography of Vasubandhu reports that the president of the council convoked by Kanishka sent envoys to find out Ashvaghosha, so that he might embellish the Vibhasha or commentary on Buddhist Gospel submitted to the deliberations of the Holy Synod. At that time Ashvaghosha was living in Kashmir and when the import of the principles of the commentary was fixed he turned it section by section into literary shape. The composition was completed at the end of twelve years. The literary merits of the *Sutralankara* justify the flattering encomium. They suffice to guarantee the authenticity of the work. Through two successive translations into two such diverse languages as Chinese and French, so far removed from the Hindu genius, the *Sutralankara* preserves its imperishable qualities, the narrative art, the vigorous imagination, the lyrical power and the suppleness of style. To describe Ashvaghosha in worthy terms we have only to borrow the beautiful words which he lends to a Bhikshu in the presence of the emperor Ashoka:

"When I speak of the good acts of the Buddha the crowd listen to me with joy. Their faces beam with happiness. Exalting the virtues of the Buddha I have destroyed the heretics. In the front of all men I have expounded the true path, the joy universal. As in the full autumnal moon all delight in me. To exalt the virtues of the Buddha all the centuries are not sufficient. But I will not stop doing it till my tongue turns dry. For the art of speaking well is my father and I regard eloquence as my mother."

**His method and themes.**

It was a dangerous undertaking. The literature of instruction borders on the nauseating and Ashvaghosha wanted to instruct at all costs. He did not attempt either to surprise the conscience or to disguise the lesson. This is his process. At first he proposes a moral theme. He illustrates it by a story. If necessary he adds another moral and finally the conclusion. The truths which he inculcates run in a narrow circle. They relate to the power of previous acts or *karma*, the importance of charity, the respect for observances, the vanity of the world, the errors of heresies, the perfection of the Buddha and the sanctity of the Law. But Ashvaghosha was not afraid of rehearsing the same themes. Sure of his art and sustained by an ardent faith he renewed himself without effort. Take only the stanzas on death which are strewn about in profusion over the book.

It is doubtful whether a Tertullian or a Bossuet could have spoken with greater grandeur or with a more noble realism. If it is the moral which above all counts for Ashvaghosha he is too much of an artist to sacrifice the narrative. He chooses his subject in every direction. He treats of all the strata of tradition and every class of society. Sometimes the Buddha himself is a hero of his story. Sometimes it is one of his disciples or a simple monk or an outcast *chandala* or a courtesan or a servant or a robber or an emperor. How can one read without emotion the conversion of Niti, the scavenger, in the 43rd story? He sees the Buddha coming into a street in the town of Sharavasti, and seized with shame at the sight of his superhuman majesty, flies from street to street and everywhere the Buddha appears before him collected and serene! At last he is caught in a blind alley. Here the Buddha calls him by his name. Could the Buddha call by his name a vile creature like himself? Could it not be that there was another person of the same name with himself? Perhaps the Buddha called the other one. His doubts are set at rest by the Master himself calling upon him to enter religious life which he does and the scene ends with the powerful king Prasenajit prostrating himself at the feet of the Buddha and the lowly sweeper, the new convert to Buddhism. Equally powerful dramatic effect is produced by the 20th story. Frightened and menaced by the success of a Buddhist preacher who captivated crowds and who preached against the joys of the world, "a daughter of Joy" goes with a sumptuous retinue to exercise her charms upon an assembly that had gathered together to hear an exposition of the Law. At her sight the attention of the listeners relaxes. They waver. The preacher, the master of the law, espies the courtesan. No sooner does his glance fall on her than the skin and the flesh of the woman drop from her. There remain only white bones and discovered intestines. Disgust seizes hold of the spectators. The skeleton joins its ghastly hands to implore pardon. The lesson goes home to the heart of the audience, and the fallen woman is converted. On another occasion, in the 40th story a robber finishes by blessing the Law. He was passing by the door of a Bhikshu. He knocks at the door. The Bhikshu does not open it. "Pass thy hand," he shouts to him, "through this small hole and I will give you something." The robber puts his unsuspecting hand. through. The Bhikshu catches hold of it and ties it to a post, takes a stick and starts vigorously belabouring the thief. With the first blow he repeats the first Buddhist formula, "refuge in the Buddha." The robber hastens to repeat the formula; similarly "refuge in the Law" and "refuge in the community." Then the thief thinks within himself: How many formulas of refuge are there with this holy man? If there are many I shall not be able to see any more this India. Assuredly it will mean the end of my life." When the Bhikshu is satisfied that the transgressor has repented he initiates him. "The perfect One, the sublime One is really omniscient. If he had taught four formulas of Refuge to his disciples that would have done for me. But the Buddha probably foresaw my case and it was to prevent my death that he has taught his disciples three refuges and not four." We see that the ardour of faith did not exclude humour from the monastery of the Buddhist.

**Authorship established.**

We have upto now spoken only of the merits of the contents of the translated work of Ashvaghosha. A fortunate accident enables us to appreciate at least to some extent the shape of the Sanskrit original. Now we have a large collection of Buddhist tales preserved in Sanskrit. It was discovered in Nepal. It is called the *Divyavadana*. Huber has been able to trace the origins of three of the stories in our Chinese translation of the *Sutralankara* to this Sanskrit *Divyavadana*. All the three stories have for their hero either Ashoka or his spiritual adviser Upagupta. They have found admittance into the *Divyavadana* through the *Ashokavadana* which embodied all the stories of the Ashoka cycle. These fragments in the original Sanskrit sufficiently establish that "the style and the versification of the *Sutralankara* are not unworthy of the author who was the first to compose a *Mahakavya*." Our investigations might proceed further in this direction if it was necessary to confirm the authorship of the *Sutralankara*. But Ashvaghosha has taken the care to put his signature, so to say, to his handiwork after the Hindu fashion. The *Sutralankara* twice cites the *Buddhacarita*. In the 43rd story Ashvaghosha represents the Buddha in one of his begging rounds in Shravasti. Here Ashvaghosha cannot resist the temptation of recalling a similar scene touching the entrance of the Buddha into Rajagrha, "as has been related in the *Buddhacarita*." The descriptions in the story and in the *Buddhacarita* correspond in detail.

In the forty-seventh story, the subject of which is the conversion of Upali, Ashvaghosha again begins by recalling without apparent reason, the conversion of the three Kashyapas and their companions, about a thousand people, who followed the Buddha to Kapilavastu "as has been related at length in the Buddhacarita." The reference has no justification except as a pretext to bring in the quotation. For the *Buddhacarita* relates in fact at length the conversion of the Kashyapas and the arrival of the Master with a following of one thousand men at his natal city. A third time the author follows his own *Life of the Buddha*, which we know in the original Sanskrit as the *Buddhacarita* and which in the Chinese is called *Fo-pen-hing*. The occasion was the lamentation of Sudatta when the Buddha is about to leave Sharavasti. The Chinese version of the *Buddhacarita* is the only one which could be used with reference to this part of the Buddha's career. But it has nothing in connection with this episode. It is to be noted here that the translator of the Chinese rendering, *Kumarajiva*, in referring to the *Life of the Buddha* here does not use the title *Fo-pen-hing* which he had employed in the two other references we mentioned above. Evidently he has probably in mind another Sanskrit work dealing with the life of the Buddha which also was translated into Chinese.

With Ashvaghosha begins the list of the literary writers of India. The only names of authors which to our knowledge preceded him are connected with technical works. And none of them permits of being assigned even an approximately correct date. Hence we can measure the importance of his work, the *Sutralankara*, as the first chronological landmark along with the sister compilation of the *Buddhacarita* in the nebulous chaos of the literary history of India. The least reliable data which we can extract from them are of inestimable value. Some of the events and facts which we can thus establish with certainty are the following :

The geographical horizon of the *Sutralankara* embraces the whole of India since it stretches as far as Ceylon, but it is the north-western India which alone is placed in full light. In the Gangetic province the author mentions Pataliputra and Mathura. But in the basin of the Indus he mentions Shakala, Takshashila, Avanti, Ashmaka, Gandhara and Pushkalavati. Two other names are hard to restore to their original shapes from the Chinese translation. The country of Ki-pin, which has so often embarrassed Indologists because it answers at once to Kashmir and to the country of Kapisha, permits of being localised in our book with some chance of certainty.

For in the seventy-sixth story, the Vihara or the monastery of Revata is situated in this territory. Now the Sanskrit text of the *Mahaprajnaparamita Shastra* which passes for a compilation of the patriarch Nagarjuna, and which was translated from Sanskrit into Chinese between 402 and 405 by Kumarajiva, gives the following description of this monastery :—

"The Buddha Shayamuni resided in Jambudvipa. He was born in the country Kippi-lo. He travelled much about the six great cities of eastern India. Once upon a time, he started from here for southern India. He lived in the house of the house-holder Kotikarna who received his homage. Once he proceeded for a short time to northern India to the country of the Yuetche to subjugate the Dragon King Apalala, and finally he went to the west of the Yuetche to conquer the Rakshasi. The Buddha here passed the night in a cave, and to this day the shadow of the Buddha is preserved here. If you enter into it to have a look you see nothing. When you come out of the hole and are at a distance from it you see brilliant signs as if the Buddha himself were there. He proceeded wishing to visit the King of Ki-pin on the mount of the Rishi Revata. He lived there for a time. He mastered the Rishi. Said the Rishi: 'I am happy at your arrival. I wish that the Buddha may give me a hair and a nail of his in order to raise a *stupa* over it for worshipping.' These have been preserved to this day."

The Chinese author here adds a note to the effect that at the foot of the mountain is situated the monastery and reproduces what he calls the exact pronunciation.

From the accounts of the Chinese pilgrims who visited India we learn of the miracles performed by the Buddha in the countries beyond the Indus. These are recorded in the Vinaya or the disciplinary code of the Mula Saravastivadis in the section devoted to medicinals herbs. The *Divya-vadana*, one of the important Sanskrit Buddhist texts, twice refers to them in the episodes belonging to the cycle ofAshoka, first in the classic story of Pamshupradana, and secondly, in the still more celebrated account which has much more of history than legend of Prince Kunala. In Chinese we have several versions and they reproduce faithfully the catalogue of the miraculous conversions. One of these which dates from 281-306 fixes also the locality of the occurrence:

"The Bhagavat subjugated and converted the Naga Apalala in Udayana; the head of the Brahmacharis in Kipin; Chandala in Kien-to-wei (which we are unable to trace to the Sanskrit original); and Gopala in Gandhara." In fact, we know from the accounts of the Chinese voyagers that the Dragon Apalala lived near the source of the Svat and that the cavern of the shadow of the Buddha, which was a witness to the victory of the Buddha over Gopala, was in the neighbourhood of Nagarahara near modern Jalalabad, to the west of the confluence of the Svat and the Kabul-rud. The third stage, therefore, has to be looked for in the continuation of the same direction, that is in the country of Kapisha. According to Hieun-tsang by the side of the shadow cavern there was a *stupa* enclosing the hair and nails of the Tatathagata, a frequent appellation of the Buddha. The Kunalavadana mentions mount Revataka alongside of Mahavana which is skirted by the Indus on its right bank below Attok.

The unidentified kingdom of Siu-ho-to, the scene of Story 39, takes us to the same region. It was there that, according to the narrative of the traveller Fa-hien, King Shibi purchased a dove at the price of his own flesh. The touching occurrence is recounted at length in the 64th Story and we know by the researches of Sir Aurel Stein that this is the country which corresponds to the modern Bunner. A further addition to our knowledge of ancient geography is furnished by Story 45. The Chinese *Han* is undoubtedly the Sanskrit China which takes us to the north of the Himalayas, the tracts subject to Chinese influences. Similarly the Ta-tsin of Story 90 continues the geographical horizon of ancient India towards Hellenic Asia, Ta-tsin being the translation of the *Sanskrit Yavana* of the Indians. If Ashvaghosha was a native of Central India there is no doubt that at the time when he composed his *Sutralankara* he was living on the confines of North Western India.

**The personae of the Story Book.**

The personages of the *Sutralȧnkara* are most frequently anonymous. They are Brahmans, ascetics, monks, merchants, painters, jewellers, washermen, iron-smiths and so on giving a clue to the inner life of the great Indian public as it lived and died in those days about whom we hear so little in the voluminous religious books of the Brahmans. Sometimes in our collection of sermons the Buddha and his disciples are brought on the scene. Some of the heroes are easily identifiable as historical personages. Asoka, the great Maurya emperor, is the hero of three tales. He is referred to in a fourth. His spiritual adviser Upagupta, one of the patriarchs of Buddhism, is the hero of another story. Both the ruler and his guide are placed definitely a hundred years after the Buddha. Upagupta became a monk "a hundred years after the disappearance of the Buddha." Elsewhere we are told that a master of the Law who had lived in the time of Buddha Kashyapa reappeared" a hundred years after the *Parinirvana* of the Buddha Shakyamuni under the reign of King Asoka." This interval of one century we find to be also fixed by a prophesy occurring in the *Vinaya* or the disciplinary code of the Mula Sarvastivada in which we are told that Asoka must take birth a hundred years after the Parinirvana.

Kanishka himself is the hero of two of the stories (14 and 31). In these he plays an instructive and honourable part. In the first he addresses a lofty lesson of charity to his minister Devadharma. In the second, deceived by his piety he salutes what he considers to be a *stupa* of the Budha, but in reality pays homage to a Jain one, which immediately breaks to pieces " because it did not deserve the homage of a king." The first episode takes place when Kanishka proceeds to the city which bears his name, the city of Kanishkapura founded by the Indo-Sythian king in Kashmir. To this day it bears the name in a scarcely altered form Kanispore. It is situated to the south-west of Lake Woollar in the *Baramula defile* (Stein, Raja-Tarangini, vol. II, p. 22.). The presence of Kanishka in the *Sutralankar* does not seem to contradict the unanimous tradition which attaches Ashvaghosha to the court of Kanishka. It is permissible to recognise in these two stories a delicate homage, which is by no means flattery addressed by the Buddhist doctor to the protector of his church. Story 15 is founded on the traditional avarice of King Nanda, who ruled over Gangetic India at the time of the invasion of Alexander and who preceded the Maurya dynasty. He had for his minister Vararuci whom we find in the introduction to the *Brahatkatha.* It is not without interest for literary history to see the tradition fixing the epoch of Ashvaghosha. Vararuci is in fact one of the great names of the literary tradition of India. He is the reputed author of a number of books of diverse classes, but especially of a grammar of the Prakrit languages called *Prakrita-Prakasha.* The Brahatkatha identifies him with Katyuyana and mixes up in his adventures two other personages connected with ancient Hindu grammar, Vyadi and Pannini. The Tibetan Tanjur preserves a collection of a hundred stanzas called the *Shatagatha* under the name of Vararuci. Finally, Sylvain Levi has found in the *Maha-*

*yanavalarashastra*, which was translated into Chinese between 397 and 439, several stanzas of a Buddhacarita as composed by the Bhikshu Vararuci. By the way, these stanzas refer to a transcendent Mahayana. One of them tells us that all the Shakyas, including not only disciples like Annanda and Aniruddha, but the inveterate enemy of the Buddha. Devadatta, are everyone of them Bodhisattvas. Another stanza speaks of the two kinds of *avivyda* or ignorance, the one mundane and the other supermundane. Our anthologies quote a dozen of the stanzas as the work of Vararuci and the Mahabhashya mentions a poem by Vararuci. *Vararucha Kavya* (Pannini 4, 3, 101). It is most significant to find in this story of the *Sutralankara* that Vararuci addresses these stanzas to the King Nanda which have a great resemblance to the style of Ashvaghosha, with his favourite regular refrain. The princes mentioned in our story-book which remain unidentified are Induvarma and Suryavarma of Avanti with their ministers Baudhayanamitra, Sudravarma of Shakala, Vallabha of Mathura, and a prince whose name cannot be successfully retraced from the Chinese to the original Sanskrit, a prince who belonged to Takshashila which the Greeks called Taxila, the spot marked by to-day's village of Sarai-kala, one hour's journey from Rawalpindi, which has yielded to the archæologicall excavators magnificent specimens of Græco-Buddhistic art.

**The grade of civilisation.**

The social condition of India, as represented in the *Sutralankara*, had attained a high standard of civilisation. There was intense intellectual activity throughout the country. The great Brahmanic epics were already known. Ashvaghosha's other work, the *Buddhacarita*, is also familiar with both the *Ramayana* and the *Mahabharata*. There are references to the Kings Nahusha, Yayati, Sagara, Dilipa. The edifying importance of this Brahmanic poems seems to be taken as admitted. A simple headman of an Indian village in what are Central Provinces listens to the recital of the *Mahabharata* and the *Ramayana* delivered by the Brahmans. Attracted by their promise which guarantees the heaven to the brave who die in the battle as well as to the pious men who burn themselves he prepares at once to mount a burning pile of wood. Fortunately for him a Buddhist Bhikshu turns up and demonstrates to him the futility of the promise of the Brahmans and eventually succeeds in converting him to Buddhism. The philosophical doctrines of the Samkhya and the Vaisheshika schools have already been constituted in their manuals. Ashvaghosha combats these Brahmanical dogmas with incisive vigour. He attacks the gods of the Brahmans and exposes their weaknesses with remorseless vigour. He shows them up as violent and cruel. Their power is only due to their good *karma*. The tradition that Ashvaghosha himself was a worshipper of Mahesha and latterly turned a Buddhist is derived probably from the first story in the collection in which an adherent of the sect of Mahesha renounces it for Buddhism. Among the religious sects of non-Buddhistic persuasion are the Nirgranthas or Jainas, the adversaries whom Ashvaghosha detests with greater virulence than Brahmans. In one story the King Kanishka is made to be enraged against the Jaina rivals of the Buddhists. From the inscriptions at Mathura we learn that the Jainas were flourishing under the Indo-Scythian kings. The number of the sects which were considered heretic attests the religious activities of the times. Ashvaghosha enumerates quite a number of them. The ornate diction which Ashvaghosha was the first to venture to apply to the otherwise insipid sutras of the Buddhists no doubt flourished amongst the non-Buddhistic creeds. In one place the king Asoka is made to say: "The heretics are able exponents of literary adornment and rhetoric." The Brahmans still love to preserve the monopoly of grammar and writing, but already "the other castes also possess the science." Literature seems to have entered into daily life. "The teaching of the Buddha has spread through writing over the world." It is most remarkable that the civilisation of India could boast of the use of palimpsests. One of the most charming stories mentions them. Up to now we had no other indication from any source whatever that the Hindus like the Greeks used this material for writing. This is an indication which will have to be reckoned with in our study of ancient manuscripts of India.

The Arts.

The arts were fully flourishing at the period. Comedians are frequently mentioned. In one story a pathetic instance of a painter's piety is afforded. He belonged to Pushkalavati and had gone on business to the country of Ashmaka where he was decorating a monastery. In one story we meet with an inebriated artist who, on coming to his senses, destroys the lamentable production of his hour of drunkenness and proceeds to produce some excellent work. In one place the king Shibi, who had disfigured and mutilated himself with his own hands to offer the members of his own body in charity, is compared to a beautiful statue disfigured by rain. In another place we have an exhaustive catalogue of the number of sciences which an accomplished heir to the throne was expected to possess. The list differs from the sixty-four classical arts mentioned in another place. It is of particular interest and may be reproduced in full.

"The Veda, archery, medicine, sacrifices, astronomy, grammar, the origin of writing, the performance of sacrifices, eloquence, rhetoric, the art of love, interest, purity of families, the ten names, computation, chess, dice, the study of origins, music and song, the art of playing on the conch, dancing and laughter, the art of the prestidigitarian, education, the making of garlands of flowers, massage, the science of precious stones and valuable materials for clothing, silk, sealing, weaving, wax work, strategy, sewing, sculpture, painting, literature. arrangement of garlands, interpretation of dreams, interpretation of the flight of birds, horoscopes of boys and girls, the training of elephants, the art of playing on the tambourine, the rules of battle array, the domesticating of horses, the carrying of the lance, jumping, running, and fording a river."

**Vindication of a neglected School.**

Whatever the interest of the *Sutralankara* in connection with its title, it is as a Buddhistic document that it is of capital importance. The study of Buddhism is even to this day unconsciously vitiated by the rivalry of two traditions, that of the north and of the south; the one founded on Sanskrit, quasi-Sanskrit, Chinese and Tibetan texts, the other based on the Pali texts. The genius of Burnouf knew how to maintain an equilibrium between the two competitors. Since his days all manner of factors have conspired to disturb the equipoise. In spite of worthy resistance Pali orthodoxy has usurped the science of Buddhism. Ceylon, the cradle of Pali, has been regarded as the authentic heir to the Master's doctrine disfigured by the rival tradition. The work of Ashvaghosha brings forward fresh information for a process of revision of our judgment. Expressly inspired by the original *sutras*, nourished by the words of the Buddha which he quotes on every page, he places before us in full light the condition of the Buddhist canon at the court of the barbarian prince, under whose auspices the text of the northern canon is alleged to have been settled about the beginning of the Christian era. It is therefore proper that we should analyse one by one the stories in this collection of sermons for the purposes of our enquiry.

**Preserved in China though lost in India.**

With the invocation with which according to the Buddhistic usage he opens his *Sutralankara*. Ashvaghosha makes his profession of faith, Like all the Buddhists in the first place he adores the Three Jewels, *viz.*, the Buddha, the Law and the Community. Next he addresses his homage to the assembly of the Sa-po-che-po, which is the transcription in Chinese symbols of the Hindu term Sarvastivadi, which means "those who believe in the existence of everything." This transcription differs somewhat from the more usual and more correct one. But we have to remember that the monk who translated the original Sanskrit into the Chinese, Kumarajiva, was an inhabitant of Karashar, in Chinese Turkestan, and that he had never been to India so that his Sanskrit pronunciation was naturally not of the best. Sylvain Levi carefully explains the process by which the Indian, Central Asian and Chinese Buddhists evolved a system of transliteration of Hindu names in the terms of the Chinese symbols. The Sarvastivadi school was one of the most prosperous in the world of Buddhism. It was powerful throughout India, but the Chinese pilgrims found it equally flourishing in Central Asia and in the Indian Archipelago. The Vinaya, or the disciplinary code of this school which is generally known as the Vinaya of the Ten Recitations, was translated into Chinese as early as 404. The translator was just our Kumarajiva who had a collaborator in Punyatara. We may note in passing that another branch of the same school which was called the primæval Sarvastivadis, Arya-mula-Sarvastivadis, possessed an enormous Vinaya in Sanskrit which was translated into Chinese under the direction of the famous Yi-tsing between 703 and 710 and a century later into Tibetan. It is a noteworthy coincidence in the history of Buddhistic researches that Eduard Huber and Sylvain Levi, both French scholars, at one and the same time working independently, discovered fragments of this Vinaya in their original form in the Sanskrit *Divyavadana*.

**His renowned predecessors.**

Ashvaghosha mentions some of his illustrious predecessors and pays homage to them along with the Sarvastivadi *samgha*. He invokes "the Bhikshus Fou-na and Parshava, the masters of the sastras Mi-tche". Sylvain Levi corrects this translation of Huber's and brings to light some of the renowned among Ashvaghosha's predecessors. The Chinese symbols Fou-na might represent the Sanskrit Purna, the fuller transcription of which in Chinese is Fou-lou-na. It frequently occurs in the name of Purna Maitrayaniputra. Further the same symbols in the same *Sutralankara* serve to transcribe the name, in an authentic and incontestible manner, of the disciple Purna (p. 325). Now Purna is not an unknown personage. Both the Sanskrit and the Tibetan tradition regard Purna as the author of the *Dhatukayapada*, one of the seven classics of the Abhidharma of the Sarvastivadis. The work was translated into Chinese by Hiuan-tsang who attributes it to Vasumitra, the president of the Council convoked by Kanishka (Takakusu, p. 75,108). This substitution is significant. For thus Purna enters into the group of the doctors patronised by the Indo-Scythian school. On the other hand, the learned Tibetan Bu-ston mentions Purnica assisted by Vasumitra and five hundred *arhats*, at the head of the redactors of the canon fixed by the Council of Kanishka (Schiefner, p. 298). Purnika is another form of the name Purna. The two doctors, therefore, again come in contact. But Wassilief who translated this passage from Bu-ston added in parenthesis next after the name of Purnika: (Parshivika). Slyvain Levi not having the text of Bu-ston is unable to state whether Bu-ston or Wassilief is responsible for this. However, this time again we meet Purna and Parshva associated as in the *Sutralankara.* Hiuan-tsang mentions in Kashmir a convent where Purna, the master of the Sastras, composed a commentary on the *Vibhishasastra.* The *Vibhishasastra* was the principal work of the Council of Kanishka. It was for the editing of it that Ashvaghosha was officially requisitioned. We are still in the same circle of authors and their works; but we might go further and take a more decisive step. A learned Chinese in a compilation of about 520 drew up two lists slightly divergent representing the filiation of the Sarvastivadi doctrine. Ashvaghosha figures in both. In one list he occurs twice. List No. 1 has Kattyayana, Vasumitra, Krishna, Parshva, Ashvaghosha, Kumarata, Vira, Ghosha, Purna, Ashvaghosha. List No. 2 comprises Kattyayana, Vasumitra, Krishna, Parshva, Ashvaghosha, Ghosha, Purna.

Thus we meet with Purna in the authentic tradition of the *Sarvastivadis* alongside of Ashvaghosha either as the second successor of the first Ashvaghosha or as the predecessor of the second. And he occurs again in a similar disguise which has thrown sinologists off the scent. Since the beginning of Chinese and Buddhist studies Remusat drew up a list of thirty-three primæval patriarchs which he had abstracted from a Japanese cyclopædia (*Melanges asiatiques* 1,113).

This list having become classical has been reproduced by Lassen in his *Indian Antiquity* (vol. 2, supplement 2). Since then the Sanskrit transcriptions of Chinese names communicated by Stanislas Julien to Lassen have been regarded as authoritative. The best of the Sanskrit-Chinese scholars Eitel, Edkins, Nanjio have tamely copied them. This list has: Parshvika, Punyayashas, Ashvaghosha.

The original Chinese from which Julien restored Punyayashas is Fou-na-yache. This is in fact the name of the eleventh patriarch mentioned in a history of Buddhism written in 1345. But we have a list of patriarchs of a much more ancient date in a Sanskrit work translated into Chinese in 472. Here the person placed between Parshiva and Ashvaghosha is Fou-na-che. In this Fou-na is quite positive. The transcription proposed by Julien is inadmissible. Punyayashas will not do. The correct restoration is Purna which is a customary abbreviation of a type known in grammar as Bhimavat, of either Purnasha or Purnashayas. Now both the Chinese works just mentioned attribute the conversion of Ashvaghosha to Purna while the biography of Ashvaghosha ascribes it to Parshva. Once more we find Purna and Parshva in close association just as in the invocation in the *Sutralankara*. They are so closely allied in fact that one of them is substituted for the other.

Parshva or Parshvika is better known. There is no equivocation regarding his personality. Both the Chinese Hiuan-tsang and the Tibetan Taranath attest the preponderating influence which he exercised on Kanishka and the part which he took in the convocation of the Council as well as in the compilation of the works. He was a native of Gandhara. The convent built for him by Kanishka where he resided in Kashmir was shown to the pilgrim. It had a commemoration tablet. He frequently bears the title of Bhikshu which is also attache d to his name in the *Sutralankara*. Further he is also styled the Elder as in the biography of Ashvaghosha.

As regards Mi-tche, Sylvain Levi again differs from Huber. According to the former it is derived from the Sanskrit Mecha. He is designated as the sixth patriarch. Lassen on the authority of Julien establishes the hypothetical Sanskrit name Micchaka, but this word is not known in Sanskrit. Wassilief has corrected the transcription in Mechaka. Mechaka is the predecessor of Vasumitra, the president of the Council of Kanishka and Vasumitra is separated from Parshva by two patriarchs, namely, Buddha Nandi and Buddha Mitra. In the lists of the Sarvastivadi filiation Mechaka occupies quite a different rank. In both the lists Mechaka floats in the neighbourhood of Ashvaghosha. Thus the name is proved to be Mechaka and the invocation may be established to be addressed to Purna, Parshva, and Mechaka, the masters of the Sastras. These three predecessors of Ashvaghosha are all of them glorious adepts of the Sarvastivadi school. Reverence to them shown by Ashvaghosha further evinces that the author of the *Sutralankara* was an adherent of the same school.

# APPENDIX III.

## MOST ANCIENT BUDDHIST RECORDS.

By M. Winternitz.

### The Pali Canon: The Lamp-post of Indian Chronological Records.

The Vedic literature leads us directly to pre-historic times. And even as regards the beginnings of epic poetry of India we despair of all time data. Only with the Buddhist literature we enter into clear daylight of history. Even the obscurity of the history of the Vedas and the epic literature is to a certain extent lightened by this illumination.. The age of the Buddha lends itself to determination and it provides us with a certain point from which we can reckon the rise of the Buddhist literature. Gautama, the Buddha, was born about 480 B. C. and a well authenticated tradition makes him die at the age of eighty. As a young man of twenty-nine he is believed to have embraced the life of a roaming ascetic and commenced to seek the way to salvation. After severe inner struggle, he started as a man of ripe age to proclaim the doctrine discovered by him. In the period between 525 and 480 B. C., therefore, the literary production of the Buddha must have issued,—the founding and the propagation of that Indian creed which was destined to be one of the three great world religions. The land of the Ganges in North-Western India was the seat of his activity. Here, in wealthy Magadha or modern Bihar and Kosala or modern Oudh, he went forth from place to place preaching his doctrine and winning to himself an increasing number of adherents.

Does a written record belong also to these operations extending for several decades? Decidedly not. In the *Tipitaka*, the Pali canon of the Buddhists, most of the speeches and maxims are put in the mouth of the Buddha himself. It is also precisely and circumstantially related where and on what occasion the Master held a particular dialogue or made a certain speech. How much of all these is traceable to the Buddha himself will perhaps never be definitely determined, for Gautama Buddha left behind as little in the shape of written record as did the Brahmanic sages Yajnavalkya, Shandilya or Shaunaka. But just as the speeches and dicta of these wise men have been to a great extent actually embodied as tradition in the *Upanishads*, so also undoubtedly many of the discourses and utterances of the Buddha were accurately preserved in their memory by the disciples and bequeathed to posterity. Deliverances like the celebrated sermon at Benares on the "four noble truths" and the "noble eight-fold path," which occur not only in many places in the Pali canon, but also in Buddhist texts, composed in Sanskrit in self-same words; much of the parting exhortation delivered by the Master to his disciples preserved in the *Mahaparinibbanasutta*, many of the verses and brief dicta in the *Dhammapada*, in the *Udana*, in the *Itivuttaka* and in more or less similar Sanskrit texts of Nepal as well as in Tibetan and Chinese translations,—these we can look upon as emanating from the Buddha himself, without exposing ourselves to the charge of undue credulity. Gautama Buddha not only preached his new doctrine of sorrow and the end of sorrow but founded a regular Order. He gathered round himself a body of monks who led a holy life in the sense taught by the Master and according to settled prescriptions in the hope of reaching the end of all sorrows, the coveted *Nirvana*. Accordingly many of the rules and ordinances enacted for this order of monks, for instance, the ten prohibitions for the mendicant friars technically called the *dasasila*, and probably also the well-known confessional litany, the *Patimokkha*, are derived directly from the Buddha,

From the age of the Buddha, therefore, no written record has reached us appertaining to the Buddhist literature known to us. On the other hand, individual texts incorporated in this literature may with justification be regarded as the word of the Buddha. Moreover, among the earliest disciples of the Buddha there were doubtless several eminent leaders and many of the discourses, dicta and poems embalmed in our collection probably had for their author some one or other of these prime acolytes.

Almost the entire oldest literature of the Buddhists consists of collections of discources or dialogues, of dicta, of songs, of stories and of a disciplinary code. And the Pali *Tipitaka* is nothing but an enormous corpus of these collections. It is manifest that such collected records can represent only the close of a literary activity spread over a long anterior period and that the components must necessarily be assigned to diverse periods of time. According to the Buddhist tradition one such final redaction of Buddhist records took place at a very early period in the history of Buddhism. Indeed, it is reported that a few weeks after the decease of the Buddha, in the city of Rajagraha, modern Rajgir, one of the personal disciples of the Buddha summoned together an assembly of monks, known as the first Buddhist Council, with a view to establish a canon of the religion (dhamma) and the disciplinary code (vinaya). Now against the trustworthiness of this report in its earliest shape, as descended to us in the *Tipitaka* itself, speaks the circumstance that it makes too gross a demand on our credulity. In a word, we are asked to believe that the two great sections of the *Tipitaka* relating to the doctrine and discipline of the Buddha entitled the *Suttapitaka* and the *Vinayapitaka* were composed essentially in the form and shape as we find them to-day in our Pali canon shortly after the demise of the Buddha,—a proposition impossible in itself. Nevertheless we have no right to assume that this tradition rests on no basis whatever. Probably it is reared on a reminiscence of the not unlikely fact that the elders of the faith gathered together soon after the passing of the Master with a view to unity on the main points of his doctrine and discipline. But for a composition of a canon of the sacred texts of the kind of our *Tipitaka* immediately after the death of the Buddha the period elapsed was certainly too brief.

More credible is the tradition regarding the second Council which is reported to have taken place a hundred years after the death of the Buddha at Vesali. To follow our most ancient account, the only object of this assembly was to condemn the ten errors which had crept into the disciplinary code. It is only in later reports of the Council that we are told that a revision of the doctrine was accomplished at a session which was held for eight months. If we rely on the older report we must assume it as a historical fact that about a hundred years after the decease of the Buddha a schism had arisen which had occasioned so much perturbation that a large council of monks had to be convened to arrive at a decision as regards the legality of certain disputed points. This, however, presumes that at that early date there were already established definite regulations for the solution of questions of this nature and those could only be a canon of rescripts for the conduct of life of the monks of a character and nature corresponding to those of the *Vinayapitaka* now extant. Thus in the course of the first century after the Buddha there must have been built up at least a fundamental basis for the text of a regular canon, if not a canon itself. An actual canon of the sacred texts was probably established only at the third council which was summoned at the time of the celebrated king Asoka, to follow the account of the Ceylonese chroniclers, whose narrative, if embellished with legends, is in the main entirely deserving of credence. That, as these chronicles relate, at the time the Buddhist Order had already split into numerous sects which necessitated an established canon for the orthodox believers, that is to say, for those who wanted to pass for adherents of the original doctrine,—this is antecedently and sufficiently probable. Not less likely is it that this redaction took place at the time of king Asoka, the greatest of patrons and adherents of the Buddhist Order. Asoka himself turns against the schismatics in one of his rock edicts. He must, therefore, have found it incumbent on himself to determine what was the real religion of the Buddha. On the other hand, however, he was so impartial,— tolerance of other creeds he especially enjoins in his other edicts—that he did not summon the council for the establishment of the canon himself but left it to the spiritual leaders. Accordingly, to follow the tradition, it was not the king but the learned and venerated monk Tissa Moggliputta who, in 236, after the death of the Buddha, called an assembly of a thousand monks at the city of Pataliputra, modern Patna, to fix a canon of the texts of the pristine religion. Now the "true religion" was for him one represented by the *Theravada*, which is to say, "the doctrine of the elders," the immediate disciples of the Buddha,– the school to which the sect of the Vibhajjavadis professed to adhere. Tissa, who was the president of the council, was a member of this sect and it was his canon which in the sessions lasting for nine months was determined at the council of Pataliputra. Credible likewise is the tradition that the same Tissa composed and incorporated with the canon the book of *Kathavatthu* in which the heretical doctrines of the period are repudiated.

Again it was Tissa, at least if we give credence to the chronicles of Ceylon, who sent out the first missionaries to the north and south and paved the way for the propagation of

Buddhism in foreign lands. A pupil of Tissa was the great Mahinda, the younger brother, or according to another tradition, the son of Asoka, who brought to Ceylon Buddhism and the Buddhist texts from Northern India. We can easily understand that legends grew round the person of this apostle to Ceylon. Should we, however, decline to believe the chroniclers who assert that Mahinda and the monks who accompanied him flew straight from India to Ceylon in the air like flamingoes, we need not reject the tradition *en bloc*, but must assume that at the root of the many legends lay the historical fact that Mahinda actually was the introducer of Buddhism into Ceylon and that emigrating into the island he brought with him the texts of the canon. These texts were,—and this sounds entirely trustworthy,—at first only orally communicated and were not committed to writing till in the first Christian century under the Singalese king Vattagamini.

Now according to the view of the Buddhists of Ceylon the canon which was composed at the third council imported by Mahinda to Ceylon and committed to record under Vattagamani was identical with our Pali canon or the *Tipitaka*, which we possess to this day. This *Tipitaka*,—the term means *three baskets*—consists of what are called the three *pitakas* or " baskets," namely:

1. *Vinayapitaka*, the basket of ecclesiastical discipline. This section consists of that which relates to the monastic order (Sangha), the regulations of the order, prescriptions for the daily life of the monks and nuns and the like.

2. *Suttapitaka*, "the basket of Suttas." The Pali word *sutta* corresponds to the Sanskrit *sutra*, but among the Buddhists it lost its ancient connotation of " brief rules " and here it is equivalent to doctrinal text or doctrinal exposition. very one of the larger or smaller expositions, often in the

form of a dialogue on one or more aspects of the religion, "Dhamma," is designated *sutta*. This *Suttapitaka* consists of five *nikayas*, that is to say, large groups of such *suttas*.

3. *Abhidhammabitaka*, "basket of scholastics." The texts comprised in this section, treat as well as those of the *Suttapitaka*, of the religion, *Dhamma*. But they do so in a more scholastic method and the form of dry enumerations, and divisions which have principally reference to the psychological basis of Buddhist ethics.

The Kathavattu ascribed by tradition to Tissa is found in our Pali canon as a section of the *Abhidhammapitaka*. But the latter is demonstrably the youngest component of our *Tipitaka*, for it repeatedly presupposes the texts of the *Suttapitaka* as is well known. Besides the more ancient texts, for instance, in the reports regarding the Council of Rajagaha speak invariably only of *Dhamma* and *Vinaya* and never of an *Abhidhamma*. It was, therefore, *per se* quite conceivable that the members of the third Council when they prepared a codex of the existing texts relegated to the end the texts of *Abhidhammapitaka* as those which were composed the last and added to them as a supplement the work of Tissa.

Nevertheless we cannot concede it offhand to the believing Buddhists of Ceylon that the canon established at the third Council is quite the same as the one now before us in the Pali *Tipitaka*.

In the first place the language of the *Tipitaka* is scarcely the same as that of the canon of the third century B.C. The latter could only be the Magadhi, the dialect of the province of Magadha, modern Behar. It was the home tongue of the Buddha who doubtless first preached in this idiom. Likewise the monks who fixed the canon in Pataliputra, the capital of Magadha, employed the Magadhi idiom. Traces of this Magadhi canon can still be perceived in our Pali corpus. But Pali, the ecclesiastical language of the Buddhists of Ceylon, Siam and Burma is designated by the latter themselves as Magadhi, although it essentially differs from the latter which is otherwise known to us from inscriptions, literary works, and grammars. At any rate it corresponds equally little with any other dialect known to us. Pali is just a language of literature which has been exclusively employed as such only by the Buddhists and has sprung like every literature language more or less from an admixture of several dialects. Obviously such a literary tongue, although it represents a kind of compromise between diverse vernaculars, is ultimately derived from one definite dialect. And this the Magadhi can very well be, so that the tradition which makes Pali and Magadhi synonymous is not to be accepted literally, but at the same time it rests on a historical basis. In the early period of Buddhism very little weight was attached to the linguistic form of texts. The tradition has handed down to us the wording of the Buddha that he was concerned only with the sense and not with the phraseology and in the *Vinayapitaka* the Buddha declines to have his word translated into a uniform sacred tongue like the Sanskrit. On the contrary he holds it necessary that each one should learn the holy word in the exposition composed in his own tongue. The literary language, Pali, could accordingly have developed only gradually and was probably fixed only when it was reduced to writing in Ceylon under Vattagamini. The monks of Ceylon at all events attached importance to the conserving of the texts in the language once for all determined and to transmit the same to posterity. And as regards the language, these monks have with rare fidelity preserved for, and bequeath to, us the contents of the texts of the *Tipitaka* recorded in the Pali tongue for the last two thousand years. But prior to this being given a definite shape in Pali and its arrival in Ceylon it is possible that it was subjected to alteration even as regards its contents. Both as regards the language and the contents, therefore, our Pali *Tipitaka* approaches very near to the canon established under Asoka but is not identical with the latter. For we must concede that in the period from the third to the first century B.C. when the commitment to writing took place and possibly at a still later date the texts underwent transformation, and possibly commentaries have invaded the texts and got mixed up with the latter. The original corpus as well as the components have probably grown since then in volume. Centuries have indeed not passed over them without leaving a mark. And it is only in this way that we can explain the numerous contradictions in the body of the canon as well as the repeated occurrence of older and younger tradition in juxtaposition and the frequent appearance of the same texts in more than one collection.

With these reservations and limitations, however, we can affirm that the body of our *Palilipitaka* as a whole cannot be so very divergent from the Magadhi canon of the third century B.C. For this above all we have a warrant in the inscriptions of the king Asoka. It is not only that his edicts preach the same spirit as the oldest of the *Suttas* in our Pali canon, but in them there are verbal echoes of the texts of our canon and quotations which with trifling divergence are to be found in our texts. There is still something more. In the edict of Bairat or Bhabra dating from 249 B. C., the king says to the monks of Magadha :

"All that the Buddha, the Lord, has spoken he has spoken well."

He proceeds to especially recommend for their study seven texts of which he mentions titles. These texts partly bear the same title and are partly referable to similar headings in our *Suttapitaka*.

From the second century B.C. and partly from the period of Asoka himself date moreover the celebrated *stupas* or

Topes of Bharhut and Sanchi, the stone sculptures of which are embellished with valuable reliefs and inscriptions. On the reliefs we find representations of Buddhist legends and stories the titles of most of which are also there subscribed. And these titles leave no doubt whatever that the reliefs represent illustrations to the *Book of Jataka* or the history of the previous births of the Buddha,—a book which forms a section of the *Tipitaka*. On the monuments of Sanchi, however, we find votive tablets in which monks are assigned the distinction of *Panchanikayika* or the master of the five *Nikayas*, *Petika* or the master of the *Pitakas*, and *Dhammakathika* the preacher of religion and to a nun is applied the designation of *Suttatikini* which means one who knows or teaches the *suttas*. It follows, therefore, that about the middle of the third century B.C. there was a corpus of Buddhist texts which was designated *Pitakas* and divided into five *nikayas*, that there were *suttas* in which the *Dhamma* or the religion of the Buddha was promulgated, that many of these *suttas* coincided with those in our *Tipitaka*, that besides, *Jatakas* exactly of the kind perpetuated in our *Tipitaka* appertained to the Buddhist literature as a component,—in brief, that in the time of king Asoka there must have existed a Buddhist canon which at least so far as the *Suttapitaka* is concerned could not have been dissimilar to our Pali canon.

The most ancient literary testimony of the existence of the three baskets or a triad of *pitakas* (pitakattyam) and of the *nikayas* is to be found for the first time in the *Milindapanha*, a work the genuine portion of which may be surmised to belong to the commencement of the first Christian century. But the entire remaining Buddhist literature outside the Pali canon in our possession shows that the texts incorporated in the latter reach back to an age of great antiquity not widely separated from the age of the Buddha himself and may be regarded at all events as the most genuine evidence of the original doctrine of the Buddha and of Buddhism of the first two centuries after the passing away of the Buddha.

This is demonstrated in the first place by the non-canonic Pali literature which comprises the dialogue of *Milindapanha*, the chronicles of Ceylon called *Dipavansa* and *Mahavansa* and a rich literature of scholastic commentaries related to the *Tipitaka*. All these books pre-supposes the existence of the *Tipitaka* at least in the first Christian century.

But the Buddhist Sanskrit literature also witnesses to the antiquity and the authenticity of the Pali tradition. To this belonged a literature of diverse varieties and different sects composed partly in classical Sanskrit and partly in a "mixed Sanskrit." One of these sects had also a canon of its own in Sanskrit of which most recently fragments have been made known. It is seen that this canon has not been translated from Pali but that it most brilliantly corroborates the authenticity of the Pali canon. For notwithstanding numerous deviations in the texts and in the arrangement there is such an amount of verbal agreement between the Sanskrit and Pali canons that we are compelled to assume a unity of tradition underlying both the records. But even Sanskrit works of the Buddhists of Nepal as well as the books of various Buddhist sects known to us only from Tibetan and Chinese versions enable us not only to determine a common stock of doctrine but also of original texts which are in accord with the tradition of the Pali canon in all essentials. The more this Buddhist Sanskrit literature becomes available to us and the more deeply we institute comparisons between it and the Pali canon the more it becomes evident that Oldenberg is only right when he claims that "the Pali replica which is naturally not immaculately correct must however be adjudged as eminently good,"

Moreover, no canon and no Buddhist text has come down to us from antiquity as remote as that of the Pali canon, of the first Christian century before Christ, in which the great Buddhist king Asoka is yet nowhere referred to. In language, style and contents the Pali texts are in harmonious continuation of the *Upanishads*, while the Buddhist Sanskrit literature much rather reminds us of the Puranas. Finally the fact that in these traditional texts committed to writing in Ceylon there is no allusion to the island further confirms it that therein we have to deal with "no canon of the Buddhists of Ceylon" but a canon of that Buddhist sect of India which has in fact preserved the most of ancient Buddhism; and this doctrine can with some justice be designated as the *Theravada* or the teaching of the first disciples of the Buddha. But not only as a source of our knowledge of Buddhism but also,—and this appeals to us directly—from a purely literary standpoint the Pali texts surpass all other evidences of Buddhist literature, and this will be manifest only from a survey of these writings.

# APPENDIX IV.

## BUDDHIST DRAMA.

By M. Winternitz.

According to the *Majjhimasila* section, a certain ancient tract in the Buddhist canon, which is preserved in the *Brahmajalasutta* and in the *Tevijjasutta* of the Dighanikaya, the Buddhist monks were forbidden to participate in all varieties of public entertainments including dancing, singing, recitation, animal fights and similar shows. Here is also interdicted the *pekkha* by which generally a dramatic performance is understood. It is doubtful, however, whether *pekkha*, which is the Sanskrit *preksha*, actually indicated a dramatic performance. In the *Vinayapitaka* also (Suttavibhanga to Sanghadisesa 13, Cullavagga 1, 13, 1-2) the enjoyment of dances, sport and music is forbidden to the monks, although there is no reference to theatrical performances. Accordingly it is at best questionable whether at the period when the Buddhist canon was compiled there already existed a theatre and the exhibition of dramatic pieces was carried out.

(The Natas who are frequently mentioned in our *Jataka Book* are wandering minstrels and dancers and not dramatic performers. Jataka No. 212, 291, 432; Fick Social Division in North-Eastern India in Buddha's time p. 188.)

In the Jatakas as well as in the Sagathavagga of the Samyuttanikaya, in the *Suttanipata*, and in the *Thera* and *Therigathas* there is not an insignificant number of ballads in the form of dialogues. They consist partly of *gathas* and partly of a combination of *gathas* and brief prose passages. The best known examples are the *Padhanasutta* and the *Pabajjasutta* in the *Suttanipata* (Windisch, Mara and Buddha, p. 1 and p. 245). But versification of entirely similar kind is represented by the poems in the *Mara-samyutta* and *Bhikkhunisamyatta*, the Chaddanta Jataka (No. 514), the Ummadanti Jataka (No. 527), the Maha-janaka Jataka (No. 539), the Candakinnara Jataka (No. 485), the ballads of the robber chieftain Angulimala in the *Theragatha* (866 ff) and also in *Majjhimanikaya* (86), the ballads of the nun Sundari in the *Therigatha* (312 ff) and many others. All these poems are uncommonly dramatic. Leon Feer calls the Chaddanta Jataka a veritable drama (JA 5 p. 47) and I have myself said of the Ummadanti Jataka that we might as well designate it a small drama (my history of Indian Literature ii, p. 114). However, to my mind, there is nothing which would justify our classing this species of poems as "small dramas," as is done by J. Charpentier in consonance with the theories of L. von Schroeder and J. Hertel (WZKM 23,33). It is quite possible, perhaps probable, that these varieties were sung to the accompaniment of a string instrument but that they were executed as real dramas and that in their dramatic performance action and imitation were brought into play,—for this we have no evidence in the entire Buddhist tradition.

On the other hand, it is conceivable that there are such dialogues, epic and lyrical poems to which nothing was wanting to make them dramas except the action; and a real theatre may easily take its rise here. Nevertheless we have the first positive testimony to the existence of Buddhist dramas in the *Avadanashataka* which belongs to the second Christian century. In Avadana No. 75 it is actually related how actors performed a *Baudhamnakatam* before a king, in which the director (natacarya) appeared in the costume of the Buddha. Sylvain Levi long ago called attention to this passage as well as to the performance of Buddhistic dramas in the present times in Tibet, China,

Ceylon and Burma. (Le Theatre Indian p. 319). In Burma of to-day as a solemn preliminary to the initiation of a Buddhist novice the Vessantarajataka is performed as a theatrical piece and the initiation itself is a formal drama.

We have preserved to us a complete Buddhist drama in the original Sanskrit which dates from the seventh century. It is the drama of Nagananda ascribed to king Shri Harsha. During the same period was issued the drama of *Lokananda* by the poet and grammarian Candragomi of which we have only the Tibetan translation. Perhaps it is identical with the adaptation of the Vishvantara Jataka mentioned by I-tsing (Sylvain Levi DEFEO, 1903, p. 41; I-tsing, a Record of the Buddhist Religion translated by Takakusu p. 164). We can only conjecture that in a much earlier age Buddhist legends were turned into dramatic pieces. When I-tsing (p. 165) immediately after the mention of the dramatic poems of Shiladitya (Shri Harsha) and of Candragomi goes on to say Ashvagosha also wrote "lyrical poems": we are to understand thereby similar lyrical dramatic pieces. That appears at least to be so from the context. At any rate, in the *Sutralankara* of Asavagosha, in the piece relating to Mara, who appears in the costume of the Buddha and like a consummate artist represents the Buddha so true to life that the holy Upagupta sinks down in adoration before him, we have a poem which is so uncommonly dramatic that it is evidently a recapitulation of a drama. Ed. Huber (DEFEO, 1904, p. 414) has established that this poem which is to be found in the *Divyavadana* (p. 356) and which has been translated by Windisch (*Mara und Buddha*, p. 161) originally belonged to the *Sutralankara* of Ashvagosha. From this we can surmise that in Ashvagosha's time a species of dramatic poems must have flourished. This conjecture is turned into proved fact by the discovery which Luders has made. It is now demonstrated that not only a variety of dramatic poesy, but actual dramas, which in their technique hardly differed from those of Kalidasa, used to be performed in the second century. Among the valuable manuscript treasures recovered from Turfan there is a palm leaf which on paleographical grounds seems to belong to the Kushana period. Luders, to whom belongs the credit of bringing it to light, is inclined to agree with Fleet and Franke that the Vikrama era of 57 B.C. was founded by Kaniska. If we admit even the second century as the time of Kaniska which would seem to be more accurate —then the Luders' Fragments are the oldest Indian manuscripts yet discovered. If they are of extraordinary importance on that score, they are almost of epoch-making significance in virtue of their contents in the literary history of India. For they contain fragments of a regular Indian drama. Luders has separated pieces of two different dramas. In the first appear three allegorical figures Buddhi, Dhriti, Kirti, which remind us of the *Probodhacandrodya* of Krishnamishra and the Buddha himself appears surrounded by a brilliant halo (prabhamandalena diptena). Now since the halo was first introduced into India by Greek artists (Foucher JA 1903 p. 298 and *L'art greco-bouddhique du Gandhara* p. 622), this drama must appertain to the age of the Gandhara art, which synchronises with the first Christian century, and must therefore flourished at the latter age, (Grunwedel *Buddhist Art in India*, German edition, p. 81; Foucher ibid p. 49).

The second drama is in such a fragmentary condition that it does not permit of its being completely identified. But it is of vast importance on account of the personæ, among whom we notice Vidushaka and other typical figures that remind us of the Mricchakatika. That the technique of the drama had completely developed is shown by the division into acts which are preceded by a prelude by the co-mingling of prose and verse, the latter in the meter of classical Sanskrit and the alternation of Sanskrit with Prakrit. Luders has devoted a penetrating examination to the Prakrit of the fragments, which leads to the conclusion important to the history of Indian languages that here alongside of Sanskrit stand three dialects which are of the same phonetic stage as Pali and the vernaculars used in the older inscriptions and which may be regarded as the precursors of the well-known three Prakrit idioms, Magadhi, Ardhamagadhi, and Shauraseni. Thus the language likewise testifies here to an older stratum of the classical drama. On the other hand, so far as we can judge from the fragments, the technique of the scenic art is so developed that we cannot regard them as the beginnings of dramatic composition, but must assume a preceding course of tolerably long evolution.

As regards the authors of the drama, Luders surmises that they belong to the circle of which the propelling centre was Ashvaghosha. This conjecture has been apparently confirmed. Hardly had the surmise been in print when Luders discovered three passages in the palm leaves of Turfan in which he came across the fragment of a drama by Ashvaghosha. It represents fortunately the concluding portion of a nine-act drama with its colophon which bears the title of *Shariputraprakarana* and which exhibits the name of the author Ashvaghosha in an unequivocal way. Ashvaghosha, who is known as the prominent poet among the Buddhists, here works into a drama the legend of the initiation into the order of Shariputra and Maudgalyayana,—a legend which is already so beautifully related in the Mahavagga of the *Vinayapitaka*.

# APPENDIX V.

## TREASURE TROVE OF ANCIENT LITERATURES.[1]

### *1. The discovery—Scientific expeditions.*

The country of East Turkestan has been one of eternal unrest since the beginning of the second century before Christ. Historical notices especially by the Chinese, supplemented by our finds, show that it had as guests one after another Indian clans, Tocharians, Huns, Scythians, East Iranians, Tibetans, Turks, the people of Kirgez and Mongols. The picture of the country as it was in the seventh century, that is, at a time when the majority of the MSS. now discovered were written, is drawn for us by Hiuen-tsang. He went on a pilgrimage to India in 629. His object was to see the cities between which the Founder of his faith travelled, and to acquire some of the holy books. He chose the northern route and passed through Chotjo, the capital of modern Turfan. On his return he traversed Kashgar, Yarkand, and Khotan. On the eastern confines of Khotan begins the desert, where the sand is kept shifting by the perpetual movement of the wind. The only landmarks visible are the whitened bones of pack-animals. Hereabout lay the ancient kingdom of Tokhara—already in ruins—and beyond was the silence of death. Flourishing life was, however, visible towards Khotan. All along, Buddhism was the dominant religion. Many thousands of monks lived in the monasteries of the countries, the northern side belonging to the school of the Sarvastivadis, Yarkand and Khotan being Mahayanists. The Chinese traveller has noted for us the various characteristics of the people who had nothing in common, except their religion.

[1] This paper is mostly a translation of Luder's *Uber die literarischen Funde von Ostturkestan.*

They were various as regards dress, customs, manners languages and modes of writing. The last was borrowed no doubt from India in each case. A new period of culture began for the country with the appearance of the Turkish clan of the Uigurs. They absorbed the inhabitants and united them into a people known to this day by their name. East-Turkestan in the matter of religion was only a province of India. Then side by side with Buddhism appeared Nestorian Christianity and Manichæism. The ruler of Turfan was the first to embrace it. Soon after came upon the scene a new arrival which showed itself to be stronger than Buddhism, Christianity, or the doctrine of Manes. The first conversions to Islam took place in Kashgar and the first Islamic dynasties took their rise there. The older faiths continued their existence, but there was no stemming the tide of Islam. From the fourteenth century onwards Turkestan became definitely Muhammadan. China acquired the country in 1758 without altering its religion.

The words of the Buddha, of the Christ, and of Manes ceased to be heard; yet the works which embody them survived. Ruins of monasteries, which are proved to be Christian from wall-paintings, inscriptions, and the find of MSS., have come to light in the capital of Turfan. In the centre of the city there was a large Manichæan colony. In this part was discovered a wall-painting, which is the most valuable find of an original fresco in the Berlin collection. It is the picture of a Manichæan priest, surrounded by believers, men and women, in their characteristic dress. The building was ransacked by the peasants in search of buried treasures when the German scientific expedition arrived. It appeared just at the moment when the real treasure would have been destroyed. The place abounds in traces of Buddhistic monuments. Without the help of illustrations it is difficult to gain an idea of the architecture of the times—the temples, the stupas, the monasteries. The art of Gandhara was transferred from its home in India to Central Asia. Over all a strong Iranian influence is noticeable. The further we come down the stream of time, the more mixed and complex becomes the style and the problems of civilisation studied by Stein, Grunwedel and Le Coq. It will require several decades to study the entire collection of finds. Philologists and archæologists will not be the least interested investigators.

The first find of MSS. by a European, which gave the impetus to further archæological search in Central Asia, was a bark MS. which was found by two Turks in 1890 in a ruined stupa. They sold it to Lieut. Bower, who was then the British Resident at Kucha. Bower presented the find to the Asiatic Society of Calcutta. The next year, Dr. Hoernle, the Secretary of the Society, published a report on the MS. which evoked considerable interest. The antiquity of the MS. was noteworthy. Indian MSS., according to the western standard, are relatively young. The destructive effect of climate and the pest of insects require their continual renovation. The oldest MSS., preserved in Nepal on palm leaves, date back to the beginning of the eleventh century. Only two palm leaves were hitherto known which had crossed the Indian border in 609 and reached Japan through China. They were preserved there in the celebrated monastery of Horiuzi, as venerable relics. The Bower MS. however was a considerable and complete one. It was written in the Gupta character, and hence had come undoubtedly from North-West India, and dated at the latest from the fifth century. Later investigations have proved that it must date from the second half of the fourth century. The possibility of such a discovery incited to further research. The Russian Archæological Society asked the Russian Consul-General in Kashgar, and the British Government commissioned the political agents in

Kashmir, Ladak, and Kashgar, to look out for similar MSS. Thus have been acquired the MSS. which are known as the Petrovski, the Macartney and the Weber. They are housed either at Petrograd or Calcutta. They belong to a large find made soon after the discovery of the Bower MS. by Turkish peasants in Kucha. For a long while the collection had remained in the house of the local Kazi, as a plaything which amused his children!

Meanwhile there was another discovery in 1892. The French traveller Dutrenil de Rhins found three MSS. in Khotan which he despatched to Paris. In 1897 Senart made known their contents and value. By now we are quite used to surprises from Central Asia. At that time, however, Senart's communication created a sensation in the Aryan section of the Oriental Congress held in Paris. The find represented a Kharoshti MS. The Kharoshti character till then had been known only from inscriptions in the outermost boundary of North-West India. Epigraphical comparison proved the date of the MS. to be the second century. As to its contents, it was a recension of the Pali *Dhammapada* in a Prakrit dialect, which was till then unknown in literary compositions. The manuscript was only a fragment. Another portion of the same MS. was brought to Petrograd.

The impetus given by an accident transformed itself into systematic research. The Russians were first on the scene. In 1898 Klementz set to work on this spot and the next year Radloff started the initiative which formed an International Association for Investigation in Central and Eastern Asia. What surprise awaited the seeker was shown by the results of the labours of Sir Aurel Stein supported by the British Government in the country round Khotan in 1901. Stein's personal travels led to a secondary discovery. He found out and exposed the manufacture and sale by Turks of fabricated MSS.

Stein's success led to the German expedition under Grunwedel and Huth to Turfan in 1902. Meanwhile with the exertions of Pischel there was formed a German Committee of Research which, with State help, in 1904 and 1907 sent out two expeditions under the leadership of Le Coq and Grunwedel. And Kucha and Turfan were thoroughly searched. The result was brilliant. In 1906-1908 Stein set out on his second journey. His most beautiful discoveries he made in the territory of Tun-huang. He came across a portion, altogether forgotten till then, of the great wall built by the Chinese as a protection against the incursions of the Huns. Here a windfall awaited him in the shape of a literary treasure. A few years before Stein's arrival, a Taoist priest in the hall of the Thousand Buddhas, or Tun-haung as it is called, discovered among the caves a cellar which had been walled up. It contained a huge library of thousands of MSS. To judge by the date of the MSS., the cellar must have been closed up in the beginning of the eleventh century. Stein secured a considerable portion of the treasure. A portion fell to the lot of the French scholar Pelliot, who journeyed to Turkestan in 1906-07. Even Japan was not behindhand. In 1902 it sent a Buddhist priest who made excavations with some success. To preserve the remains of the Tun-huang library from destruction, he despatched them to the National Library of Peking. Thus, in addition to archæological discoveries, there has been collected a huge mass of MSS. and block-prints in the libraries and museums of Petrograd, London, Oxford, Calcutta, Berlin, Paris, Tokio and Peking. Almost every material used for writing purposes is represented—palm-leaf, birchbark, wood, bamboo, leather, paper and silk. The number of alphabets represented is very large. The languages in which these MSS. are written are counted by the dozen, including several of which, till the other day, we had no knowledge.

Among the first finds which reached Calcutta and Petrograd, there were fragments of MSS. written in a variety of the Indian Brahmi character. The language, however, was not Samskrit. The writing was tolerably clear and Hoernle succeeded in deciphering Indian names and expressions of Buddhistic terminology and Indian medical terms. Next Leumann proved that we had here to do with two different tongues. The merit of discovering the exact nature of the first of these belongs to Sieg and Siegling, who in 1907 proved its Aryan character from the names of domestic animals, parts of the body, terms of relationship, and figures. The name of this language was the Tocharian. It was mentioned in the colophon of a MS. deciphered by F. W. K. Muller. The manuscript represented the Turkish version of a Tocharian translation from a Samskrit original. One dialect of it seems to have been widely common. Caravan passes written in it have been discovered, and dated and deciphered by Pelliot and Sylvain Levi. Further results may be expected from the studies of Mironov and Meillet. There is a vast number of MSS. which represent translation and redaction of Samskrit works relating to Buddhism and medicine. There are also some Buddhistic dramas; they can be traced to Indian models, as is shown by the mention of the Vidushaka.

The second new language is represented by two groups of texts, and is studied especially by Staiel-Holstein and Konow. The first represents business papers, mostly dated, though the current era is not known. The second group embodies Buddhist texts, partly dated. While the Tocharian fragments are of works belonging to the Sarvastivadi school, the texts of the second language belong to the later

Mahayanist literature—for example the *Vajrachedika*, the *Aparimitayu-sutra*, the *Suvarna praphasa Sutra, Samghata Sutra*, and the *Adhyardhashatika prajnaparamita.*

*II. New-old Tongues—Resurrection of dead languages—The lost creed of Manes—Pahlavi the religious and secular idiom of mediæval Iran.*

In 1904, F. W. K. Muller succeeded in deciphering a couple of fragments of paper, letter, and silk, originating from Turfan. He declared the alphabet to be a variety of the Estrangelo, the language as Middle Persian or Pahlavi, and the contents as pieces from Manichæan literature believed to have been lost. This was the commencement of a long series of brilliant discoveries, the results of which have been registered in contributions to learned journals. A heap of dogmatic and liturgical works has been recovered of the religion of Manes, which spread from further Asia to China, and in spite of sanguinary persecutions of centuries asserted itself on the coast of the Mediterranean as a rival to Christianity. It is, though but débris, a priceless possession, because for the first time we perceive here from its own books the doctrine, for a representation of which, up to now, we had to rely on the hostile writings of Augustine, the *Acta Archelai*, the formula of abjuration of the Greek Church and the celebrated *Fihrist*, a kind of detailed catalogue of contemporary Arabic literature by an-Nadhim. So far as can be ascertained the principles of the doctrine have been correctly characterised: here the ethical and physical elements have been indissolubly united in a fantastic fashion. Kessler was inclined to see in it a preponderating influence from Babylonian sources, and now it can be asserted as certain that at least the immediate basis of Manichæism was the religion of Zoroaster. Apart from the pronounced dualism which is common to both the religions, the names bear witness to this. Here we find the whole mythology of the *Avesta* reproduced. A fragment from the *Shapurakan*, composed by Manes himself, makes mention of Mihir, and the demons Az, Ahriman, the Parikas and the 'Azhidahaka. In a fragment which according to the superscription belongs to a hymn of Manes himself, he is named as a son of God Zarvan, who represents Time in Zoroastrianism and who in later times is exalted as the highest Principle. In a hymn, Fredon is invoked together with Mihir. Fredon is the Thrætaona of the *Avesta* and the Faridun of the *Shahname*. Many of the Zoroastrian angels like Srosh and Vohumano occur side by side with Jesus. For Manes claimed to be the perfector of Christianity. In the fragment discovered by Muller, Manes calls himself the apostle of Jesus, as has already been told us by Augustine. To judge, however, from the fragments, the syncretism of the Christian elements has not been perfectly achieved. There has been no complete amalgamation. The different layers of belief lie one over another. Thus the description of the end of the world in the *Shapurakan* presupposes the Day of Judgment and has a close connection with the words of the *Gospel of Matthew*. Further Christian influences are evidenced by reference to the history of the crucifixion and resurrection of Christ.

Manes acknowledged the Buddha as also a predecessor of his. Clear evidences of Buddhistic influence, however, only appear in the fragments belonging to later times, like the confession of sins. It is quite possible, therefore, that what we meet with here is a later development of Central Asian Manichæism. Probably here in the ancient soil of Buddhism it took the Buddhist colour, just as in the West it assumed a Christian tinge.

In their exterior get-up Manichæan MSS. are distinguished by the great care bestowed on them. Many are adorned with pictures, which must be regarded as magnificent specimens of miniature-painting. This taste for artistic book ornament was a legacy from old Iran. Augustine, as we know, turned with flaming wrath against the bibliophiles. Manes' name has been connected from ancient times with painting, and legend ascribes to him the knowledge of secret signs. In Persian he is always known as Manes the painter.

From the philological standpoint the Iranian writings fall into three groups. The first group is composed in a dialect which comes very near to the Pahlavi, the official language of the Sasanian empire. We know this language from a few inscriptions and texts of the Zoroastrian religion, and especially from a translation in it of the *Avesta.* Accordingly, the texts from Turkestan publishėd by Muller and Salemann indicate an infinite advance of our knowledge. The writings on the monuments known up to now are wholly uncommon. They do not give back the pronunciation of the time, and they employ Aramaic cryptograms for ordinary words, so that, for example, people wrote *Malka* while they read *Shah* or King. In the script of the fragments recently discovered this method is avoided, so that here for the first time we find an actual presentment of the proper Middle Persian language.

The second group is composed in the dialect of North-Western Persia, which no doubt was the language of the Arsacides who proceeded from these regions and who preceded in sovereignty the Sasanians. Andreas surmises that the so-called Chaldeo-Pahlavi, which appears in the inscriptions of the Sasanian kings, is identical with this tongue. He has now in hand a rich amount of inscription material for the investigation of the question, and we may hope in the near future to hear from himself the confirmation of this theory.

The third group occupies the premier position in importance, if not in number. It is written partly in the Manichæan and partly in a younger alphabet, called the Uigurian. Andreas sees in this the Soghdian dialect. It was only an accident which has preserved for us in al-Beruni the names of the months current in this language. The discovery of the Soghdian has led to another important discovery. F. W. K. Muller has ingeniously succeeded in showing that in the celebrated polyglot inscription of Kara-Balgassum, which informs us of the introduction of Manichæism into the land of Uigurs, the difficult text in a character which was up to now regarded as Uigurian is in reality composed in Soghdian. He also demonstrates that the Iranian terms in Chinese astronomical writings of the eighth century do not belong to modern Persian but to the Soghdian idiom.

Another find furnishes a proof to the fact that Soghdian was used not only by the Manichæans, but was the common language of intercourse of all the Iranian inhabitants of Turkestan, while to Pahlavi was assigned the rôle of a written language.

Among the MSS. which are acquired in the northern parts are found pages in Syriac writing ;and language, which have been published by Sachau. They are connected with the hymns of Nestorian Christianity. The activity of the Nestorian missions, which starting from Assyria and Babylonia spread into the interior of China, is attested further by 12 leaves from a charming little book, the Pahlavi translation of the *Psalms* with the canon of Mar-Abba which to this day is in use in the Nestorian church. The MS., to judge from the characters, must date from the middle of the sixth century. But the translation lies some 150 years before the oldest MS. of the Peshita Psalter, and promises to prove of the greatest importance for the history of the text criticism of the Syriac originals. Then, in Syriac writing, but in a language which owing to certain peculiarities can be designated as a younger phase of Manichæan Soghdian, considerable fragments relating to Christian confessions of faith, legends, and acts of the martyrs are found. The major portion has been edited by Muller. They show that the Christians employed the Pahlavi and the Soghdian languages for the spread of their doctrine quite as much as their Manichæan rivals.

Also the third religion, Buddhism, made use of the Soghdian for its propaganda. The Berlin collection possesses fragments of the *Vajrachedika* the *Suvarnaprahasa*, etc. The cave of Tun-huang is, however, a peculiar treasury of Buddhistic Soghdian texts which are written in a particular alphabet of Aramaic origin. Among the texts published by Gouthiot, the most interesting is that of the *Vesantarajataka*, the gem of didactic story-literature (forgotten in India but known to every child in Burma and Ceylon), which we find here in a new version. Gouthiot has deciphered also the oldest form of this writing as well as language, which was found by Stein in the desert between Tung-hung and Lop-nor, along with Chinese documents of the beginning of the first century. Above all there can be no doubt as to the character of the Soghdian. It was the language of the Iranian population of Samarkand and Ferghana, and was spoken as a kind of *lingua franca* from the first to the ninth centuries in Turkestan and farther in Mongolia and China. From a Buddhist MS. of Stein's, it appears that it was written in Singangu. An echo of the Soghdian is still found in certain modern dialects in the higher valleys of the Pamir. Especially the Yaghnobi can lay claim to the designation of modern Soghdian.

When it is further mentioned that the Stein collection also contains a document in Hebrew letters, and written, according to Margoliouth, in the year 100 of the Hegira, the most ancient Judo-Persian piece of writing, which at the same time is also the most ancient piece of writing in modern Persian, it must suffice to measure the importance of the Turkestan finds for the Iranist; and yet Turkish philology is in greater debt to the country. Up to now there was almost an entire dearth of its ancient literature. The earliest Turkish book known to us was the *Kutadgu-bilig*, written at Kashgar in 1069. Now we have acquired an ample collection of MSS. and block-prints in the land of the Uigurs, which is 200 years older in language and in character than that book. A splendid number of old Turki texts which, however, represent only a small portion of what we possess, have been edited by Radloff, Thomsen, Muller, Le Coq, and Stonner.

*III. Enormous Buddhist Samskrit literature in original and vernacular versions—Great discovery of the century; Pali* not *the mother tongue of Buddhism; Pali represents translation from perished vernacular.*

The varieties of scripts employed in these manuscripts are as curious as their contents. We meet with a Manichæan Estrangelo, the Uigurian alphabet, the Brahmi, the Runes of a particular kind, (which the genius of Thomsen was able to read twenty years ago for the first time on the stones at Orkhon and Jenissei). From the standpoint of their contents the texts fall into three divisions. The Christian literature has up to now been very sparsely encountered, the largest document dealing with the adoration the Magi who are here described after the manner of the Apocrypha. Among Buddhist texts, those of a comparatively later date occupy a large place—the *Saddharma pundarika*, the *Suvarna prahasa Sutra*, (of which both Berlin and Petrograd boast of complete texts), passages from the diaries of travellers, from the peculiar species of literature, not always of a cheerful nature, the

Dharanis, and the penitential formulas with their lively portraiture of all manner of imaginable sins. They bear a strong resemblance to the Zoroastrian *Patets*. Then there are again fragments of works with interlineal versions, which are not without value for the originals, since though they are somewhat younger in age they reflect the oldest accessible texts. From the standpoint of history and literature the most interesting of our acquisitions are the miscellania of Indian legends. Who could have ever conceived an expectation of coming across in Turfan the old legends of the *Mahabharata* related by Bimbasena or more correctly Bhimasena and his fight with the demon Hidimba, or of the *svayamvara* of Indian princesses? We have confessional formulas of the Manichæans which are without doubt framed after the Buddhist exemplars, like the *Khuastuanift* which is valuable even in its dogmatic contents, and another which witnesses to a considerable tolerance of Buddhism. In this text, in the same breath, are enumerated the sins committed by one against one's own brother in religion as well as the sins shared in Viharas dedicated to Shakyamuni! Further, our inventory of the treasure trove has to notice fragments of hymns, sermons, divine judgments, and dogmatic transactions; next, a small complete book of prognostications or a dream book in the Rune script. It bears resemblance to similar products of China, but is of Manichæan origin. A special value is to be ascribed to two leaves from Berlin which from their exterior can be marked as Manichæan and not Buddhistic. The first relates to the setting out of the Bodhisattva or as he is here called, the Bodisav, on the path of renunciation, and those who meet him. The other contains the revolting story of the youth who in his intoxication embraces the dead body of a woman. It is of Buddhistic origin and S. Oldenburg has shown that it occurs as the first parable in the Persian version of the legend of *Balaam and Joasaph.* This discovery as good as confirms the conjecture of Muller and Le Coq, to which the peculiar name Bodisav had led them, that here we have to do with the vestiges of the Manichæan version of the celebrated Buddhist romance. But it is not at all impossible that the original was a Manichæan work possibly in the Soghdian language. It would constitute a remarkable instance of involuntary syncretism if the Manichæans had contributed to the turning of the founder of Buddhism into a Christian saint.

There is hardly a single nation among those of the East Asiatic continent possessing any civilisation of its own, which has not left literary traces in Turkestan. Muller has in certain fragments recognised the script employed by the Hephthalites or White Huns on their coins. We have Mongolian letters and xylographs in the enigmatical Tangutian written language. Tibetan manuscripts are numerous of which only a few, the fragment of a sutra and a couple of religious songs, have been brought out by Barnett and Francke. The number of Chinese writings is enormous. The oldest of these excavated from the sand by Stein are now before the public in a magnificent work by Chavannes. Of the paper manuscripts a few go back to the second Christian century. They are at any rate the oldest paper documents in the world. A large majority of the documents are on wooden tablets. Some are one bamboo chips : they mark the condition of the oldest Chinese books. The wooden pieces, the oldest of which date from 98 B. C., come from the archives of the garrisons stationed here in the outermost west of the empire on the Great Wall. Here are gathered the detailed particulars regarding the daily life of the military colonies in the first centuries of Christ. They deal with the duties, the wages, the equipments of the soldiers, an optical telegraphic service, a postal department ; and, a complement to the picture of the realities of the day, a poem of later days describing the miseries and dangers of the frontier legions guarding against the barbarians of the West. The mass of later Chinese manuscripts seems to belong to works of the Buddhist canon and to business documents. A stranger has sometimes strayed into the collection as is shown by the "Lost Books in the Stone Chamber of Tun-huang," published five years ago in Peking. It is a pleasant sign that China is willing not merely to guard the ancient literary treasure entrusted to her, but also to make it useful.

For us, in India, the manuscripts in Indian languages are of supreme importance. Historic interest is claimed before all by documents on leather and wood discovered by Stein on the Niya river. They contain, as is evidenced by the publications of Rapson and Boyer, dispositions and reports of local authorities, instructions, regulations, official and private correspondence—all inscribed in the Kharoshti script and drawn up in a Prakrit dialect. The date of the Prakrit documents is fixed by the Chinese wooden tablets which have been mixed with the latter, and one of which is dated A. D. 269. In the third century, therefore, there were Indians in Khotan of Gandhara origin who were living mixed with a Chinese population. It is, therefore, not improbable that an historic fact lies at the basis of the legend according to which Khotan in the days of Ashoka was colonised by Chinese emigrants under the banished son of the Emperor as well as by the inhabitants of Takshashila whom the Indian king, wounded over the blinding of his son Kunala which they had not prevented, had ordered to be banished to the deserts to the north of the Himalayas. In the circle of these Indian colonies lies also the Kharoshti manuscript of the *Dhammapada* which is known after Detrenil de Rhins. Professor Luder thinks that it is by no means a private anthology, but the remnant of a particular tradition of the word of the Buddha which up to now has undoubtedly remained the only one of its kind.

Since the time of Pischel, who deciphered the first pages of the xylograph of the *Samyuktagama*, the remnants of the Buddhist canonical literature in Samskrit have been infinitely multiplied. What up to now has been placed before the public out of the *Vinaya* and *Dharma* of the Buddhist Samskrit canon by Sylvain Levi, Finot and de la Vallee Poussin is only a small portion of the salvage. Of the *Udanavarga*, which seems to have been unquestionably the most favourite Samskrit Buddhist work, 500 leaves are preserved in the Berlin collection alone, out of fragments and leaves belonging to some 100 manuscripts, so that the text is almost completely restored. Pischel recognised that these vestiges belong to the canon of the school of the Sarvastivadis lost in the original Samskrit. He already noticed that the Samskrit texts were not translations from the Pali canon, which is the only canon preserved intact to us. A penetrating research has revealed that both the Samskrit and Pali canon are traceable to a common source which, as is proved by mistakes in the translations, was drawn up in the Eastern dialect which was spoken as the common idiom in the territory of the Buddha's activity. THIS IS AN EVENT WHICH IS OF DECISIVE CONSEQUENCE IN THE HISTORY OF BUDDHISM. We are now in a position to restore the Samskrit canon from the débris of tradition. It existed in the pre-Christian centuries in Magadha. That, however, is not equivalent to saying that we have come upon the original word of the Buddha. What the Buddha himself exactly taught will always remain a subject of speculation although Professor Luder believes we are not yet justified in resigning ourselves to the position of *ignorabimus*. That, however, which the Church thought He taught at a time to which no direct documents go back, is now in our hands, thanks to the Turkestan discoveries.

Another region in literature has now been made accessible from this quarter—the pre-classical Samskrit poetry. Thirty years ago the Kavya appeared to begin with Kalidasa who was placed in the sixth century. Before that seemed to lie centuries of complete sterility and Max Muller coined the phrase about "Sanskrit renaissance." To-day we are positive that Kalidasa lived in the beginning of the fifth century, that his name signifies the zenith of courtly poetry, and that it was preceded by a spring. Inscriptions and a couple of lucky discoveries in India have given us an idea of the beginnings of the Kavya. Turkestan intimates to us the existence of an unsuspected wealth of hymns, epics, romances and anthologies which in the majority belong probably to this period. The material is always religious but the form is that of the secular Kavya. This differentiates the poetry from the old Buddhistic, though the old Church did not by any means stand hostile to poetry.

[ The present writer may be allowed to dwell for a moment—a moment only—on the brilliant confirmation of the discovery of the Buddhist canon in Samskrit. A short eight years ago his refusal to look upon Pali as the prime word of the Buddha, and Samskrit Buddhist books as later fabrications, drew on him a storm of indignation from Burmese monasteries. Unfortunately for the time being the excavator's spade is left for the shrapnel; else it were easy to make a present to the Shwe-da-gon shrine of an anthology of Samskrit Buddhism as voluminous as any in Pali issued from Leipzig or New York.]

*IV. The hiatus in classical Samskrit literature supplied—Buddhist poetry or drama in Samskrit—Matriceta and Ashvaghosha the forerunners of Kalidasa—Authenticity and verification of Tibetan treasures.*

People appropriated the popular species of poetry called the Gathas by putting over it a Buddhistic veneer. The first age of profound religious passion gave rise to a number of poets who, however, had not the ambition to hand down their names to posterity. Many of the strophes which were placed in the mouth of the Buddha himself or his disciples are among the finest produced by the literature of any age. But only when Samskrit was given the position of a church language, instead of the popular dialect, doubtless with a view to a wider spreading of the doctrine, it was that poetry began to be composed according to the rules of the Samskrit court singers. Our manuscripts prove how much under the influence of this artificial poetry gradually the ear of the monk himself in the Turkestan monasteries was refined. Scholars were constantly at work improving upon the old translations of canonical works which were in many ways crude and unpolished. They laboured to reduce the text in language and metre to the stricter requirements of later ages.

Two names belonging to this early period are mentioned in the Middle Ages with enthusiastic admiration, Matriceta and Ashvaghosha. Both belong as it seems to the beginning of the second century. Matriceta's fame is based on his two hymns to the Buddha, which according to I-tsing in the seventh century every monk in India learnt by heart, whether he was attached to the *Hinayana* or the *Mahayana*, and gave rise to the legend that the author in his previous birth had rejoiced the Buddha with his songs as a nightingale. They were up to now known only from Tibetan and Chinese translations. From the fragments in the Berlin collection about two-thirds of their text has been restored. The work of Matriceta has great value in the history of the Samskrit literature as the earliest example of Buddhistic lyrics; although the enthusiasm with which the Chinese Buddhist scholar and translator I-tsing speaks thereof is not altogether intelligible to us. Dogmatic punctiliousness can scarcely compensate us for the monotony with which synonym after synonym has been heaped. Also the *alankaras* which constitute the regular decoration of a *kavya* are only sparingly employed. Incomparably higher as a poet at any rate stands Ashvaghosha. Fragments of his epic, the *Buddha carita* and the *Saundarananda* in the original Samskrit are found in Turkestan. Here we have also palm leaves eaten up and ruined on which was inscribed the *Sutra alankara* which is at present known only from its Chinese translation. A French version of the Chinese rendering was done by Huber. The ruined remains, however, give us an idea of the style of Ashvaghosha. We likewise possess a wholly unexpected fund of remnants of dramas of which at least one in the colophon is expressly designated as Ashvaghosha's work. One of the two palm leaf writings in which it is preserved to us is a palimpsest prepared in central Asia. The other was probably written in northern India during the lifetime of the poet. It represents the oldest Brahmi manuscript we know. One leaf has come out of a dramatic allegory in which Wisdom, Endurance, and Fame entertained themselves on the virtues of the Buddha. Probably it is an epilogue or an interlude. A fragment represents a comic piece in which the principal part seems to have been played by a courtesan. The drama which undoubtedly is a production of Ashvaghosha treats of the story of the two chief disciples of the master, Shariputra and Maudgalyayana, up to the time of their conversion to Buddhism. The fragments do not suffice to enable us to judge of the individuality of Ashvaghosha although they furnish valuable suggestions for a general history of the Indian theatre. We here come across, apart from divergences of little consequence, forms as in the classical period. The speeches are in prose intermixed with verse. The women and the inferior *dramatis personae* speak a Prakrit dialect which undoubtedly stands here on a more ancient phonetic level. The comic person of the piece, the Vidushaka, is also here a Brahman perpetually suffering from hunger in the company of the hero, and the manner of his jokes is the same as in *Shakuntala.* All this demonstrates that the Indian drama at the close of the first Christian century was fully developed in all its characteristics and this has been completely established by the discovery in Southern India of the dramas of Bhasa, by Ganapati Shastri. Bhasa is one of the poets mentioned by Kalidasa as his predecessor.

It is a variegated picture this, presented to us by research in Turkestan. It is all still almost in confusion, the flickering light of accident. It will require years of labour before we are able to judge of the whole huge collection. The question with some is whether the results will be commensurate to the labour. There are many in the West who have hardly any appreciation for the work of scholars engaged on the investigation of peoples and speeches of Southern and Eastern Asia. But the sinologues' views at least must count. Chinese is a "colonial language." The Samskritist, however, is something more than a tranquil man who worships dead deities worlds apart. These gods are not dead. The knowledge which Gautama Buddha acquired in the holy night under the *Bodhi* tree is still the *credo* of millions of mankind, and thousands and thousands of lips still repeat the prayer at sunrise composed by a Rishi thousands of years ago. Nor are those countries far from us. Only 18 days' journey divides the heart of Europe from Colombo, in whose harbour steamers from their journey to the ends of the earth take shelter. The world has become narrower, the people of Asia have been brought close to us and will be brought still closer. Whether this will be peaceful or will lead to strife, this nobody knows. It is nevertheless our duty to endeavour to study hte ancient systems of culture, to endeavour to appreciate them in the only possible way—that of historical research. In the history of this research the discovery of the Ancient and Middle Ages of Turkestan constitutes only a single chapter but that happens to be one of the most important.

# APPENDIX VI.

## THE INSCRIPTION OF ARA.[1]

BY PROF. H. LUDERS, PH.D., (BERLIN.)

The Kharoshthi inscription treated of here was discovered in a well in a *nala* called Ara, 2 miles from Bagnilab. It is now in the museum at Lahore. Mr. R. D. Banerji was the first to bring it to our notice. In publishing it (*ante*, vol. XXXVII, p. 58),[2] he expressed the expectation that I should succeed in completely deciphering the text. I regret that I am not able wholly to respond to the expectation. The last line of the inscription remains obscure though the script is here partly quite clear. I believe, however, to have been able to read so far the remaining portion of the inscription with the help of the impression which I owe to the kindness of Dr. Fleet, that at the most there will remain doubt as regards the two names in the fourth line.

In order to show what I owe to my predecessor I reproduce here his reading of the text of the inscription. I consider it superfluous to go into every point in detail in which I differ from him: in most cases an inspection suffices to determine the text. Let me, however, make one observation: Banerji believes the inscription to be broken towards the left end, and that the final words of all lines except the first are missing. This assumption is wholly without foundation. Only the last line is incomplete at the end. Banerji reads :—

1. *Maharajasa rajatirajasa devaputrasa pa*(?) *thadharasa* . . .
2. *Vasishpaputrasa Kanishkasa samvatsarae eka chatari* (*se*) . . . .

[1] Translated by Mr. G. K. Nariman from the *Sitzungsberichte der Preussischen Akademie der Wissenschaften*, 1912, pp. 824 ff., and revised by the author.

[2] *Indian Antiquary*.

3. *sam* XX, XX, 1, *Chetasa masasa diva* 4, 1 *atra divasami Namikha* . . . .

4. . . . . *na pusha puria pumana mabarathi Ratakha-puta* . . . .

5. *atmanasa sabharva putrasa anugatyarthae savya* . . . .

6. . . . . *rae himachala*. Khipama . . . .

I read :—

1. *Maharajasa rajatirajasa devaputrasa* [*ka*] *i* [*sa*] *rasa*[1]

2. *Vajheshkaputrasa*[2] *Kanishkasa sambatsarae*[3] *ekachapar*[*i*]

3. [*sae*][4] *sam* 20 20 1 *Jethasa masasa di* 20[5] 4 1 *i* [*se*] *divasach-hunami kha*[*n*]*e*[6]

4. *kupe* [*Da*]*shaverana*[7] *Poshapuriaputrana matarapitarana puya-*

5. *e Namda*[*sa sa*]*bharya*[*sa*[8] *sa*] *putrasa anugraharthae sarva* . . [*pa*]*na*[9]

6. [*ja*] *tisha hitae*[10] *ima chala*[*khiyama*[11] . . .

1. To the reading of this word we shall revert later on.

2. The second *akshara* can in my opinion be only *jhe*; the reading *si* is at all events excluded. As regards the reading of the third *akshara*, there may be different views at first sight. As *shka* occurs in the name of Kanishka, Vasishka, Huvishka, and as exactly the same symbol occurs in the Zeda inscription in the name *Kanishkasa*, one might feel tempted to read *shka*. On the other hand *shpa* is suggested by the fact that in the ligature *shka*, in the word *Kanishkasa* which follows immediately after, the *ka* is joined to the *sha* in a different way. But, I think, we shall decide for *shka* when we take it into consideration that in the Kharoshthi script the same symbol on the same stone shows often widely different forms.

3. I have already given the correct reading of the date of the year in *Jour. R. As. Soc.*, 1909, p. 652. The ligature *tsa* is not new as Banerji thinks. It occurs, not to mention uncertain cases, in the word *samvatsaraye* in the Taxila inscription of Patika (*Ep. Ind.* 4, 54; Buhler: *samvatsaraye*), and in the Mahaban inscription (*Jour. As.* IX, 4, 514; Senart: *samvatsaray*), and in *bhetsiti* and *matsana* in the MS. Dutreuil de Rhins, as was shown ten years ago by Franke (*Pali und Sanskrit*, p. 96 f.)

4. The *i* of *ri* is not clear.

5. After the symbol for 20 there is a hole in the stone.

6. The *n* has crumbled away. The sign for *e* is attached below as in *de* in line 1, in *e* generally, and probably also in *ve* in line 4.

7. The *da* is uncertain.

8. The *sa* at the end of the word and the following *sa* are not quite distinct, but perfectly certain.

9. The *akshara* after *sarva* is totally destroyed, and the *pa* is uncertain. Shall we read *sarvasapana*?

10. The *hi* is not certain.

11. After *khiyama* there are three or four illegible *aksharas*.

**Translation.**

"(During the reign) of *Maharaja*, *Rajatiraja*, *Devaputra*, *Kaisara* Kanishka, the son of Vajheshka, in the forty-first year,—in the year 41,—on the 25th day of the month of Jetha (Jyaishtha), in this moment of the day, the dug well of the Dashaveras, the Poshapuria sons, for the worship of father and mother, in order to show favour to Namda together with his wife and his son, and to all beings (?). For the welfare of these (?) . . . ."[3]

The inscription reports the sinking of the well in which it was found, by a number of persons who called themselves Dashaveras, if that name has been correctly read, and who are further characterised as Poshapuriaputra. Since it is said later on that the work was undertaken for the worship of father and mother, Dashavera can only be the family name indicating here a number of brothers belonging to it. The expression ' Poshapuriaputra" one would be at first sight inclined to understand as "sons of Poshapuria"; but Poshapuria would be a very strange personal name. I therefore believe that *putra* is here employed in the frequently occurring sense of ' member of,' ' belonging to,'[4] and that Poshapuria is derived from the name of the city of Poshapura, which is equal to Purushapura, the modern Peshawar. As for the form *posa* it can be authenticated from Pali writings.

*Khane*[5] is no doubt derived from *khan* in the sense of "dug"; whether it is an adjective or a participle (Sk. *khatah*) should be left an open question. *Khane kupe* seems to have been used as a contrast to the natural fountains. The expression is of interest inasmuch as it enables us to explain a passage in the enigmatical inscription of Zeda. There occur after the date *sam 10 1 Ashadasa masasa di 20 Utaraphaguna ise chhunami*, the characters which Senart[6] reads: "*[bha] nam u[ka]* . . . . *chasa ma* . . *kasa Kanishkasa raja[mi]* . . . *[dadabhai] da[na]mukha*"; and which are read by Boyer[7] as:

[3] The final portion is not clear to me.

[4] Compare *e. g.*, *nigamaputa* in the Bhattiprolu inscriptions and other instances, ZDMG. 58, p. 693 f.

[5] I adhere to the usual transcript of the two *na* signs without expressing that I consider them as absolutely correct.

[6] *Jo. As.* VIII. 15, 137.

[7] *Ibid* X. 3, 466.

"*khanam usphamu . . chasa mardakasa Kanishkasa rajami[to] yadalabhai danamukha.*" Now the impression before me clearly shows that the three first *aksharas* of this passage are exactly the same as those following the date in our inscription. Even the *e* of *ne* is joined to the *matrika* in exactly the same way as here.[8] That the fourth character is neither *ka* nor *spha* but *e*, can now hardly be disputed.[9] The words thereafter I read as : *Veradasa mardakasa.* They are pretty clear in the impression except the second *akshara* which may as well be *ro.* As regards the five *aksharas* coming after *rajami*, I can for the present only say that they can in no case be read as *toyadalabha*. Therefore the reading that we get is : *khane kue Veradasa mardakasa Kanishkasa rajami.* . . . . *i danamukha.* The form *kue* instead of *kupe* is found also in the Paja inscription[10] and in the Muchai inscription.[11]

Much more important than the contents proper of the inscription is its date. Until now the numerous dates of the inscriptions of the Kushana period presented no difficulty at least in so far as the succession of the kings is concerned. They yielded for Kanishka the years 3-11, for Vasishka 24-28, for Huvishka 33-60, for Vasudeva 74-98. Here we suddenly find Kanishka in the year 41.

To explain this contradiction it may be alleged that in the text of the inscription we find nothing to show that Kanishka was on the throne in the year 41. *Kanishkasa sambatsarae ekachaparisae* literally means " in the year 41 of Kanishka,' and one might find in it the sense, " in the year 41 of the era

---

[8] It seems that both Senart and Boyer have regarded the right hook of *ku* as a portion of the preceding symbol. Otherwise I am unable to explain the reading *nam u.*

[9] See my remarks *Jour. R. As. Soc.* 1909, pp. 647 ff.

[10] *Ante*, 37, 65.

[11] *Ibid*, 37, 64; *Jour. R. As. Soc.* 1909, 664.

founded by Kanishka." Now it is self-evident that the combination of the number of a year with the name of a king in the genitive case originally indicated the year of the reign of that king but I need cite no instance to show that later on in a similar way people combined the names of the reigning king with the number of the year of the current era; and that must be also the case here. Kanishka receives here his whole title, and even a statement about his descent is added. And people generally do not speak in this fashion about a king that was long dead especially when they are silent as regards the name of the reigning king. That explanation, therefore, seems to me out of the question. Another possibility is afforded by the assumption that Kanishka was a contemporary ruler of Vasishka and Huvishka. Banerji has expressed this view. Accordingly Kanishka, between the years 10[12] and 24, would have handed over the rule of India to Vasishka, who afterwards was succeeded by Huvishka, and himself confined his rule to the northern part of his empire. This does not appear to be probable, because all other sources are silent. We should above all expect that in the titles of Vasishka and Huvishka there should appear an indication of a certain relation of dependence. But in the inscription of Isapur and Sanchi, Vasishka bears the title of *maharaja rajatiraja devaputra shahi.*[13] That for Huvishka up to the year 40 only the title of *Maharaja devaputra* can be ascertained as far as the inscriptions go, is probably a matter of accident. In the inscription of the Naga statue of Chargaon of Sam 40[14] and in the inscription of the Wardak vase of Sam 51[15], we find that he is called *maharaja rajatiraja*, and in the Mathura inscription of Sam 60[16] *maharaja rajatiraja devaputra*. Under these circumstances, it seems to me more probable that the Kanishka of

---

[12] This is the date of an inscription in the British Museum which apparently was found in the country about Mathura, (see *Ep. Ind.* IX. 239 ff.)

[13] *Jour. R. As. Soc.*, 1910, 1313; *Ep. Ind.* II. 369.

[14] VOGEL, *Catalogue of the Archæological Museum at Mathura*, p. 88.

[15] *Jour. R. As. Soc.*, XX. 255 ff.

[16] *Ep. Ind.* I, 386.

our inscription is not identical with the celebrated Kanīshka. I lay no stress on the fact that Kanishka here bears a title which is not applied to him anywhere else. But the characterisation as the son of Vajheshka, which too does not appear anywhere else, gives an impression, to me at least, that it was added with a view to differentiate this Kanishka from the other king, his name-sake. Now the name Vajheshka or Vajheshka sounds so near Vasishka that I look upon both forms only as an attempt to reproduce in an Indian alphabet one and the same barbaric name.[17] These two forms at any rate are closer to each other than, for instance, the various shapes in which the name of Huvishka occurs in inscriptions and on coins. Now, cannot the Kanishka of our inscription be the son of the successor of the great Kanishka? He would be probably in that case his grandson, which would well agree with the name, because grandsons are, as is well known, often named after the grandfathers. The course of events then would be something like this. Kanishka was followed by Vasishka between the years 11 and 24. After Vasishka's death, which occurred probably soon after Sam 28[18], there was a division of the empire. Kanishka II took possession of the northern portion of the kingdom. In India proper, Huvishka made himself king. The reign of Kanishka II endured at least as far as Sam 41, the date of our inscription. But before Sam 52 Huvishka must have recovered the authority of the northern portion of the empire, for in this year he is mentioned as king in the Kharoshthi inscription which was found at Wardak to the south-west of Kabul.

[17] *Jh* and *s* may have been used to express a *z*; compare the writing *Jhoilasa* in Kharoshthi by the ride of ZΩΙΛΟΥ on the coins of Zoilos (Gardner, *Coins of Greek and Scythic Kings in Bactria and India*, p. 52f., 170). It need hardly be noted that the notation *e* or *i* before the *shka* makes no difference.

[18] In case the Mathura inscription (*Ep. Ind.* II. 206, No. 26) is dated in Sam 29 and in the reign of Huvishka.

I do not misapprehend the problematic nature of the construction I have proposed: whether it is correct will depend on further discoveries for which we are fortunately justified in entertaining hopes.

The inscription which presents us with so many new difficulties carries us, however, in my opinion, by means of one word further towards the solution of a question which for the last few years has considerably occupied Indian historical research. This word is the fourth title of Kanishka which I read as *kaisarasa*. This reading appears to me to be absolutely certain, although the upper portion of some letters on the stone have been injured. Banerji read it *pa* (?) *thadarasa*. I must at once concede that the first *akshara* can be *pa*. But it is equally possible that the upper portion of the symbol has been broken away, just as has been the case with the preceding symbol which undoubtedly is *sa*. In that case the *akshara* can only be *ka*. The second *akshara* can be nothing but *i*. The hook at the top of the symbol is perfectly visible in the impression and makes the reading *that* impossible. Of the third *akshara* only the lower portion has been preserved. Comparing the remnant with the last *sa* of the word, one can have no doubt but that it was a *sa*. The lection *dha* is simply impossible. The two last *aksharas* are manifestly *rasa*. Thus we can either read *paisarasa* or *kaisarasa*; and it is obvious that only the latter can be the right reading.

The title of *kaisara* has not up to now been traced to Indian soil, and it would be incredible if we had to deal with a national dynasty. But the Kushana kings drew their titles from all parts of the world. They call themselves *maharaja*: this is the genuine Indian title. They call themselves *rajatiraja*: this obviously is the translation of the Middle Persian royal designation *shaonano shao* which we meet with on the coins of Kanishka, Huvishka, and Vasudeva. The third title *devaputra* is, as has been long known, the rendering of the Chinese *t'ien-tzu*, 'son of heaven.' And now to these has been added the Roman appellation of Cæsar. It may be asked: why this heaping up of epithets? For this too we have an answer: These were calculated to mark the monarch as the lord of the whole world. *Maharaja* is the king of India, the ruler of the South. As against him we have *rajatiraja*, the king of the Northern country. That properly speaking Iran lies to the North-West of India, and not exactly to the North, need not be considered as prejudicial to our explanation, inasmuch as we have to deal here with the cardinal points in a general way only. The term *devaputra* marks the ruler of the East. To him is opposed the *kaisara* or sovereign of the West. Thus the Kushana king is a *sarvalogaisvara*, as runs the title on the coins of the two Kadphises. This idea appears to be an Indian one. I need only call to mind the *digvijaya* which was the ideal and aspiration of every Hindu ruler. In this connection there is an interesting passage in the Chinese translation of the *Dasaviharanasutra* of A. D. 392. I quote it according to the version of Professor Sylvain Levi.[19] In the *Ien-feou-ti* (Jambudvipa) there are. . . . four sons of heaven (*t'ien-tzeu*). In the East there is the son of heaven of the Tsin (the Eastern Tsin 317-420); the population is highly prosperous. In the South there is the son of heaven of the kingdom of *T'ien-tchou* (India); the land produces many celebrated elephants. In the West there is the son of heaven of the Ta-ts'in (the Roman Empire); the country produces gold, silver, and precious stones in abundance. In the North-West there is the son of heaven of the Yue-tchi; the land produces many good horses." This passage is almost a commentary on the significance of the royal titles in our inscription.

---

[19] *Jour. As.* IX 9, 24, note.

We have seen above that there is some doubt as regards the personality denominated here as *kaisara*. It is immaterial to the chronological inference which we may draw from the use of these titles. No one will deny that this inscription dates from the Kushana period and its date *Sam* 41 belongs to that series of dates which run from 3 to 98. The beginning of the era which the reckoning has for its basis is uncertain. The theory which was advanced first by Cunningham that the Khushana era is identical with the Malava-Vikrama era of 57 B. C. has found in Dr. Fleet an energetic defender. Professor O. Franke has attempted to support and I too have agreed to it. But the word *kaisara* overthrows this hypothesis. The idea that so early as in the year 16 B.C. a Central Asian or Indian ruler should have assumed the title of Cæsar is naturally incredible. With the possibility of transferring the beginning of the era, and consequently Kanishka, to pre-Christian times falls likewise the possibility of placing the succession of kings from Kanishka to Vasudeva before Kujala-Kadphises[20], whose conquests, according to Professor Chavannes[21] and Professor Franke,[22] took place in the first post-Christian century. In these respects I am now entirely at one with Professor Oldenberg, who has recently treated the whole problem in a penetrating way.[23] The exact determination of the era however depends before all on the question whether we should identify the king of the Ta-Yue-chi, Po-t'iao, who sent in the year 229 A.D. an embassy to China, with Vasudeva, the successor of Huvishka.[24] In that case the era would start at the earliest with 130 and at the latest with 168 A.D. None of the

---

[20] Fleet, *Jour. R. As. Soc.* 1903, p. 334, 1907, p. 1048; Franke. *Beitrage aus Chines ischenquellen sur Kenntnis* der. *Turkvolker*, &c., p. 93 ff.

[21] *T'oung Pao*, S. II. Vol. VIII, p. 191, note 1. [22] *Beitrage*, p. 72.

[23] *Zur Frage nach der Ara des Kanishka., N. G. GW. Phil. Hist. KL.* 1911, pp. 427 ff.

[24] *T'oung Pao*, S. II. Vol. V., p. 489.

grounds which Oldenburg has adduced against this supposition is decisive. On the other hand, the identification of Po-t'iao with Vasudeva is, as observed by Chavannes, merely permissible and not necessary; besides there still remains the possibility that a later and another Vasudeva is meant. Accordingly a *consensus omnium* can hardly be attained at once, and final decision will vary according to the evidential value attached to the Chinese data. Our inscription has, however perceptibly narrowed the bounds of the possible, a fact the value of which, under the prevailing circumstances, is not to be underestimated.

**Postscript.**

After I had already written the above paper, I received the July number of *Jour. R. As. Soc.* containing the first half of the essay by J. Kennedy, on the "Secret of Kanishka." The author supports the theory of Fleet and Franke. So far as I see there is nothing in the essay which invalidates the clear evidence of our inscription. This is not the place to enter into details; only one word I shall say regarding the argument upon which Kennedy seems to place chief reliance. Kennedy argues thus (p. 667) :—"We must date Kanishka either 100 years before 50 A. D. or after 100 A. D. (strictly speaking after 120 A. D.). Now the legends on his coin are in Greek. The use of Greek as a language of every-day life however ceased in the country to the East of the Euphrates partly before and partly soon after the close of the first Christian century. Hence Kanishka cannot be placed in the second century, but must belong to a period prior to the Christian times."

Now before me lie a pair of foreign coins: a nickel coin from Switzerland of 1900 and a penny of 1897. The inscription on the former reads: *Confœderatio Helvetica.* On the penny stands *Victoria. Dei. Gra. Britt. Regina. Fid. Def. Ind. Imp.* I pity the historian of the fourth millennium who will draw from the coins the conclusion that about the year 1900 Latin was the languge of daily life in the mountains of Switzerland and in the British Isles.

---

# APPENDIX VII.

## THE SOURCES OF THE DIVYAVADANA.

### Chinese Translations of Sanskrit-Buddhist Literature.

---

The *Divyavadana* is a collection of pious tales which differ too considerably in style and language from each other to be attributed to a single author. Ed. Huber and Sylvain Levi more or less simultaneously established the sources of these tales collected together in the *Divyavadana*. By an examination of three of the tales, namely, Mara and Upagupta (p. 357), Yashas (p. 382) and the Gift of the Half Mango (p. 430) Huber comes to certain definite conclusions. The negligence with which these sources have been put together was noted so long ago as by Burnouf in his *Introduction to the History of Indian Buddhism*. The story of Mara and Upagupta is translated also by Windisch in his *Mara und Buddha* (pp. 163-176). Already here Windisch noted the characteristics of a drama. "The legend is," he says, "prettily and didactically related with dramatic circumstance. But the dialogue between Upagupta and Mara is not in the simple verse of the Pali legends, but is partly in the more artistic meters such as are employed in the Sanskrit drama. Along with the *shloka* and *arya* we find such meters as Praharshini, Vasantalilaka, Shardulavikridita and even Suvadana. We are reminded of a drama also by the theatrical show, especially the manner in which Mara appears in the costume of the Buddha." Speyer had also noted that the form *sahiya* in place of the usual *sahaya*, which is found in the Asoka legends in the *Divyavadana*, is also to be met with in the *Buddhacarita*. This was a particularly happy discovery of Speyer's (WZKM 16, p. 2). As a matter of fact, Ashvaghosha, the author of the *Buddhacarita*, has composed, as we know, another work called the *Sutralankara*, which is preserved only in a Chinese translation made by Kumarjiva about 495. And the three stories of the *Divyavadana* under examination are precisely found there. The importance of the Chinese translation consists in this: that with its help we can correct the Sanskrit text of the *Divyavadana* as we shall see later on. Now the question is: Did the stories originally belong to *Sutralankara*, or did there exist a third work upon which both Ashvaghosha and the editor of the *Divyavadana* could draw? Ashvaghosha was a learned poet. His *Buddhacarita* is perhaps the first in date as a *kavya*, and both I-tsing and Taranatha agree in pointing to him as a peerless poet. In the story of Mara and Upagupta, the Elder asks Mara to show him the features of the Buddha; Mara agrees to do this: "I will show him to you in the same form which I created in order to *shuram vancayitum*."

Windisch not being acquainted with the Chinese, translates the last phrase as "in order to deceive the hero." But the real sense of the passage is recovered only when we place back the story of Mara and Upagupta in the book from which it was drawn, namely, the *Sutralankara*. There it is preceded by another story where also Mara plays a great part. It is the story of the householder Shura. Shura is a miserly man of wealth, who refuses to give alms to the disciples of the Buddha. The Buddha personally goes to his house, preaches him the Law and makes him see the sacred Truths. Mara is thereby put to shame. As soon as the Buddha has withdrawn, Mara himself puts on the guise of the Buddha and appears before Shura. Next follows a description in verse of the majestic appearance of the false Buddha, who thus addresses Shura: "While I was explaining to you the Law, I made mistakes in certain points." He proceeds then to deliver a sermon which is anything but orthodox. Shura makes him out. "You are the Wicked One. It is in vain that you hide the jackass in the skin of a tiger; although his appearance may deceive the eye he is found out as soon as he begins to bray." It is evident, then that in the *Divyavadana* we should take Shura as a proper name, and not as a common name meaning hero. Further on, in his comparison of the Sanskrit text with the Chinese, Huber notes that the Chinese translator has noticed the play on the word "Asoka," which signifies the name of an emperor and the name of a tree, a pun, which has escaped both Burnouf and the English editors of the *Divyavadana*.

Thus at least three of the tales in the *Divyavadana* have been borrowed from the *Sutralankara* of Ashvaghosha. But the latter is far from being the principal source upon which the anonymous compiler of the *Divyavadana* had drawn. Already the English editors notice that the collection was a part of a *Vinayapitaka*. They saw that the stories related to a school of Buddhism different from Pali. According to a Tibetan authority quoted by Barth (RHR 41, p. 171), of the four schools of Buddhism only one, that of the Sarvastivadi, employed Sanskrit in its liturgy; the Mahasanghikas used corrupt Sanskrit, the Sthaviras or Theravadis employed Paishaci and the Mahasammatiyas used the Apabhramsha. And since the fragments of the *Vinayapitaka* recently found are in Sanskrit, *a priori* they must belong to the *Vinayapitaka* of the Sarvastivadis, and this is in fact the conclusion which Huber establishes. Now the Chinese canon, which has preserved the "basket of discipline" of several schools, furnishes a means of verifying the hypothesis. The result of Huber's researches is that at least eighteen out of the thirty-eight stories of the *Divyavadana* are taken from the Sarvastivadi *vinaya*.

The compiler has treated, in fact, the *Vinayapitaka* of the Sarvastivadis in the same manner in which the author of the *Mahavastu* has dealt with the *Vinayapitaka* of the Mahasanghikas. Only the redactor of the *Divyavadana* had not the grace, like the author of the *Mahavastu*, to acknowledge his debt. On the other hand, in taking his loans the compiler has been faithful, rather too faithful. He wrenches sometimes the stories along with the ligatures preceding and following them in the original Sanskrit *Vinayapitaka.* The divergence between the Sanskrit and the Chinese lies only in two points. In the first place, the translator, who was the celebrated I-tsing and who rendered the original Sanskrit into Chinese, commits minor mistakes. Consequently when he comes to one of the numerous *cliches* or the stereotyped series of phrases, I-tsing sometimes loses his patience and instead of reiterating the passage in Chinese, contents himself with a brief "and so on". Less frequently he uses the term corresponding to the Sanskrit *Purvavadvavat.* With these two exceptions the two tally completely. We can easily see the utility of the existence of a Chinese version, which so exactly corresponds to the Sanskrit, when we think of undertaking a translation of the *Divyavadana* into a European language. Now we shall see below some examples of how I-tsing's Chinese version helps us to restore the sometimes corrupt text of the Sanskrit *Divyavadana.*

**How Chinese helps Sanskrit.**

Huber first analyses the stories of Makandika and of Rudrayana corresponding to stories 36 and 37 in the *Divyavadana.* These two *Avadanas* were originally the section Prayashcittika 82 in the *Vinayapitaka* of the Sarvativadis corresponding to the Paccittya 83 of the Pali *Suttavibhanga.* The regulation in question referred to the prohibition on the Buddhist monks against entering the royal palace on certain occasions, In this section, the Pali makes of

*Chattapani* a proper name whereas from the Chinese it is evident that it is an adjective phrase meaning "carrying an umbrella in the hand," qualifying the monk which follows. As Huber notices it is strange that the great Buddhaghosha, the Pali commentator, has repeated the mistake more than once. In one place the Chinese translator I-tsing cannot tolerate the interminable monotony of certain repetitions and notes: "The Sanskrit text has the entire enumeration. I am afraid of wearing the reader and abridge the portion." In the light of the Chinese, Huber establishes that the *kharam* at page 577 in the *Divyavadana* renders a whole sentence senseless, and that judging by I-tsing's Chinese version the original Sanskrit should be *khaladhana* which restores sense to the corrupt sentence. At page 579 the same Chinese rendering helps us to restore *kamshi* in place of the unintelligible *kashika*. Similarly the first *shloka* in the Makandika tale (p. 515) is restored to sense with the help of the Chinese. In the same story the *upanasthaniyo* should now be read *apadasthaniya*. Further down *Sasambhramena* is a corruption for *Udakabhramena*. In the story of Svagata (*Div*. pp. 167-193) the proper name Asvatirtha is certainly a mistake. The corresponding Pali is Ambattitha which is confirmed by the Chinese which this time, instead of translating as it often does, here transcribes the proper name of An-po. At page 191 of the *Divyavadana*, the Sanskrit text should be altered into *mamudishyadbhir*. The *avadana* at page 483 has an erroneous title, *Cudapaksha*. It should be *Cudapantha*. Verses produced at page 497 are massacred in Sanskrit, but are restorable by a reference to the Chinese. At page 512 *mathurayam* must yield place to the sensible *mandurayam*. With these plenteous examples and a faithful rendering of several stories, Huber avers that I-tsing's translation testifies to the existence in India in the eighth century of the Sanskrit canon of the Sarvastivadis. "The disproportion," he proceeds, "between the dry brevity of the Pali text and the redundant prolixity of the Sanskrit recension may prove repulsive at first to the reader and might make the Sanskrit appear suspicious to him." As a matter of fact, nevertheless, the compilers of the Sanskrit canon invented nothing in the sense that they were as faithful translators as those of the Theravadi canon. The only difference is this: Whilst the Pali school habitually leave out or throw into the commentaries the pious tales which serve to illustrate the precepts of the rules, in the Sanskrit school these *avadanas* have completely invaded the text itself of the Sarvastivadi canon. Although we have not yet received from Ceylon Buddhaghosa's commentary of the *Vinaya*, we have already shown that there is not one of these stories which cannot be found again in the Pali *Atthakathas*. Windisch with his accustomed penetration, saw long ago that Buddhaghosa must be familiar with the literature of the North (*Mara und Buddha* p. 300).

To these important discoveries by Huber we may add a few notes from the accidentally simultaneous research on the same problem by Sylvain Levi (*Toung Pao*, March 1907). The *Vinaya* of the Mulasarvastivadis is also the same as the Tibetans have admitted into their canon. It constitutes the *Dul-va* of the Kanjur. The various parts of the *Dul-va*, according to Csoma, were translated from Sanskrit into Tibetan in the course of the ninth century. I-tsing's Chinese translation was made in the ninth. It is interesting to note that I-tsing expressly states that his work accords with the Mulasarvastivadi principle and should not be confounded with the teachings of any other school. The Mulasarvastivadis are to be distinguished from the simple Sarvastivadis whose *Vinaya* was translated into Chinese as early as 494 by Kumarajiva and Punyatara, under a Chinese title which is equivalent to *Dashadhyayavinaya* as distinct from the *Vinaya* of the Dharmaguptas which was called the *Vinaya* of the Four Sections, and from the *Vinaya* of the Mahishasakas which was entitled the *Vinaya* of the Fivefold Sections. According to I-tsing, the Mulasarvastivadi was a sister school to the Sthavira, the Mahasamghika and the Sammitiya, and the school itself was subdivided into four branches, *viz.*, the Sarvastivadis, the Dharmaguptas, the Mahishaskas and the Kashyapiyas. The Dharmagupta *Vinaya* was translated into Chinese in 495 by Buddhayashas; the Mahasamghika in 416 by the Indian Buddhabhadra and the celebrated Chinese Fahien; the Mahishasaka in 424 by Buddhajiva. The Chinese translation of the *Vinaya* of the Sthaviras was made between 483 and 493 and has been lost. But a portion of even the Pali *Samantapasadika* of Buddhaghosa was done into Chinese in 489 by Sanghabhadra. Among the translators there were some who had migrated from Persia, one of whom rendered into Chinese two tracts on the *Vinaya* between 148 and 170.

# APPENDIX VIII.

## INSCRIBED FRESCOS OF TURFAN.

By Ed. Huber.

---

### I.

The Buddhist art of India in Gandhara as well as in the south has preserved from early days the legend of the Brahaman Sumedha, who is subsequently to be the Shakyamuni and who receives from the Buddha Dipankara the prophecy of his future career. We come across this episode with the same features in the scriptures of the different Buddhist fraternities and that is an index which leads us to suppose that it forms a part of the ancient elements of the canon. This beautiful legend has not been excluded by posterior literature. The hagiographies of the church of Ceylon have extended their activity to the Pranidhicaryas of the Bodhisattva under each Buddha of the preceding *Kalpas.* They inform us of the spiritual progress even of the chief disciples of the Master during the age of any one of his remote forerunners. In the Pali canon the *Mahavagga* and the *Theragatha* have been continued into the *Buddhavamsa* and the *Therapadana.* We shall presently see what corresponds to these two Pali works in the northern canon in Sanskrit. For the paintings at Turfan in Central Asia, recently brought to Europe, refer to legends in this Sanskrit canon. One of these grottos there has a kind of a gallery of *Nakshatras* or the lunar mansions, each of which is surmounted by its name and diagram. They were probably intended to serve as *mangala* or auspicious marks. The *Vinayas* of the north like that of the Mahasanghikas have prescribed stanzas of good omen which the superior of monasteries had to address to visitors and who had specially to invoke upon them the protection of the 28 mansions which, in groups of 7, preside over the 4 cardinal points. These are the same stanzas which in the *Mahavastu* (iii, 305) and in *Lalitavistara* (p. 387) the Buddha addresses to Trapusa and Bhallika at the time of their departure. It is significant that it is the *Mahavastu* and not the *Lalitavistara* which accords with the recension of the Mahasanghikas which has come down to us only through the Chinese translation of Fa-hien. These pages of the *Mahavastu* by the way offer an exceptional opportunity to test the knowledge of Sanskrit possessed by this chronologically first Chinese pilgrim and his Indian collaborator. As regards the subjects which the religious painter has to represent in the different parts of the monastery from the verandah to the kitchen we have minute descriptions of them in the *Vinaya* of the Mulasarvastivadis. These texts would be useful in a translation prepared with a comparison with other Chinese and Tibetan renderings.

It was, in fact, reserved for the Buddhist art of Turkestan to employ its beautiful technical skill in the methodical utilization of the source of inspiration provided by the texts. The mission of Donner and Klementz brought some of these pictures which were discussed by Senart in 1900 in the *Journal Asiatique,* especially with reference to the Sanskrit stanzas written in the Brahmi script found on the frescos in the neighbourhood of Turfan, explanatory of the paintings which depict the Pranidhicaryas.

More frescos have been discovered by Grunwendel and the finest amongst them found in the temple of Bazaklik have been reproduced in the magnificent *Chotscho* by Von le Coq. Each of them, except one, has a Sanskrit *shloka* to identify the individual scene.

Luders has studied these stanzas. He started with the hypothesis that the *shlokas* formed part of a whole poem which has perished. He supposes that the original from which these bits of verse have been drawn could be recovered from two texts which have been already indicated in his exploration of the *Mahavastu* by Barth (*Journal des Savants*, August-October, 1899.) These texts are the Pali *Buddhavamsa* and the *Bahubuddhasutra* in the *Mahavastu* (iii. 224-250). However, the texts and the stanzas in the frescos have nothing common between them except the general narrative. The proper names and the circumstances which have led each time to the *Pranidhana* or solemn vow of the future Buddhas are different in the *Mahavastu*, in the *Boddhavamsa* and in the frescos. Starting with the fact that on the frescos of Turkestan the *Pranidhanas* of the Bodhisattva are distributed over three Asamkheyakalpas, and that, on the other hand, the monasteries to the north of the Tarim desert belonged since the days of the visit of Hiuan-tsang to the Sarvastivadi school, Luders concludes that the third recension of the *shlokas* which we have in the frescos must be related also to this school. And this arrangement of the distribution over three Asamkheyakalpas is noticeable only in the *Divyavadana*. However, considering the corrupt composition of the stanzas, Luders doubts whether they were actually borrowed from a canonical work of the Sarvastivadis, and is inclined to think that here we have to deal with a debased Sanskrit which was current at a latter period in the barbarous monasteries of Turfan. As a matter of fact, at this period there was no barrier between the church of Turkestan and that of nothern India. I have already shown that the geographical horizon of the text from which the compilators of the *Divyavadana* have borrowed extended beyond the Pamirs and the same holds good of the redactors of the *Mahavastu*. However, the stanzas on the frescos of

Turfan are not much farther removed from the Sanskrit of Panini than the language of the *Divyavadana.* If really there is no difference between them it can be explained on the assumption that the *shlokas* have been inscribed by an illiterate painter who did not understand them and actually this seems to have been the case, because as Luders has indicated more than once, the subject represented is quite different from the *shloka* which is expected to explain it.

These stanzas then have issued from the same work on which is based the *Divyavadana* itself, namely, the *Vinaya* of the Mula Sarvastivadis. They are followed by the beautiful tale of Sudhana and the Kinnari which is retained by the compilator of the *Divyavadana* chrestomathy. The stanzas are addressed to Ananda and the subject is divided into three *Kalpas* just as in the fragments of Turfan. At the close of the fragments it is stated in prose, "Here are the names of the Buddhas," analogous to the *samaptam bahubuddhasutram* of the *Mahavastu.* The next chapter contains also in verse a recension of the *Therapadana.* Here also, as in the case of the *Buddhavamsa*, the proper names in the stories of the past and the other circumstances do not agree with the Pali version.

The interest which it has for the iconography of Central Asia would justify a translation of this *Buddhavamsa* of the Mula Sarvastivadis. But it would be better to produce the translation from the Tibetan text. For the Chinese translators of the Tang dynasty have rarely succeeded in comprising into their stanzas the whole expression of the Sanskrit verse even when they were able to understand the latter. Besides the proper names which they translated in their own fashion are difficult of reproduction.

(Huber gives here a striking illustration of the important service which Chinese renders to Buddhistic studies. With the Chinese renderings of the original texts before him he corrects the errors of the scribes and painters who have preserved the scriptural verses in the frescos of Turfan.)

Every section of the Sanskrit *Vinaya*, when closely examined, reveals the same features. There are few fundamental differences with the Pali. As Barth has put it, the Triple Basket of the Mula Sarvastivadis had no cover and that it continued to absorb material from outside. The same conclusion can be arrived at by a comparison of the three diverse translations of the *Vinaya* of this school, namely, the portions borrowed by the *Divyavadana*, the Tibetan translation of the 9th century and the Chinese of the 8th. The divergencies can be illustrated by an example. The long story of Simhala, which is given in its entirety by the Tibetan and the Chinese translators, has been abridged in the *Divyavadana* (p. 524) into a simple reference to the *Rakshisasutra*. Again where the manuscript of the Tibetans gives the whole history of Rashtrapala that of I-tsing quotes only the title. On the other hand, numerous tales in Chinese and Tibetan are thus disposed of: "Place here such and such *sutra* and such and such chapter of this or that *Nikaya*." This problem, although it is more in the domain of the literary history than theology, attracted the attention of the doctors of the old Indian church. Thus Vasubandhu in his *Gathasamgraha* has no hesitation in placing the *Avadanas* and the *Jatakas* in the *Vinayapitaka*. One more important piece of information we gather from a work of Nagarjuna translated by Kumarajiva about 400 A.D. which was a voluminous commentary on the *Mahapranaparamita* and which lays down, "There are two recensions of the *Vinaya*, the *Vinaya of Mathura* which contains the *Avadanas* and the *Jataka* and has eighty chapters; the *Vinaya of Kashmir* which rejects the *Jatakas* of the *Avadana* and preserves only what is essential which is divided into ten chapters." But what were these *Vinayas of Kashmir* and *Mathura*? Here we enter only upon the domain of hypothesis.

## A BHARHUT SCULPTURE.

### II.

The identification, one by one, of the archæological monuments of India every day proves with greater certainty that all Buddhism, even of the ancient epochs, has not been included within the limited scope of the canonical texts. Oldenberg has already indicated that two scenes in the legend of the Buddha, which are depicted at Bharhut, are strangers to the Pali canon, namely, the ascension to the heaven of the Thirty-three gods,—a scene which is represented also at Sachi,—and the great miracle of Shravasti. It is possible to add one more scene of this class.

One of the bas-reliefs at Bharhut represents a group of musicians accompanying with their instruments the movements of a troupe of dancers in the front of two edifices: one on the right, the palace of Indra, from the balcony of which the god looks down upon the festival, surrounded by his women, while from the upper stories the servants show their heads from the windows; the other to the left of the *chaitya* through the open door of which we notice laid on the altar the tuft of hair of the Bodhisattva.

The dome of the *chaitya* bears an inscription in the Ashoka characters which reads thus: *Sudhammadeva sabha Bhagavato chudamaha.* Cunningham taking the word "maha" in the sense of "great," translated it to be "the great headdress (relic) of Buddha in the Assembly-hall of the Devas." (*The Stupa of Bharhut*, p. 126), and it does not seem that this translation in spite of its queerness has been criticised. This inscription on the *stupa* of Bharhut does not bear the solitary instance of the expression *Chudamaha* in Buddhist literature. The same term is employed in the

*Lalitavistara* when, after having described how the Bodhisattva cut off his hair and threw it up in the air where it was received by the Thirty-three gods, it adds: "And to this day, among the Thirty-three gods, the festival of the tuft of the hair is celebrated," which the Tibetan translates word for word including the term "festival" leaving no room for doubt for the meaning of the expression (Foucaux, Part I, p. 195). And, as fortune would have it, it is a case where I-tsing has for once at the same time correctly understood, and entirely translated, the passage in the *Vinaya* of the Mula Sarvastivadis. The Chinese affords final confirmation: "Shakra Devanamindra seizes in the air the hair of the Bodhisattva and carries it to the Thirty-three gods; the Thirty-three gods are gathered together who all do homage to the hair circumambulating it." (*Tripitaka*, Tokyo xvii, 3, 16 b, 14).

On the other hand, the *Mahavastu* uses the same expression when it relates almost in the same phraseology as the *Lalitavistara* that the tuft of the hair, cut off by the Bodhisattva having been received by Indra, the Thirty-three gods celebrate a festival in its honour (II, pp. 165-166). Finally, the festival of the tuft of the hair of the Bodhisattva among the Thirty-three gods is further mentioned expressly in the *Abinhishkramana Sutra*, which is a long life of the Buddha translated into Chinese towards the sixth century by Jnanagupta (*Tripitaka*, Tokyo xiii, 7, 69b 19-20). It is here related that the Bodhisattva cut with his sabre his hair which was taken up by Indra, then the Bodhisattva was shaved by the Shuddhavasas and that Indra again gathered up the hair which fell under the razor. "Shakra received it and carried it to the heaven of the Thirty-three gods where it was worshipped. Since this day he commanded all the gods to celebrate this occasion as a festival for the adoration of the tuft of hair of the Buddha, the observance of which has not been interrupted to this day." Further, the word ". maha", although it appears rare in the vocabulary of Buddhist Sanskrit, is not otherwise absolutely unknown. The *Divyavadana* supplies an instance (p. 579). We may remember the long description of the voyage of Katyayana beyond India and the Oxus. At the place which is called Lambaka, the apostle leaves behind at his departure his copper goblet *kamshika*, as a souvenir to the goddess of Roruka, who raises a *stupa* and celebrates a festival in which the inhabitants of the place take part. The English editors of the *Divyavadana* hesitate between *kashika* and *kushi*; but the true reading is *kamshi* as I have already indicated (BEFEO vi, p. 15). The Chinese and Tibetan translations support this correction of the Sanskrit text. The Chinese translator of the Mula Sarvastivadis has slightly altered the order of the text, and in doing so, has omitted the passage relating to the piece which probably he had not sufficiently understood (*Tripitaka*, Tokyo xvii, 98b 15). But the Tibetan, always faithful to the letter of the text which he translates, exactly follows the Sanskrit (Kanjur red edition *Vinaya*, viii, 120 b). The Tibetan word *Bu-ston* shows the meaning which the translator attached to the Sanskrit *maha*, namely, that of a festival.

This scene has been discovered by Foucher among the bas-reliefs of Boro-Boudour at Java and it affords archæological confirmation to the identification which is proposed here for the bas-relief of Bharhut. At Boro-Boudour also we see the men in gaiety, the musicians and dancers who enter the sanctuary. It is in brief, allowance being made for the differences of technique, an exact counterpart of the bas-relief of Bharhut.

Thus we find at Bharhut a figure representation of the annual festival observed by the Thirty-three gods to commemorate the cutting of the topmost hair of the Bodhisattva. But the legend is unknown in the Pali canon. Besides we know how sober the latter is in details as regards the life of the Bodhisattva. Not only have I not discovered myself this legend in the canonical text, but it has not been mentioned in the two great Buddhistic compilations of Indo-China belonging to a later period—compilations which have been made so conscientiously and carefully and in which are embodied not only the cononical texts but also the commentaries and the super-commentaries of these texts and in which minor variants are invariably noted. Neither the Burmese Jinathapakasani nor the Siamese Pathamasambodhi make mention of it. In fact, in the Pali canon itself the later texts like *Nidanakatha* are not aware of it. According to it the hair of the Buddha, when it was cut off and tossed up into the air, was immediately seized by Indra who conveyed it to heaven where a *stupa* for it was erected; but it has no knowledge of the festival annually celebrated in commemoration of this event in the abode of the Thirty-three gods.

It is, therefore, a subject exclusively appertaining to the tradition of the north which is represented at Bharhut. "But the tradition of the north" is a vague term under which are hidden a number of diverse things. We shall get at something more precise when we succeed in determining the schools to which these legends appropriately belong. Unfortunately this is not easy to achieve. The *Lalitavistara* takes us to the Sarvastivadis, the other texts have been extracted from the *Vinaya* of the Mula Sarvastivadis; the *Mahavastu* is attached to the school of the Mahasanghikas. Finally, the *Abhinishkramana Sutra* has issued from the Dharmagupta school. The festival of the tuft of the Buddha's hair is mentioned in no other *Vinaya* of the diverse schools translated into Chinese. So all the great sects of Northern India are cognisant of this legend. Since, on the other hand, the *Abhinishkramana Sutra* which almost always indicates in detail the divergencies of the principal schools makes no mention of it, it appears that its author held the festival to be common to all the schools known to him. But on the other hand we have to note that the Gandhara school seems not to have known much, or at least not to have represented the scene of the shearing of the hair (Foucher *l'Art greco-bouddhique*, p. 365).

We need not draw a general conclusion from such uncertain circumstances. However, it is the accumulation of details of this class which alone will perhaps permit us one day to substantiate all the *a priori* discussions, so complicated, regarding the subject of the relative age of the traditions of the different schools by more precise knowledge. For the present, all that can be said is that our opinion confirms what other indices lead us to suspect in the fragmentary state of our knowledge of Indian Buddhism. The recent date of a document which acquaints us with a legend does not by any means lead to the conclusion of the recentness of the formation of the legend itself.

## KING KANISHKA AND THE MULA SARVASTIVADIS.

### III.

It is well known that the canon of the Pali *Theravadis* was crystallised at a sufficiently early period; their *Vinaya*, after it was drawn up in Pali, could hardly receive any new elements except in the shape of commentaries; but that of the Mula Sarvastivadis remained long after it had been drawn up in Sanskrit open to all the extraneous influences and did not cease being amplified till it grew into the enormous compilation which lost in Sanskrit has been preserved to us only in Chinese and Tibetan translations. Now, up to what date did the *Vinaya* of the Mula Sarvastivadis continue to enrich itself with fresh texts? The Chinese translation dates from the seventh century and the Tibetan from the ninth. Both are too late in date to give us any information on the point. Their constant exact harmony demonstrates that there was a limit to their expansiveness and that from a certain period a definite text of the *Vinaya* was substituted which thenceforth remained identical till the date of its disappearance. This period was prior to the seventh century, but prior by how much? The problem remains yet unsolved.

In the section treating of medicaments (*Tripitaka*, Tokyo xvii, 4) there is placed in the mouth of the Buddha a prediction concerning king Kanishka. Unfortunately I have not got with me the Tibetan translation. The Buddha goes to the abode of the Yakshas, to the city of Rohitaka, which is described at such length in the *Divyavadana* (pp. 107-108). From there, accompanied by Vajrapani, he proceeds to subjugate Apalala the *Naga* and to show his prowess otherwise. " Bhagavat having again arrived at the village of Dry-tree, he sees in this village a young boy playing at the making of an earthen *stupa*." Bhagavat sees him and speaks to Vajrapani, "Do you see this young boy who is at play making a *stupa?*" Vajrapani replies, "I see him". The Buddha says "After my Nirvana, this child who is playing at the building of a *stupa* of earth, will be the king Kanishka and he will found a great *stupa* which will be designated the *stupa* of Kanishka; and he will spread the religion of the Buddha."

As we may observe, the basis of the legend has nothing of originality. It is hardly anything beyond a clumsy repetition of the prophecy touching the king Ashoka; the handful of dust which the future Ashoka offers to the Buddha is here replaced by the earthen *stupa* on account of the *stupa* which in his future life the child who is to be Kanishka is to build. The only interest which it possesses beyond the mention of king Kanishka is the connection with a well-known monument which the Buddhist pilgrims visited and which was actually built by Kanishka, namely, the temple now discovered in the ruins of Shajikidheri.

This little fact, added to a certain number of others, tend to show that the *Vinaya* of the Mula Sarvastivadis underwent a kind of re-handling about the beginning of the Christian era. The word "dinara" which implies Græco-Roman influence, has been already pointed out. I have also shown in the incorporation in the *Vinaya* of some of the stories of Ashvaghosha. When discussing the actual date of the king Kanishka we may say that the mention of his name carries us to the same period.

# APPENDIX IX.

## THE MEDICAL SCIENCE OF BUDDHISTS.

---

The celebrated Bower manuscripts were found in a Buddhist *stupa* in Kashgaria. They were probably written by Hindu emigrants. They are in the Indian Gupta characters. On paleographical grounds they should date from 450 A. D. The material on which they are written is birch-bark which is cut into long strips like the palm leaves of southern and western India. The manuscripts embody seven Sanskrit texts, three of which are purely of medical contents. The first medicinal work contains an eulogy on garlic and various recipes especially for eye diseases. The second, which is a much more voluminous work and is entitled the *Navanitaka* or the quintessence, treats in fourteen chapters of powder butter decoctions, oil, mixed recipes, clyster, elixirs, aphrodisiacs, ointments for the eye, hair dyes, of *terminalia chebula*, bitumen, plumbago, and care of children. The third work contains fourteen prescriptions in seventy-two verses. The sixth text, which is a charm against the bite of a cobra, has also a medicinal character. The language of these books is more archaic than that of *Charaka* and *Sushruta*. We owe the decipherment and translation to Hoernle. The same scholar has been busy with another work relating mostly to Indian prescriptions or medical formulæ and which is even more ancient than the Bower manuscripts. In the text represented by the Macartney manuscript, written in 350, and which is a paper manuscript unfortunately in a bad state of preservation, we come across several familiar herbs like *arka*, *priyangu* and also gold, silver, iron, copper and tin. The great importance of the Bower manuscripts for the history of Indian medicine lies in this: that they positively establish the existence of the medical science of the Indians as early as in the fourth and fifth centuries and puts an end to the scepticism regarding the trustworthiness of the Arabic sources touching upon them. The principles of the three fundamental humours, that of digestion, that of the influence of the seasons, the forms of medicinal remedies, the names of the diseases all appear here just as in the later works, while many of the longer prescriptions in the Bower manuscripts appear in their entirety in the better known medical *Samhitas*. It is noteworthy that quicksilver, opium and small-pox are not yet mentioned.

These Bower manuscripts come to us from the Buddhist source as is most clearly shown by the sixth and the seventh texts which several times make mention of Bhagava, Tathagatha, Buddha and so on. Vagabata has traces of Buddhistic propensities which explain its transplantation to Tibet as well as the complete absorption of the Indian science of medicine by that country. The Tibetan system of the science of healing can be traced back only to Buddhist medicine. The exhaustive accounts of the Buddhist pilgrim I-tsing (671-695) on the then condition of Indian therapeutics including medicinal herbs, the three fundamental principles, diagnosis, fasts, etc., accord not only with the contents of our standard works like *Charaka* and *Sushruta* as well as the Bower manuscripts ; but the Chinese traveller's account includes extracts from a sermon which is a *sutra* dealing with medicine ascribed to the Buddha himself. The Buddhist king Buddhasa of Ceylon in the 4th century cured the sick, appointed physicians with fixed stipends, established hospitals and wrote the medical manual called *Saratthasangaha*. Charaka is reputed to be the body-physician of Kanishka, but whether it was the celebrated physician or a namesake of his is hard to determine. Nagarjuna too lived about the same time. Besides being credited with several medical treatises he is the reputed compiler of an edition of *Sushruta* to whom also is ascribed a medical formula on a pillar in Pataliputra. The hospitals with physicians for men and animals founded by King Asoka in the third century are well known. A good deal of medical knowledge is revealed by the Pali *Mahavagga*. It refers to eye ointments, nose cures, oils, butter decoctions, *lotus* stalks, myrabolams, salts, assafœtida, cupping, diaphoretics and even to laparatomy cf the later works, but to no metal preparations as yet.

# APPENDIX X.

## THE ABHIDHARMA KOSHA VYAKHYA.

It is a striking testimony to the genius of Engene Burnouf who examined with profundity the three great religions of the world simultaneously, Brahmanism, Buddhism and Zoroastrianism, that since 1844 when he wrote his Introduction to the History of Indian Buddhism, still a mine of unantiquated information, very little fresh light has been thrown on the *magnum opus* of Vasubandhu, the author of Abhidharma kosha and on Yashomitra, his commentator. Minayeff, Sylvain Levi, Max Walleser and Vallee Poussin have excavated extracts from Yashomitra's *Vyakhya* or commentary which still exists in the Sanskrit original, the *kosha* itself having survived to us only in Chinese and Tibetan translations. Manuscripts of the Vyakhya are to be found at least in Cambridge and Paris and it would be worthy of any patron of Indian learning to secure the services of an erudite scholar like Sylvain Levi to prepare a critical edition with an illuminating introduction similar to his prefixed to the Alankarasutra of Asanga.

Burnouf calls the Abhidharma kosha an inexhaustible mine of valuable information on the speculative side of Buddhism. As regards Yashomitra's expository art, an example may be interesting: "This is the view of those who follow the Abhidharma, but it is not that of ourselves, the Sautrantikas. The tradition informs us, in fact, of the existence of other works on the Abhidharma like, for instance, the Jnana prasthana of Katyayaniputra; Prakaranapada of the Elder Vasumitra; Vijnana kaya of the Elder Devasharma; the Dharmaskandha of Shariputra; Prajnapti Shastra of Maudgalyayana; Dhatukaya of Purna, Sangitiparyaya of

Maha Kushthila. Now what is the meaning of the word Sautrantikas? This is the appellation of those who take for their authority the sutras and not the books. But if they do not take for their authority the books how do they admit the triple division of the text into sutra, vinaya and Abhidharma pitakas? In fact, the Abhidharma is spoken of in the sutras in connection with the question of a monk familiar with the Tripitakas. And this is not surprising since there are several sutras like the arthavinishcaya and others under the heading of Abhidharma in which Abhidharma is defined. To reply to this objection our author (Vasubandu) says: Abhidharma was expounded by Bhagavad along with other subjects."

The text leaves no doubt as to the meaning of the term Sautrantikas. It is a designation of those who follow the doctrine according to which the authority of the sutra is paramount.

The designation of Vaibhashika is not less familiar to our author. The commentary also cites the Yogacaras. Yashomitra is also acquainted with the Madhyamikas, one of the four great sects of which we have detailed information of a historical nature, the three others being Sautrantikas, Vaibhashikas and Yogacaras.

The Abhidharma kosha enjoys considerable authority among all the religious sects of the Buddhists since it is considered to be the corpus of a large number of elucidated texts and its author Vasubandhu was called a sage like unto the second Buddha. Yashomitra's commentary or Vyakhaya is known as the Sphutartha. In a cursory analysis of the work our attention is directed to three principal points. First, the system of the commentator; secondly, the indications which he gives of works not connected with the subject of his commentary; and thirdly, his treatment of the subject itself.

As regards the system of Yashomitra, he belongs to the superior school of Indian exegetics. He possesses all the resources of the Sanskrit language of which he makes an excellent use for the elucidation of Vasubandhu's text. His. glosses are grammatically correct, and philosophically acute. In his diction he follows the grammatical school of Panini. In his philosophy he pursues the canonical sutra texts. He expressly denominates himself "Sautrantika." We do not naturally possess all the authorities on which he relies. Yashomitra's labours represent that service to Buddhism which is rendered by the philosophical treatises of the Brahmanas to the Vedas which they cite at every step. Yashomitra assumes the triple division of the Buddhist scriptures,—the three Baskets or Tripitakas. He refers pretty frequently to lost works. To the more eminent of his authorities he prefixes the epithet Arya (noble) or Sthavira (Elder). They were the apostles or the early fathers of the Buddhist Church according to the sanctity of their dicta. The quotations of Yashomitra are sometimes exhaustive at others brief. They witness to his immense reading and orthodoxy. A fascinating study is afforded by the comparison of texts of the authorities quoted by Yashomitra with the Pali scriptures. Vallee Poussin has unearthed a number of passages of verbal identity. That the strict definition of the primitive body of Buddhist scriptures was not rigidly adhered to but that the expounders of the Vinaya Sutra and Abhidharma proceeded more or less in a general way is established by the legend of Sumagadha which in the Tibetan is incorporated with the sutra literature, whereas according to Yashomitra it related to the Vinaya. The concord, however, between the Sanskrit and the Tibetan is perfect.

Among the noteworthy Elders alluded to is Ashvajit, so generally to be met with in the Sanskrit texts from Nepal. We also come across Dharmatrata and Buddhadeva. Further, we encounter more frequently Gunamati and his disciple Vasumitra who both preceded out Yashomitra as expositors of Vasubandhu's Abhidharma khosha. Next we notice Samghbhadra, Bhadanta Shrilabaha, Arya Dharmagupta, Acharya Manoratha and Bhadanta Ghoshaka. Bhandanta signifies that the name following it belongs to a Buddhist particularly respectable for his learning. And Yashomitra thus comments on the specific Buddhist term:

"Bhandanta, says the text; this is a certain Elder of the school of sutras or it was his own name. But Bhagavad-vishesha alleges that this title is a designation of the Elder Dharmatrata. To this we on our part reply: The Elder Dharmatrata maintains the existence of things past and future, he belongs neither to the school of the sutras nor to the school of Darshtantikas; (after further elaborate argument Yashomitra concludes) all this goes to show that Bhandanta of our text means to suggest a person of the sutra school other than Dharmatrata. It suggests a certain Elder or a monk whose name has not been specified."

There are two or three titles of books which seem to be of non-Buddhistic origin, *e. g.*, Nirgrantha sastra, which was probably a Jaina work. There is also an allusion to the Shatarudriya of Vyasa, no doubt a Brahmanical treatise.

Among the heretical sects mentioned by Yashomitra are Pandaras, Pashupatas, and Kapalikas. Moreover he refutes the Vaisheshikas. He admits that the Buddhists were by no means agreed on a number of disputed philosophical questions. At the same time he mentions its existence where unanimity among the Buddhists prevailed. He states, for example, that the *hemanta* or winter (November-December) is the first of the seasons for all Buddhists. Those schools which he cites the most often either for the purpose of refutation or for entering his own doctrinal protest are the Buddhists of Kashmir and Ceylon and the Vatsiputriyas. The Kashmiras are of frequent occurrence. They are stigmatised as Outsiders. They are described as recent arrivals from Kashmir. But the expression here used is ambiguous, for it may as well mean the Westerners. Any way it is clear that our book was produced in India and probably in a province to the east of Kashmir. In one passage the Ceylon Buddhists are thus referred to: "The text (of Vasubandhu) says in *all the other books*, which means to say, that in the books of the Buddhists of Ceylon and others." From this it is evident that the Ceylon *nikayas* were known to the Buddhists of the north and that they were of sufficient importance in the eye of the latter to be cited by them. It appears that there were certain Vatsiputriyas who were also Madhyamikas. From the fact that Yashomitra mentions and combats the views of Nagarjuna or Nagasena it is clear that he lived posterior to the times of the founder of the new school. The third Buddhist Council is referred to as the *Tritiyam Dharmasamgitam*.

The method of Yashomitra does not lend itself to a reconstruction of the text of Vasubandhu, his own exposition being so co-mingled with the words of the author whom he interprets. Vasubandhu's own work was itself in the nature of a commentary for Yashomitra states: "Many of the sutras have been omitted because the exegesis of the texts has been lost and, accordingly, the Master has written no commentary." The Master is obviously Vasubandhu.

At the lowest estimate Yashomitra's *Vyakhya* is a compilation of texts and philosophical interpretations. The contents of the volume are: The chief characteristics of beings, of conditions or of laws,—for the word "Dharma" signifies all these things; the senses, the elements, sensation and perception; the sequence of acts and effect; the affections, hatred, error and other moral modifications; human birth, destiny, the fruit of works, and the passage of man along diverse paths of existence; the various degrees of virtue and intelligence to which man can attain in this world; the action of the organs of sense in respect of perception and the conditions which accelerate or retard the said action; man and woman considered from the physical standpoint; passions and the necessity of suppressing them; on pleasure and pain and the necessity of breaking away from them for the attainment of Nirvana which is the perfection of absolute repose; the conditions of human existence and the functions of the organs; *pravritti*, or action and *nirvirtti* or quiescence; the various degrees of humanity with regard to education and the relative perfection of human senses, supernatural faculties; the passage of superior intelligence through the various degrees of existence; the devas and the numerous classes into which they are divided; the infernos and the worlds. These subjects, none of which is examined in a consecutive method nor in a dogmatical manner, are jumbled up and the same matter is discussed in several connections in the work. The doctrine of the book is manifestly that of the most ancient school of Buddhism which was atheistic. On the question of the existence of God it has a very striking passage which leaves no doubt as to the tendency of the work or at least the belief of the commentator Yashomitra. It illustrates how the celebrated critic discusses questions when he permits himself the liberty to digress :—

"The creatures are created neither by Ishvara, nor by Purusha (spirit) nor by Pradhana (matter). If God was the sole cause, whether that God was Mahadeva, Vasudeva or another, whether spirit or matter, owing to the simple fact of the existence of such a primordial cause the world would have been created in its totality at once and at the same time. For it cannot be admitted that there should be a cause without an effect; but we see the creatures coming into existence not simultaneously but successively, some from wombs, some from buds. Hence we have got to conclude that there is a series of causes and that God is not the sole cause. But it is objected that this diversity of causes is due to the volition of the Deity, who says, "Let now such and such a creature be born, let another creature be born in such and such a way." It is in this way that is to be explained the phenomenon of the appearance of creatures and that it is proved that God is the cause of them all. To this we reply that to admit several acts of volition in God is to admit several causes and that to make this admission is to destroy the first hypothesis according to which there is one primordial cause. Moreover this plurality of causes could not have been produced except at one and the same time since God, the source of the distinct acts of volition which have produced this variety of causes, is Himself alone and indivisible. The sons of Shakya hold that the evolution of the world has no beginning."

This passage is remarkable in many ways. It shows how far removed was the theory which it expresses from the pantheistic naturalism of the Brahmanic creeds. The fact that Yashomitra cites the Shaivites, the Vaishnavites, and other theistic schools, but does not combat the later analogous Buddhistic creed of the Adibuddha which was tantamount to a sort of monotheism, demonstrates the non-existence of the said sect in Buddhism in his time. "These considerations lead me to think," concludes Burnouf, that the work of Vasubandhu (Vasumitra is obviously an oversight on Burnouf's part) with the commentary of Yashomitra which accompanies it, are both anterior in time to the period when was established in Buddhism the creed of a Supreme God." (For attack on theists see Shantideva's Bodhi, c. v. p. 135.)

Bendall (Catalogue of Buddhist Manuscripts, p. 25) describing the Cambridge Manuscript of Abhidharma kosha Vyakhya by Yashomitra, says that it is an accurate copy. The accuracy and the great value of the work may be judged from the fact that, firstly, it was the only copy of the work existing in Nepal, and secondly, that the owner before parting with it had a copy made for himself. The Abhidharma kosha was translated into Chinese in 553 and again in 654.

The contents of the *Vyakhya* are somewhat differently set forth by Rajendralal Mitra (Nepal. Bud. p. 4.)

# APPENDIX XI.

## REFERENCE TO BUDDHISM IN BRAHMANICAL AND JAIN WRITINGS.

References to the Buddha and his Order are very rare in Sanskrit literature, so scarce are they that though Holtzmann (Geschichte und Kritik des Mahabharata, p. 103) has collected a few passages in which Buddhism is referred to, he is inclined to believe that the Brahmans deliberately effaced all memory of the Buddha, appropriating to themselves all that was convenient in his particular teaching. In all Ramayana the Buddha is mentioned in one place only which, however, is regarded as an interpolation by Schlegel and Weber. There is scarcely anything specially Buddhistic in the 20th chapter of Shankaravijaya which is devoted to Buddhamatanirakarana. The Sarvadarshana Sangraha gives but a belated version of Gautama's doctrine.

The *Harshacarita* (p. 265-6) has naturally more references to Buddhism because king Harsha was partial to the faith. But the particular passage which I have in mind I am inclined to look upon (with all diffidence) more as a derisive allusion than appreciation of the doctrine. The three refuges are mentioned as having been resorted to by monkeys; the law as being expounded by *Mayanas*, and it is the owls which repeat the *Bodhisatvajataka* while the explaining of the *Kosha* is left to mere parrots. Here and there, however, we must not omit to mention some glimpses of unaffected admiration. "The doctrine of Shakya Muni is the family home of pity," (p. 244). "Calm in mind like Buddha himself," (p. 56). The Buddha doctrine which "drives away worldly passions" (text p. 288). There is also a reference to the *Sarvastivadi* school in Bana's Kadambari (text p. 106, Translation p. 112). It may be incidentally noted that it is difficult to see why Professor K. B. Pathak contends that "Bana is misunderstood and mistranslated by Professor Macdonnell", when he speaks of "pious parrots expounding the Buddhist dictionary." The text has "*paramopasakaihishukaihiapi shakya shaskana kushalaih kosham samupiadishadbhihi* (Harshacarita p. 317). The *Kosha* is undoubtedly the *Abhidharma kosha* of Vasubandhu as the learned professor has himself noticed. The Buddha is referred to in the Bhagavata purana (1, 3, 24) and Vishnu purana (III, 17, 18) derogatorily. However, there is one book in Sanskrit which treats of the Buddha and his doctrine without hostility or derision. It is the *Buddhavatara* of Kshemendra. The Sotapatti, the Sakkadagami, the Anagami and the Arahat of the Pali are enumerated and the Saddharma described without animus and the Buddha is spoken of in his favourite role of spiritual healer "bhavabhishag Bhagavan babhashe." (63). I came across more than one MS. of interest in this respect in the numerous catalogues of Sanskrit MSS. in the various Indian libraries. Among the books acquired for Government by the late Dr. Peterson we notice three Buddhist tracts including the *Nyayabindu tika* (407.) As regards Dharmottar's commentary on the Nyayabindu there is the pathetic note by the Professor. Examining the Jain bhandar he says with reference to the book: "It is the only Buddhist work in the old library (of Shantinath at Cambay). I have already tried to convey to the reader something of that sense of ruin and desolation which must flow into the mind of him who, in this empty temple, turns over these records of human faith and love and sorrow. Here in the midst of it all is one solitary survival of a still older shade of a yet greater religion," a remark as true to-day as it was when Peterson noted that the recovery of this book was a new justification of the importance which has been attached to these records, as "it is a fresh pledge of the inestimable wealth which still lies buried below the surface in India." (p. 33). In the same report there is a notice of a Jaina work called the *Darsana sara* containing a virulent attack on the Buddhists charging them not only with consumption of animal food—not a groundless accusation—but also of spirituous liquor which is a calumny "idi loe chhorita paktiyam sangha savajam." A *Buddhashatra* is mentioned by Oppert in his Sanskrit MSS. in Southern India (I, 2914) and a *Baudhadhikara* of which unfortunately there are no details. The XIth volume of notices of Sanskrit MSS, Calcutta, has a Buddhist work in the index. The reference to Volume III, p. 332, shows it to be a book which seems to have four commentaries and super-commentaries on it. In the same catalogue there is an *Arya Vasundhara* which is in the form of a complete Mahayana Sutra beginning with *evam maya shrutam* and ending with the inevitable *Bhagavato bhashitam abhyanandan* (Notices of Sanskrit MSS. 2nd series Volume III, p. 19). See further the note by Vallee Poussin (JRAS 1901, 307) on the Buddhist sutras quoted by Brahmana authors.

The following are further stray references :—

"Here now come forward the Madhyamikas who teach that there is nothing but a universal Void. This theory of universal "Nothing" is the real purport of Sugata's doctrine; the theories of the momentariness of existence, etc. which employ the acknowledgment of the reality of things, were set forth by him merely as suiting the limited intellectual capacities of his pupils." Ramanuja on Vedanta Sutras, (SBE 48,514).

Kshemendra in Vallabhadeva, Peterson's edition, (pp. 26-27.)

The Buddhist mendicant Divakaramitra in Harshacarita, Mudrarakshasha, (Telang's edition 175.)

Ashvaghosha is cited by Vallabhadeva in his Subhashitavali (p. 8) where he is called Bhadanta.

According to Peterson the Chandragopi in Vallabhadeva may be Chandragomi (p. 36.)

Vallabhadeva has many verses attributed to Dharmakirti who is called Bhadanta (p. 47). There is another Bhadanta called Dhiranaga (p. 49.); and another still Bhadanta Prajashanti (p. 60). There is a poet called Bodhisattva (p.543), Rahulaka (p. 104), and Bhadanta Sura who may be our Aryashura of the Jatakamala (p. 131.)

The Sharnga-dhara-paddhati quotes Kshemendra (p. 95.) Also Dharmakirti's one shloka of a Buddhistic flavour (p. 150), Bhadanta Jnana-varma (p. 155), Vararuci (p. 473) and (p. 515), Bhadanta-varma (p. 522) and Rahulaka (p. 587).

The following Buhdhist works occur in the *Catalogus Catalogorum* of Aufrecht: *Bauddha dushana, Bauddha Dhikkara, Bauddha mata, Baudda mata dushana.*

" References to Buddhist authors in Jaina Literature," by G. K. N. Ind. Ant. 1913, (p. 241.)

According to Telang Buddhists are not found in Sanskrit literature because they are confounded with Jainas, (Telang's Mudrarakshasa, XVI, XVII).

A palm leaf MS. of Vararuci's work is still preserved in the Jain Matha at Kolhapur in which the grammarian laments the rejection of Buddhism (See Pathak's papers read before B. B. R. A. S., Bhamaha's attacks on Jinendrabuddhi, &c.)

Vinashvara-nandi is another writer whose work is also preserved in the same Matha and who salutes the Buddha in the commencement of his work. For reconstructions of Sanskrit Buddhist texts from Chinese transcriptions see " One more Buddhist hymn" by G. K. Nariman, Ind. Ant., 1913, (pp. 240-1.)

" A new list of Buddhistic Sanskrit words," by Levi and Nariman, Ind. Ant. 1913, (p. 179).

For Buddhism in Brahmanic literature see the Bhamati of Vacaspati Misra. It is curious that the views regarding Buddhism as cited and combated by these Brahmanical writers accord with Japanese Buddhism of to-day. Max Walleser is inclined to identify the *Sangiti paryaya* with the *Dhammasangani* according to the tradition of the Japanese sect of Kou-Cha-Shu which is based on the Abhidharma Kosha of Vasubandhu. (Die Philosoph Grundlage des Buddhismus p. 5).

For Shankara's refutation of Buddhism see his commentary on the Badarayana sutras, II, 2, 18-32, corresponding to pp. 546-581 in the Calcutta edition. On the doctrine of non-ego (see page 74 ) For doubts regarding the consistency of the Buddha's doctrine (see page 77). For a literal concord of the Sanskrit Abhidharma kosha with Pali sources (p. 77) see especially the passages noted by Vallee Poussin, Dogmatique Bouddhique J A., Sept.—Oct. 1902. In Hiuen-tsang's time the Mahayana was considered identical with Shunyavada (p. 102). Specific Mahayanistic influences were already at work in the later Pali literature (p. 115.) The Jnana prasthana of Katyayani is cited by the Pali school as Mahapakarana, *e. g.*, by Buddhaghosa in his *attha salini* (p. 146).

Buddhist material is at time to be met with in the Sanskrit Koshas or lexicons.

The following has been gleaned from the *Abhidhana Sangraha* of the Nirnaya Sargra Press. The Amara Kosha naturally has a good deal Buddhistic because the author was most probably not a Jaina, but a Buddhist. He refers to mithya drishti, ashrava sanshraya, chaitya, pravachana, paryaya, Maskari. *Trikanda shesha* is also rich in Buddhist terminology. It mentions karanda vyuha prajna paramita, magadhi, agama, nikaya, sutra. The *Abdhidhana Cintamani* refers to the thirty-four jatakas, ten paramitas, ten bhumis (stages); bhadanta, bhattaraka, Maskari, shunyavadi, caitya, vihara. The *Anekartha Sangraha* has avadana (1528); Katyayana and Vararuci (1639); Avalokita as a synonym of the Buddha (1738).

# APPENDIX XII.

## NOTES ON THE DIVYAVADANA.

(By G. K. N.)

The *Divyavadana* when closely studied will be found to abound in expressions, ideas and principles identical with those in the Pali *Pitakas*. This store-house of information has been thrown open to us by various scholars in connection with the several problems of Buddhism. And I will give here a few points that have struck me in my own study of the work. As is well-known and has been proved by means of the Chinese version, the *Divyavadana* is the *Vinaya* of Sarvastivadi school. The language of the *Divyavadana* though Sanskrit offends now and then against classical rules of Panini, but "these inaccuracies, like those which occur in the *Mahabharata*," may be interesting for the history of the language. *Udanam udanayati* is often found in Pali (p. 2). The component parts of the work are of unequal age. That portions of the *Divyavadana* are not very old is evident from the frequent mention in it of the art of writing, *e.g.*, *aksharani abhilikhitani* (p. 6). In this work we often find a record of the attacks on Buddhism and the great disfavour with which the Buddhistic monks were held among the Brahmans, and more especially the Jainas. The general abusive epithets are *mundakah shramanakah* (p. 13), and *amangalah* (p. 39). Whether the body of the Buddhistic scripture was originally divided into *Nikayas* as in the Pali canon is doubtful. The older term seems to be *agama* but the latter does not appear after the fifth century as alleged by Rhys Davids. We find it in the *Abhidharma-kosha-vyakhya* of Yashomitra, side by side with the term *Nikaya*. The *Divyavadana* more than once speaks of the *agama catusthaya* (p. 17). Of frequent occurrence is the term as at page 16. Several important texts corresponding to the Pali are mentioned; *shailagatha*, *munigatha* and the *arthavargiyani* (p. 20). According to the *Abhidharma-kosha-vyakkya*, '*arthavargiyani sutrani kshudrake pathyante*' whereas the corresponding Pali *Mahavagga* (V. 13, 9) refers to the Book of Eighths (*see* JRAS 1906, p. 946; but see now the illuminating recitation primitive by Sylvain Levi J A. 1915, p. 418). The celebrated verse which puzzled some scholars turns up in the *Divyavadana*, '*samyoga viprayoganam marananlashca jivitam.*' (p. 27). Another set of books is quoted at page 35, viz., *sthaviragatha*, to which corresponds no doubt the Pali *Theragatha* and the *Shailagatha*, *munigatha* and the *arthavargiyani*. The corresponding Pali of *Ehi bhikkhu cara brahmacaryam* is obvious (p. 36). That not only *nivirana* as in Pali but also the *parinirvana* was to be atttained in this life is seen from the exhortation to Purna; *Gaccha twam Purna makto mocaya tirnastaraya ashvasta ashvasaya parinirvapaya* (p. 39). Was the service of the Buddha with flowers and incense so early as is described at page 43? A glimpse of social life, mansions corresponding to the three seasons and the conventional mode of bringing up of a wealthy house holder's child can be had at page 58. As regards *Kashyapa* it is said: *Shakya muneh parinivrittasya anena shasana sangitihi krita* (p. 61) which reference to the first Council may give us some clue as to the date of the work. The usual formula in invitation to the Buddha to dinner and his acceptance of it by silence corresponds exactly to the Pali and is of frequent occurrence in this book (*e. g.* pp. 64-65), The Pali rules, however, strictly prohibit the asking for alms, but in our book the no uncommon phrase is *yadi te bhagini parityaktam akiryatam asmin patre* (pp. 67, 82, 88). The formula, *adyagrena yavajjivanam pranopetam sharanam gatam*, strictly speaking, prohibits the return of the

Bhikshu to the world, which is, however, permitted both in practice and theory in the Pali canon. That the *Divyavadana* is a *vinaya* is seen again from *etat prakaranam bhikshavo bhagavata arocayabti* (p. 84). *Bhagavan aha: tasmat anujanami*, &c. (p. 89). This has an exact counterpart in Pali almost in every *sutta*. The Buddha was given various offerings during his lifetime including lamps of which we do not meet any mention in the Pali (p. 90), *tailasya stokam yacayitva pradipam prajvalya bhagavatah cankrame dattah* (p. 90). Cankrama, of course, is the path in the monastery up and down which the monks walk for exercise. *Civarapinda-patashayana asana glana pratvaya bhaishajya parishkara* are the same as in Pali (p. 91). In Buddhistic text as a rule the Kshatriya takes precedence of the Brahmana, but in one place in our book we find: *Bhagavan bhikshugana parivrito bhikshusangho puraskritah sambahulaisca shravasti nivasibhirbanig Brahmana grihapati bhihiscasardham* (p. 93). *Bhagavata tesham ashayanushyam prakritinca jnatva tadrishi dharmadeshana krita yam shrutva*, &c. is a literal translation of the original stock on which Pali also has faithfully drawn. We have some passages about the arts and crafts of old India and the general culture of a wealthy youth is described at page 100. The great influence of the tenets of the Buddha and the corresponding fear among the Brahmans of the spread of his doctrine of celibacy is perpetuated at page 126. Here is the clear echo of the opposition effered to the Buddha whose gospel was not promulgated so smoothly and without restraint as may be inferred from the majority of the Pali books, in which sermon after sermon ends in the conversion of thousands of human and non-human beings: *Kimlyushmakam shramano Gautamah karoti, sopi pravrajito yuyam api pravrajitah bhikshacarah* (p. 126). We also see further the door being closed in the Buddha's face. Once more the *Vinaya* rule: *Bhagavato ciram dharmam deshayato*, *bhojanakalo atikrantah, Mendhako grihapatih kathayati Bhagavan kim akale kalpate. Bhagwan aha, ghrita, guda sharkara, panakani ceti* (p. 130). Thus we find here that there were certain *akala khadaniyas*, and *akola panakas*. The peculiarity of Pratyeka Buddhas is mentioned (p. 133). The Buddha's smile and its significance (p. 138). There is the complete list of the six leaders of philosophy who were the contemporaries of the Buddha whom we so often meet with in Pali, (for instance, in the *Brahmajala sutta*), *Purana kashyapa Maskari goshaliputra, Sanjayi vairattiputra, Ajita keshakambali, Kakudha katyayana* and *Nirgrantha, Jnatiputra* (p. 143).

There is an express repudiation of any desire to teach the occult spiritualism or miracles. *Aham evam shravakanam dharmam deshayami*, &c. (p. 150). On the same page we find the *dasha avashya karaniyani*. A clear polemical tone of the times is found in the *gatha* placed in the mouth of the Buddha: *Tavat avabhasate krimir yayan nodayate divakarah*, &c. (p. 163.) Note the degraded sense in which *tarkikas* are used as sophists. The same story gives an amusing description of the discomfiture of the opponents of the Buddha who, when they had heard the challenging *gatha, anyonyam vighatayanta evem ahu, tvam uttishtha tvam uttistha iti* (p. 163). Buddha's creed is summed up in the following: *Yestu Buddhanca dharmanca sanghanca sharangatah, arya satyani catvari pashyanti*, &c. (p. 164). There is a slight reference to the Jainas at page 165, which breathes of *odium theologicium. Asthanan anavaksho*, &c. (p. 175), is pure Palism. The ten *balas*, the four *vaishradays*, &c., as in Pali at page 182. That the generality of people were not free from the use of intoxicants is attested to by the 13th story where a sermon is preached against *madya-pana* and its effects on the unfortunate victim. (p. 190). *Akalpam va tishtheta kalpavasesham va.* (p. 201). This is a reference to the now celebrated passage in Pali which, according to Edmonds, has a parallel to the Eon of the New Testament. But the whole passage beginning with *yasmin Bodhisatya* at page 204 has a parallel in the *Mahavastu* (1,240) and in the *Majjhima nikaya* (III, 252) *sumatinaca trini pitakani adhitani*, (p. 253). The ninth story is specially worth studying because of its delineation of 20-7-19 Jaina hostilities. At page 258 we have a list of the Buddha's principal disciples, most of whom are to be found in Pali, *viz.*, *Anyata kaundinya*, *Ashvajit*, *Kashyapa Mahanama Bhadika*, *Shariputra*, *Maudgalyayana*, *Kashyapa*, *Yashas*, *Purna.* The stock passage describing the up-bringing of a noble child found so often in the *Avadana shataka* as well as in the Pali occurs again at page 271. A testimony to the terror of social excommunication occurs in the threat: *Nocet vayam tvam jnatimadhyat utkshipamaha*, (p, 272). There is a highly important reference to the *sthavira* or Theravada school and to their *Sutrantas.* In fact there seems to be a direct quotation from the Pali work. *Tatha sthavirairapi upanibbhadham* (read so with Oldenberg as against the meaningless " upanirbadham " of the text p. 274). There is a distinct prohibition of cultivation of miraculous powers as is laid down in Pali: *Na bhikshuna agarikasya purastat rdhir vidarshayitavya, darshayati satisaro bhavati*, (p. 270). That the *Divyavadana* is not the original book but a compilation from various sources is evident from many places especially from *esha eva grantho vistarena kartavjah*, (p. 285). Almost every Pali *Suttanta* begins with the formula *evam me sutam*, about the suspected antiquity of which attention has been drawn by Kern. The 20th chapter in fact commences with *evam maya shrutam*, (p. 290). More reference to writing and *lipi*, (pp. 300-301.) An easy way to salvation seems to have already taken root in the minds of the Buddhist community even in the lifetime of the Buddha. A candidate for salvation being advised to undergo the *pravrajya* inquires, *arya kim tatra pravrajyayam kriyate*, and is told, *yayat jivam brahmacaryam caryate*. The candidate objects, *arya, na shakyam etat, anyosti uapayah ? Bhadramukha, asti, Upasako bhava, Arya kim kriyate ? Bhadramukha, yavat jivam pranatipate prativiratih samrakshya*, &c. *Arya etadapi nashakyate, anya upayah kathaya Bhadramukha. Budhapramukham bhikshusangham bhojaya*, &c., (p. 303). The beginning of the 23rd story is unfortunately missing. But it is clear that it contains allusion to the *Anguttaranikaya* The principal divisions of the Buddhist canon are described in the same story, and mention is made of *sutra, matrika*, besides *samyukta Madhyama, dirgha* and *ekottarika agamas*, (p. 333). The *Brahmanavarga* of which Sangharakshita makes *svadhyaya*, evidently refers to a portion of the scripture, probably the chapter in the *Dhammapada*. The celebrated *Nagaropama sutra* is referred to at page 340, How far the old tradition of the acts of the Buddha was faithfully preserved upto and after the times of Ashoka is illustrated by the 27th story. As Foucher has shown the sacred spots of Buddhism were then common knowledge of both Pali and non-Pali schools. The passage beginning with *vivikatam papakaih akushslaih dharmaih* is a clear reproduction of the original text of which Pali version is of too frequent occurrence to be specified (p. 391). The "middle path" of the Buddha was ridiculed by his opponents as impossible to lead to salvation, being too worldly and luxurious. People were in fact scandalised and the hostile satire is again characteristic of the objection to the practices of Buddhism which were considered to be not sufficiently rigid to suit an ascetic life: *bhuktva annam saghratam prabhulapishitam dadhuyttamalankratam Shakyeshu indriya nigrahoyadibhavet Vindhyah plavetsagare* (p. 420). The important point to be observed is that they are, even at this comparative remote period, accused of eating flesh which is clearly in conformity with indifference on this point shown by the Buddha (p. 420). Buddha and Jaina animosities are further attested to in the 20th story, where we are told that a certain Jaina scandalised the Buddha by drawing the picture of the Buddha in the act of making obeisance to the Nirgrantha (p. 427). That India was not altogether free from religious persecution is evident from some of these old legends themselves. About Pushyamitra it is stated that he proclaimed: *yo no shramanashiro dasyati tasyaham dinara shashtam dasyami* (p. 434.) The Shadvargiyas, who are the constant instigators of mischief in Pali, occur in our book at page 489. The 36th story furnishes another example of the difficulties which the Buddha had to encounter in the propagation of his gospel. A certain Bhikshu repudiates the teaching and the discipline which he had received from the Buddha and severs his connection with Buddhism in these terms: *Idancha te patram, idancha civaram imanca shiks'am svayameva dharaya* (p. 520) Though the first line does not seem to have come down to us correctly, the manner of the Brahman and his contemptuous repudiation of Buddhism leave us no doubt of his meaning. There is another *sutra viz*, *Rakshasi sutra*, quoted at page 524. Certain portions of *Divyavadana* are of late origin, one of which is the 36th story. There we find the Buddha's discourses were not only committed to books, but that even women, *ratrau pradipena Buddhavacanam pathanti* (p. 532). The several portions of the scripture and the doctrines mentioned in the 37th story are interesting in that some at least of them have no correspondence in Pali (p. 549). In the same story we have reference to "sharirapuja" or relic worship and the erection of stupa over the relics, (p. 551). The general Pali formula is "anaityam, dukham and anatma," but we find in the *Divyavadana* the fourth factor added, *viz.*, "shunyata" (p. 568).

---

# NOTES.

**Note to p. 1.**

Formerly the mixed Sanskrit was called the Gatha dialect. Senart JA 1882, xix, 238; 1886 viii, 318; Kern SBE 21, xiv; Buhler Ep. Ind. 1, 1892, 239, 377; Ep. Ind. II, 34; Hoernle and Bhandarkar, Ind. Ant. 12, Ind. Ant. 17, 1883, p. 36; J. Wackernagel Alt. indische Grammatik, xxxix.

We owe our first knowledge about this literature which is principally found in Nepal to Brian Houghton Hodgson who lived in Nepal from 1821 to 1843 and distinguished himself equally as a statesman, geographer, zoologist, ethnographist and investigator of Indian languages and antiquities. Through his instrumentality numerous Buddhist manuscripts were deposited in the Indian and European libraries especially in Paris, where they were examined by the eminent scholar Eugene Burnouf (Introduction a la histoire du Buddhisme Indian, 1876). About the time (1874) he was making such important discoveries relating to our knowledge of Buddhist literature, the celebrated Hungarian Alexander Csoma de Koros who had made the journey from Hungary to Tibet on foot, started his enquiries into the Buddhist literature of the latter country. Shortly after him George Turnour attacked the Pali literature of Ceylon. Rajendralal Mitra reported on the contents of numerous Buddhist-Sanskrit manuscripts in his *Sanskrit-Buddhist Literature of Nepal*, 1882. C. Bendall gave us his catalogue of Buddhist Manuscripts in Cambridge, 1883.

The Tibetan translations of Sanskrit books are described by Koros in the Asiatic Researches, volume 20, 1836, and by L. Feer Annales du Musee Guimet, 1883. The principal work on Chinese translations from Sanskrit is Bunio Nanjio's Catalogue of the Chinese translation of the Buddhist Tripitaka, 1887. (Winternitz.)

### Note to p. 5.

## "OUTLINES OF MAHAYANA BUDDHISM."

(BY T. SUZUKI.)

"The first *Shiksha* forbids the killing of any living being but the Bodhisattva does not hesitate to go to war, in case the cause he espouses is right and beneficient to humanity at large (p. 71)."

The two kinds of knowledge or truth distinguished by the madhyamika philosophy (p. 95, p. 97, p. 101).

The completely neglective nature of madhyamika is illustrated by the opening Sutra:

There is no death, no birth, no destruction, no persistence, no oneness, no multitude, no coming, no departing (p. 103).

The emperor of China in 535, having become a devout Buddhist, turned to the founder of the Dhyana school in China and asked, "I have dedicated so many monasteries, copied so many sacred books and converted so many people; what do you think my merits amount to?" The master of Dhyana replied "no merit whatever" (p. 104).

The Surangamasutra was translated twice into Chinese and once entirely transliterated (p. 157).

---

### Note to p. 5.

The Atmavada or the theory of the soul is sometimes proclaimed by the Buddhists themselves apparently without their being conscious of the gross contradiction which it involves to their cardinal principle of philosophy. It is related in our Tibetan sources derived from India (Vassilief p. 57) that towards his end Dhitika convened the priests in the kingdom of Maru to an assembly to condemn the doctrine of a certain Vatsa who asserted the reality of the soul. It is the same Dhitika who came from Ujjayini and succeeded as a teacher Upagupta, the renowned contemporary of Asoka and the head of the elders at the Council of Pataliputra and a contemporary of King Milinda of Baktria. Hence the recognition of the anatmavada as decisive for adherence to Buddhism must have been set up.—N.

---

### Note to p. 5.

## DIE PHILOSOPHISCHE GRUNDLAGE DES ALTEREN BUDDHISMUS.

(BY MAX WALLESER.)

Walleser divides the development of Buddhism into three stages; the first is the primitive realistic indifferentism, the second is idealism or nihilism, that is the Shunyavada, which is associated with the name of Nagarjuna, and the third subjective idealism of the Vijnanavadis which is attributed to Asanga, the brother of Vasubandhu.

The passage which yields this remarkable information is found in the fifth chapter of the Sandhi Nirmocana (Tibetan and Chinese translations) (p. 4).—N.

---

### Note to p. 7.

Lalitavistara translated by Foucaux. Senart has discovered a bark manuscript in the Punjab containing an arithmetical treatise in the *gatha* dialect which shows that it was at one time a literary language (p. 3). According to the Mahavansa the original scriptures of Buddhism were in verse. (p. 4).—N.

**Note to p. 8.**

International Congress of Orientalists, Paris 1894.

Sanskrit-Buddhist manuscript from Burma describing Buddhist cosmology according to the Mahayana school by Herbert Baynes (p. 127).

Notes on the Pancakrama by Vallee Poussin (p. 137) and the same book report Pali inscriptions from Magadha or Behar by Cecil Bendall. The Ashatamahashri Chaitaya stotra of the King Harsha Shiladitya is given in the Chinese text and the reconstructed original Saṇskrit by Sylvain Levi (p. 189).—N.

---

**Note to p. 8.**

Le bouddhisme au Japon by J. Dautremer, RHR p. 121, 256, 1916.

Kashmir and the neighbouring countries are probably the home of the Mula Sarvastivada literature. See Sylvain Levi in the foreword to a very interesting study of his pupil Przyluski on the Buddha in the North West India (JA 1914, p. 494).

On *Pancaraksha* see the geographical list in the Mahamayuri JA 1915, 19. For an Ouigour version of the story of the *Wise man and the Fool*, see JA 1914; Pelliot proves that the Chinese Mo-ni is Mani. He makes further a most interesting observation, namely, that there is a sufficient number of Chinese texts which concern the Nestorians and the Mazdians. (JA 1914, p. 461). Shall we ever get at any of these Zoroastrian texts in Chinese in a European translation? For the Sanskrit text of the Pratimoksha of the Sarvastivadi school see Finot and Huber JA 1913, p. 465.—N.

**Note to p. 11.**

## MAHAVASTU, VOLUME I.

The full title of the book is given at page 2 which may be translated:—The Mahavastu section of the Vinayapitaka of the recension of the branch of the Mahasamghikas called the Lokottaravadis of the Madhyadesha. Brahman hospitality, the story of Malini (p. 307). Example of the Sanskrit restitution of a Pali form (p. 2, line 15.) Textual resemblance with Lalitavistara (p. 229, line 6).—N.

---

## MAHAVASTU, VOLUME II.

Shady side of Buddhist character, history of Shyama (p. 68).—N.

---

## MAHAVASTU, VOLUME III.

Example of superiority of the Sanskrit (Mahavastu) texts to the Pali, (p. 191). Example of Pali tradition interfering with the text (p. 401). Example of the Sanskrit (Mahavastu) text being superior to the Pali (p. 417).—N.

---

## MAHAVASTU.

Professor Windisch has discussed the sources of Sanskrit Mahavastu (Ed. Senart) in a special monograph *Die komposition des Mahavastu* (Leipzig, 1909) which furnishes us with a series of Pali parallels to Sanskrit Buddhistic writings. The Mahavastu is a portion of Vinayapitaka according to the recension of the Madhyadeshikas belonging to the Lokottaravadi sect of the Mahasangikas (Arya Mahasanghikanam Lokottaravadinam Madhyadeshikanam pathena vinaya pitakasya mahavastuyeadi, Vol. I, p. 2). The Madhyadesha comprises the sixteen countries of Northern India from Kamboja and Gandhara in the West to Magadha and Anga in the East. (Anguttaranikaya Tikanipata 70, 17). In this monograph we find a number of interesting parallels. The usual Pali formula of admission to the Order as in the Mahavagga (1, 6, 32) runs as follows :

"Labheyyaham bhante bhagavato santike pabhajjam, labheyam upasampadan ti, hi bhikkhu ti bhagava avoca, svakkhato dhammo, cara brahmacariyam samma dukkhassa antakiriyaya ti."

Identical phraseology is found in the corresponding Sanskrit canon as represented in the Divyavadana at p. 48, while the Mahavastu differs but little from both.

In the course of the work Professor Windisch establishes that the Mahavastu issued from the Mahavagga. This he proves by a comparison of the first twenty-four chapters of the Mahavagga with the Mahavastu which presents a number of passages of verbal identity. It may be noted that in this respect the Lalitavistara also betrays close correspondence, but it is farther removed from the Mahavagga than the Mahavastu.

In his *Studies in the Mahavastu* (Gotingen 1912) Oldenberg gives further illustations of Pali gaps supplied by Sanskrit, and interestingly points out how the transcriber of the manuscript omitted a line owing to two lines beginning with the same word (p. 131). His conclusion on comparing the Pali and Sanskrit sources of the Mahavastu seems to be that the Pali copy of the Sutras discussed is not always the more correct one when it differs from the Northern version. But the Northern text has undergone a revision, and has invested the text in numerous places with minor, and in a few places with larger, accretions and finally that where the positive standard for deciding is wanting the Pali form may be adopted as the more probably correct (p. 141).—N.

---

**Note to p. 19.**

Winternitz calls attention to a most remarkable passage in the Lalitavistara (p. 142 of translation) where Gopa the Shakya princess is expected to observe what we should call the *purdah* system.—N.

---

The Lalitavistra was translated into Chinese in 587 by Janana Gupta; but an earlier translation existed since 308. BEFEO 1905.—N.

---

**Note to p. 23.**

**BUDDHA'S GEBURT. (Birth.)**

**Example of Pali and Sanskrit parallels.**

An instance of words latterly put into the mouth of the Buddha which were not uttered by himself (p. 17). Vishnu, Shiva and other gods in the older Buddhist texts (p. 32). Pali original of portions of Mahavastu and Lalitavistara (p. 157). Here we see the influence of the doctrine of Bhakti with which we are familiar in the Bhagavad Gita and it is probable that it was the latter work which influenced the development of the Mahayana. Kern's Manual of Buddhism p. 122. (p. 4). The expression *agama* occurs also in the

Pali canon, Mahaggava ; x, 1, 2 ; 6 and Cullavagga 1, 11, 1, (p. 9.) Jataka Mala, edited by Kern, Harvard Oriental Series, Boston. 1901, translated by J. S. Speyer, 1895. Kern in the Fest Gruss to Bohtlingk, 1888. S. d'Oldenburg, JRAS 1893, 308 ; Barth, RHR 1893, 260 : Watanabe, JPTS 1909, 263. J.J. Meyer has reproduced four tales of the Jataka Mala, Lotus Verlag, Leipzig. (p. 41.)—N.

---

**Note to p. 23.**

## MARA AND BUDDHA.

The Northern books presume the existence of the Pali texts (p. 1). Pali Padhanasutta translated into the Sanskrit Lalitavistara. Probability of Sanskrit version being older than Pali (p. 40). Though the theme may be the same the Divyavadana, Lalitavistara and Mahaparinibbanasutta are not interdependent but mutually independent (p. 41). Most ancient form preserved by Lalitavistara and not by Mahaparinibbana (p. 66). Example of the correct reading preserved in Sanskrit and the currupt in Pali (p. 108). Example of a complete Sanskrit translation from Pali (p. 330).—N.

---

**Note to p. 30.**

I-tsing in his dictionary of a thousand Sanskrit-Chinese words translates the Sanskrit Parvata by po-fa-to. (BEFEO 1905 p. 301.)—N.

---

**Note to p. 39.**

## AWAKENING OF FAITH IN THE MAHAYANA.

By T. Suzuki.

Beal thought that Ashvaghosha's writings when examined would probably be found to be much tinged with a pseudo-Christian element (p. 42.)

Suzuki thinks that there is an abundance of similar thoughts and passages in Ashvaghosha and the Bhagavadgita, (p. 44.)

Kern in his history of Buddhism (German vol. 2, p. 500 foot-note) has indicated coincidences between the Bhagvadgita Saddharma-pundarika, (p. 44.)

According to Suzuki Ashvaghosha refers to Sukhavati-sutras so that the latter must at least be a couple of centuries prior to Ashvaghosha, (p. 50.)

The Lankavatarasutra was translated first into Chinese by Bhumibhadra, A. D. 443; then by Bodhiruchi A. D. 513 and lastly by Shikshananda, A. D. 700-704, (p. 65.)

An example of a great solemn vow *maha-pranidhana*, occurs in Ashvaghosha, see Suzuki (p. 142):

"May my mind be freed from all contradictions, may I abandon particularisation, may I personally attend on all Buddhas and Bodhisattvas, whom I shall pay homage to, make offerings to, revere and praise, and to whose instructions in the good doctrine (saddharma) I shall listen; may I truthfully discipline myself according to their teachings, and to the end of the future never be negligent in self-discipline; may I with innumerable expediencies (upaya) (of salvation) deliver all beings who are drowned in the sea of misery, and bring them to the highest bliss of Nirvana".—N.

---

**Note to p. 39.**

Some critical notes on Ashvaghosha's Buddhacarita by J. S. Speyer (p. 105, JRAS 1914.)

**Note to p. 39.**

Saundarananda of Ashvaghosha by Vidyushekhara Bhattacharya (p. 747, JRAS 1914.)

---

**Note to p. 39.**

Uddyotakara, a contemporary of Dharmakirti by S. C. Vidyabhushana (JRRS p. 601, 1914.)

---

**Note to p. 47.**

**AVADANASHATAKA.**

The Chinese translation is not of much use being rather free, abridged and with many omissions. The Tibetan translation is very literal and has proved of great value to Feer in his translation of the Sanskrit text into French.—N.

---

**Note to p. 60.**

Notes on the language of the Dvavimshatya vadana katha by Turner (JRAS 289, 1913.)

---

**Note to p. 62**

**AVADANA-KALPALATA.**

This work was translated into Tibetan in 1272 under the auspices of the spiritual guide of the Mogal Emperor Kublai Khan, the Tibetan version being executed with utmost literal accuracy.—N.

## Note to p. 64.

## L'INFLUENCE DU BOUDDHISME.

(BY NYANATILOKA.)

Do not be guided by rumours, by that which is written in sacred books, by reason or deductions which appear to be reasonable or logical simply because of their external appearance, by visions and reveries, by the appearance of the possible; do not believe because it is the ascetic or teacher who speaks, but when by your personal conviction you recognise that such and such things are bad and to be rejected, that they are blameworthy and that they are fit to be discarded, that they lead to evil and to suffering, then you must reject them. (Anguttara Nikaya Tikanipta 65) (p. 7.)

Offerings to the dead and the Paritta service in Japanese Buddhism, Khuddaka-Patho by K. Siedenstucker (p. 35.)

Classical example of ancient Buddhist adjuration hymn (p. 29.)—N.

---

## Note to p. 65.

## SAMGITI SUTTA.

There are three sorts of weapons :—The weapon of what is heard of the Tipitaka, the weapon of quietness (Kayaviveka : Solitude, Cittaviveka : detachment of the mind from passions, and upadhiviveka : nirvana) and the weapon pertaining to wisdom.—N.

---

## (Note to p. 79.)

On the Avatamsanka and the Mahasannipatta see Sylvain Levi Notes Chinoises sur L'Inde, (BEFEO 1905.)—N.

### Note to p. 81.

On the Patra or the Bowl of the Buddha destroyed by Hun Mihira Kula, (BEFEO 1905, p. 297.)—N.

---

### Note to p. 89.

## MADHYAMAKAVATARA.

(BY CHANDRAKIRTI.)

Translated from the Tibetan by Vallee Poussin Le Museon, volume II, No. 34.

The celebrated shloka nanyabhasaya mlecchah shakyo grahayitumyathana lankikam rte lokah cakyo grahayitum tatha is here traced to Aryadeva. Professor K. B. Pathak in his paper on Vasudeva and Patanjali (p. 2) cites a remarkably clear definition of Nirvana by two Buddhist writers Jayaditya and his commentator Jinendrabuddhi.—N.

---

### Note to p. 90.

## MADHYAMIKASUTRAS.

### With Candrakirtis Commentary.

Comparison of the Chinese and the Pali versions of the Brahmajalasutra (p. 3). Agreements of Mahavastu and Majjhima (p. 9). The dangers of Shunyavada (p. 248). Inconsistency of the permission and prohibition regarding free thought (p. 268). Rejection even of the middle path (p. 270). Vallee Poussin consistently searches for parallels which are sometimes of verbal agreement in Sanskrit and Pali. The instances I have noted are at pp. 1, 6, 9, 40, 41, 47, 63, 90, 145,

166, 297, 246, 263, 270, 292, 296, 297, 303, 306, 314, 331, (complete), 335, 348, 349, 354, 355, 361, 362, 366, 443, 451, 454, 486, 492, 498, 501, and 504.—On Jatakas in the Avadana literature see S. d'Oldenburg, JRAS, 1893, 304, and Feer les Avadanas Jatakas, JA 1884, 332. Vyakarana or exposition is the term used for the prophetic future histories. The Avadana Shataka has been edited by Speyer and translated into French by Feer who in a series of essays (JA 1878-1884) translated and discussed a number of the Avadanas. (Speyer Vol. II, Preface p. XV.) Books in which the Roman Dinarius is mentioned as the Dinara could not have been composed prior to the second Christian century, since this coin came to India only through the Greeks. See Jolly Recht. und Sitte (p. 23.)—N.

---

Not to p. 90.

## MADHYAMIKASHASTRA OF NAGARJUNA.

(Translated from Tibetan by Max Walleser.)

The older Buddhism was positive interwoven with scepticism and a goodly share of indifferentism, but the new phase which introduced itself as Mahayana, that is the great vehicle in contrast with the older or smaller vehicle of Hinayana, has by no means all the inner development which is easily understood as advanced to the denial of all phenomena, p. 3. According to Walleser the Akutobhaya commentary supplies a cue to the terminology and the dogmatics of the preceding and contemporary Hinayana texts throwing light on the obscure relation between the Pali Abhidharma and the Abhidharma Kosha of Vasubandhu, (p. IV)

Owing to the perfect precision of the Tibetan translation and the systematic persistence with which it has been adhered to, the technical expressions being invariably translated by the same equivalents, it is possible almost to reconstruct in its literal entirety the original Sanskrit text of Nagarjuna, (p. V.)—N.

---

(Note to p. 95.)

## MAHAYANA SUTRALAMKARA OF ASANGA.

The text and translation of the book are a magnificent illustration of French scholarship. The author's familiarity with Chinese and Tibetan enables him to deal with the text much more efficiently than an authority acquainted with Sanskrit alone would be in a position to do. All the gaps in the Sanskrit manuscripts are supplied from the Chinese translation which was made by the Hindu Prabhakara Mitra between 630 and 633 A.D. A noteworthy vindication of Devnagari character will be found at page 3. As I have maintained before, the Cambridge edition of the Divyavadana and other texts would have gained in popularity in India had they not been printed in the Roman character. As Sylvain Levi says the Devnagari editions reach a class of readers who are generally not taken into consideration by European scholars and yet who merit attention. The example of European editors might stimulate emulation among the lamas and save from destruction or bring to light the texts which are in danger. For Indianism, as Levi contends, is by no means an empty exercise of dilettantism. Beyond our linguistic, philological, political, religious and social problems we have to have regard for the hundreds of millions of living creatures who are affected by these problems and whose lot is connected with the success of their solution.

Throughout the text Sylvain Levi notes the numerous new words in Sanskrit unknown to our lexicons, indigenous or European, which he has encountered in this work. The future Asanga was first of all known under the name of Vasubandhu and his two younger brothers also were so called (p. 2). The Tibetan translation of the Sutralankara was also prepared by an Indian called Shakyasimha assisted by Tibetan Lotsavas or interpreters. In the text there are traces of influence of the spoken vernacular or of some language in which the epithet follows the qualifying noun (p. 12). Here as in the Divyavadana the language bristles with solecisms and barbarous phrases as judged by the standard of Panini. But the fact seems to be that Buddhist Sanskrit constantly tends to emancipation from the innumerable rules laid down by the grammarians and to make nearer approach to the spoken idiom. Two or three centuries after Asanga the Sanskrit grammar prepared by Candragomi marks the capitulation on the part of Buddhism to Brahmanic purism (p. 13). As regards the scriptural texts drawn upon by Asanga the Samyukta Agama seems to have been his favourite. Next comes the Anguttara (p. 15). Sylvain Levi holds that Asanga was influenced by the currents of foreign religious beliefs having come into contact with the professors of Zoroastrianism, Judaism, Christianity and Manicheism (p. 18).

Definition of Buddhavachana (p. 10 note). The concord of the Sanskrit texts with Pali is constantly established reference being made to the Pali canon (*e. g.* page 186 where the agreement is perfectly literal). How far a thorough knowledge of Buddhism is unattainable without Chinese and Tibetan may be judged from the French-Sanskrit, Sanskrit-French, Chinese-Sanskrit, and Tibetan-Sanskrit vocabularies appended to this book.—N.

### Note to p. 97.

Bana in his Harshacharita (p. 265-6) gives a detailed description of the various religious persuasions in his time. The monkeys who had taken the three refugees of Buddhism occupied themselves with the rituals of the Chaitya. Devout parrots versed in the Shakyashastras expounded the Khosha, which was no doubt the Abhidharma Khosha of Vasubandhu, while some Mainas after their monastic exercises, the ten Shikshapadas, lectured on the Law, and the owls recited the history of the previous births of the Buddha and the tigers under the restraining influence of the teachings of the Buddha renounced flesh food.—N.

---

### Note to p. 97.

Ettinghausen in his Harshavardhana gives the Suprabhata-stotra (p. 172) which illustrates the type of inspiring poetry not often to be met with in classical Sanskrit literature and which is an index to the piety and fervour of the Mahayanistic authors.—N.

---

### Note to p. 101.

### SHIKSHASAMUCCAYA.

The form of the book represents a type familiar to students of Indian literature. It is an author's commentary on Karikas or memorial verses written by himself. Bandall's view is that the Mahayana writers used passages which are neither translated nor adapted from the corresponding Pali text but represent the Mahayanist's handling of the common tradition of Buddhism. "A curious instance of the conscientiousness of something else than Sanskrit as the real underlying sacred language is found in the charm occurring at p. 142, 15, quoted from the Vidyadharapitaka where the conclusion is practically a sentence of Pali," (p. 14). Bandall believes in the expertness of the Tibetan translators. "When I find how wonderfully well even as late as the IXth century the Pandits who translated the Prakrit Dohakoshas into Tibetan understood the extremely difficult forms of that work, I must unhesitatingly reject Childer's supposition that the northern Buddhists were misled by ignorance of Pali (p. 14). It will be found that the confusion of forms is sometimes on the side of Pali tradition and that the Sanskrit writing Buddhism preserves the etymological one" (p. 15). Duties of married life (p. 78). Medicine includes use of spells (p. 142). Certain shastras to be avoided (p. 192). On faith (p. 5). A precept which has no parallel in the Pratimoksha as known from Pali or as yet translated from Chinese ; it illustrates a familiar posture for kings and other laymen found in Buddhist art as in the Amaravati sculptures (p. 125). Discussion on animal food prohibited with reserve (p. 131 and 137). Example of the Sanskrit text transcribed and not translated in the Tibetan version (p. 139). Snake charms (p. 141). Example of a Dharani (p. 142). Buddhist confession of sins (pp. 160-161). Traditional list of tortures in Sanskrit and Buddhist writers (p. 181). Parallel between Sanskrit and Pali enumeration of heretic schools (p. 331). Example of Mantra transliterated not translated into Sanskrit (p. 355). The number of works consulted by Shantideva is 108.—N.

---

**Note to p. 101.**

**BODHICARYAVATARA.**

TRANSLATED BY

VALLEE POUSSIN.

Against the theory of extreme self-sacrifice see the Atma-bhava-raksha.

The legends of the surrender of his eyes and his children by the Buddha are not to be imitated by others, I-tsing *Records*, 198, (p. 43). Buddhist Confession of Sins, (pp. 27-66.)

Shantideva speaks at the most with reserve regarding the magical formulas which may be held to include Tantra, Bodhi, c. v. 5, 90, (p. 45). Vallee Poussin differing from Bendall attributes only one text, *sutra samuccaya*, to Nagarjuna (p. 48.)

For the authority on which the Mahayana enjoins marriage upon the monks and the future Buddhas and ultimately leads to the excesses of the Tantras, see p. 51.

The value of force, which does not seem to exclude physical force, *virya paramita*, chapter 7 of Bodhi c. v. (p. 70).—N.

---

**BODHICARYAVATARA SANSKRIT TEXT.**

The author has composed his book not because he has anything new to convey, nor because he is an expert writer or he is officiously solicitous about others but only to please himself, (1, 2.)

On the costliest of material gifts being surpassed by a single act of devotion, (p. 33.)

Example of touching devotional hymns, (p. 48.)

Instance of the incorporation of six stanzas in the Bodhicaryavatara into the Svayambhu-purana, (p. 58.)

Buddhist confession of sins, (p. 69 *et seq.*)

Parallels between Bodhicaryavatara and Svayambhu-puran, (p. 72.)

The aspirant's desire to be the protector of the poor, leader of the caravan, to be a ship or bridge to those desiring to cross the ocean, (p. 83.)

Instead of subjugating all sensations it is easier and more desirable to control the mind just as it is infinitely more easy to protect oneself against thorns etc., by a piece of leather required to make the sole of your shoes than to cover the whole earth with leather, (p. 102). Prohibition against suffering discomfort for others, (p. 142). On the theory of *atityaga*, the contrast with the doctrine of the Hinayana, (p. 288).

Respect for Hinayana, (p. 146). The familiar posture for laymen found in Buddhist art and not prescribed in the Pratimoksha, (p. 148).

Anxiety to gain popular favour, (p. 146).

Kalyanamitra, (p. 156).

Recommendation to study the sutras, (p. 159).

Insistence on the study of Shikshasamuccaya, (p. 163).

Authority of Nagarjuna (p. 164).

To act upto and not merely to read the scriptures; the mere reading of pharmaceutical works will not effect a patient's cure, (p. 1667).

Duty of cheerfulness, (p. 172-3).

Diverse tortures, (p. 177 *et seq*.)

Non-resistance of attacks on images, stupas and the religion itself, (p. 204). Causes of want of energy, (p. 244).

Pride in being a follower of the Buddha, (p. 273).

Longing for wandering without unnatural restraint in foreign lands, (p. 267).

The vulgar, fatigued with the day's business, come home in the evening to lie down in bed like the dead, (p. 318). The two varieties of truth, (p. 341). Explanation of the doctrine of Maya or Shunyata as in the Bhagavati, (p. 379.)—N.

---

**Note to p. 104.**

**LANMAN ON PALI BOOK-TITLES.**

Buddhaghosa in explaining 22, how the Tipitaka as an aggregation of collections (nikayas) may be regarded as five-fold, says that it consists of the Digha, Majjhima, Sanyutta, Anguttara, and Khudaka, and proceeds :—Apart from the four Nikayas, all the rest, namely the entire Vinaya and Abhidamma and the fifteen aforesaid works, Khuddaka patha etc. are the words of Buddha. Then, continuing with a verse of "the ancients" he says : "And apart from these four Nikayas, Digha and so forth, the words of Buddha other than those, are held to be the Khuddaka-nikaya." (p. 685).

Different names for the same thing—Polyonymy. We have heard of the student who, undergoing examination on the Homeric question, answered that "The Iliad was not written by Homer, but by another man of the same name." In India the trouble is often the other way, it is the same man with another name. "The Hindus, even in historical documents and works, had the bad habit of designating one and the same person by different names of the same significance. Thus Vikrama-arka-Vikrama-aditya ; Surya-mati-Surya-vati." So one of the three Elders at whose request Buddhaghosa wrote the Ja. cm., is called by him (I. 1) Buddha-deva, but by the Gnvn., p. 68, Buddhapiya.—Unfortunately, this is true not only of men, but also of texts. The Dhammasangani is called Dhamma-sangaha by the great Buddhaghosa himself at D. cm. I. 17; while in the Rangoon (Mundyne ed. of Atthasalini, p. 408, lines 18-19 and 26, we read Atthasalini nama Dhammasangah-atthakatha, but in line 27, Dhammasangani-atthakatha.

The titles of such texts are justly the despair of Occidental librarians and bibliographers, who are inevitably at their wit's end in trying to perform the well-nigh impossible task of making these Oriental books available to Orientalists Perhaps we ought not to blame the Hindus. With their erudition, profound in many ways, but narrow, they had no more conception of the many-sided knowledge indispensable for a modern librarian than they had of aerial automobiles or wireless telegraphy. (pp. 693, 694).—N.

---

**Note to p. 104.**

The Maharatanakuta Dharmaparyaye Kashyapa Parivartah has been edited with notes by Baron von Steel-Holstein.

(Bulletin of the Imperial Academy of St. Petersburgh, 1909 p. 739.)—N.

---

**Note to p. 110.**

**BULLETIN de L'ACADEMIE des SCIENCES.**

ST. PETERSBURGH

*June 15, 1911.*

Notes on the Trikayastava by Baron A. von Stael-Holstein (p. 837). The Hymn has been reconstructed into its original Sanskrit form from the Chinese transcription.—N.

### Note to p. 122.

### SUBHASITA-SANGRAHA.

Although as Bandall impartially puts it a considerable portion of the contents of the book is objectionable and even sometimes repulsive to modern readers, its publication was necessary and appropriate for the right understanding of the history of Buddhism in India. *cittamatram jagat sarvam* as a dictum of Nagarjuna, quoted (p. 20). Contrasting with the original doctrine of Buddhism to conquer hatred by love stands a recommendation to conquer passion by passion (p. 50-55). Bandall styles the whole second part as an extraordinary phase of soi-disant Buddhism and publishes it "thinking it well that scholars at least should know the worst." It reads like an obscene caricature of the teaching both of earlier Buddhism and of the legitimate Yoga. Our doubt still remains unsolved, the doubt suggested by M. Barth, whether such teachings were among those officially accepted by Buddhism. Possibly in these writings we have a clue as to how Buddhism came to be discredited in India and finally disappeared. One must proclaim the law (dharma) to fulfil the highest aspirations of men (95), but a knowledge of charms (mantra, sadhana) is also necessary. These may check sin even in great sinners (96-98).—N.

---

### Note to p 125.

(Albert J. Edmund's work on *Buddhist and Christian Gospels* is invaluable, also for the indirect light thrown on the relationship between Buddhism and Zoroastrianism, Volume I, 136 ff. For the Parthian contacts see p. 68 ff: p. 150, Volume II, pp. 158, 263, 266, 273, etc., G.K.N.)

Besides Seydel, Bergh van Eysinga and Edmunds the dependence of the Christian Gospel upon the Buddhist text is assumed also by O. Pfleiderer, *Die Entstehung des Christentumus*, second edition, Munich 1907, p. 198; also Ernst Kuhn in a postcript to the book of Bergh van Eysinga (p. 102) and R. Pischel (Deutsche Litztg. 1904 September Sp. 2938 ff.) who states "the question whether Indian influences are to be found in the narrative literature of the Gospels can now no longer be denied." In diverse points K. E. Neumann is of similar views, *Reden Gotamo Buddhos* III, 112, 256A, 258A, 259A, 260A, 364A. A sort of primitive Christian connection is supposed by H. Kern (Deutsche Litztg, 1882, Sp. 1276) and R. O. Franke (Deutsche Litztg, 1901, Sp. 2757, ff.). A. Weber (The Greeks in India, SBA 1890, p. 928 f.), and H. Oldenberg. (Theolog. Litztg. 1905 Sp. 65 ff. *Aus dem Alten Indien* (p. 47 f.) still leave the question open. Wholly or almost repudiating is the attitude of T.W. Rhys Davids, SBE xi, 165 f.; J. Estlin Carpenter, The First Three Gospels, their Origin and Relations, 1890, p. 130 ff., 161, 174, 203, 237; E. Hardy, *der Buddhismus*' p. 110; E. W. Hopkins *India Old and New*, p. 120; E. Windisch *Mara and Buddha*, p. 60, 214, 312 and *Buddha's Geburt*, p. 195; La Vallee Poussin *Revue bilique* 1906, 353 and *Bouddhisme* p. 5; S. Levi *Revue critique*, 1908, volume 65, p. 382; A. B. Keith, JRAS 1910, 213; R. Garbe, *Deutsche Rundschu* Volume 144, 1910, p. 73, and Volume 149, 1911, p. 122, and *Contributions of Buddhism to Christianity*, Chicago, 1911; Edw. Lehmann Buddhism as an Indian sect and World Religion Tubingen, 1911, p. 78. Some of these authorities deny all similarities others explain them without assuming mutual dependence.—Winternitz.

---

Note to p. 126.

Edmunds I, 107, 167; Luke I, 35 Majjhima Nikaya, 38, 123. Edmunds I, 198 and Pischel, Life and Teachings of the Buddha p. 26, see no dependence here. Edmunds II, 123,

Mark IX, 2; Luke IX, 30. Rhys Davids Dialogues of the Buddha II, 146; Dutoit Life of the Buddha, p. 283. Bergh van Eysinga 21; Edmunds I, 181. The Buddhist legend was undoubtedly known in the third century B.C., consequently borrowing on the part of the Buddhists is out of question.

Luke II, 41. The similarity is greater with Lalitavistara XI than with the Nidanakatha (Rhys Davids Buddhist Birth Stories, p. 75; Jataka p. 58). See Kern *Der Buddhismus* I, 39, Bergh van Eysinga, p. 26.

Jataka volume I, p. 60; Rhys Davids Buddhist Birth Stories, p. 79; Seydel, p. 26; Bergh van Eysinga, p. 41. It is true that this kind of benedictions occurs also in the chants (Neumann, Songs of the Monks and Nuns, p. 309 note); Lehmann Der Buddhismus, p. 85). However, the similarity in detail is striking in as much as the Buddha as well Jesus remark upon what in their opinion blessedness consists of.—Winternitz.

---

**Note to p. 127.**

Matth IV, 2; Mark I, 13; Majjhima nikaya 36; Edmunds I, 192.

Matth XIV, p. 16 f.; Jataka Nr. 78; Edmunds II, 253. The Rasavahani in which similar legends occur (Lehmann p. 90) is altogether a late work.

Edmunds II, 257; Jataka Nr. 190, Matth. XIV, 24; Bergh van Eysinga, p. 45; Carpenter First Three Gospels, p. 203; Garbe Contributions, p. 12; Lehmann, p. 88. Sutralankara W. Huber, p. 119, Mark, XII, 41; Luke XXI, 1; Bergh van Eysinga 23, Lehmann, p. 88.

Seydel p. 230; J. M. Carter, JRAS 1893, 393; Bergh van Eysinga, 57; Edmunds II, 260; Seydel 232 compares the metaphor of the born blind (John IX) with the Saddharma.

Neumann, Songs of the Monks and Nuns, p. 359. There is a greater similarity between Matth, XVII, 19, where there is mention of the removal of the mountains by faith and Angattara nikaya, VI, 24, where it is said that the monk by means of his meditation can split the Himalaya. Edmunds 11, 40.– Winternitz.

---

**Note to p. 128.**

**BUDDHIST TEXTS IN JOHN BY EDMUNDS.**

On the 26th of August in the Eastern Communion and on the 27th of November in the Western we have the singular spectacle of Catholic priests commemorating the Hindu thinker as a Christian saint.—N.

---

**Note to p. 129.**

Khuddakapatho VIII translated by Winternitz, Rel. Lesebuch, p. 270, see Edmunds I, 222. Lehmann Der Buddhismus, (p. 92.)

Bergh van Eysinga, p. 77; Edmunds I, iii to 164. On the other hand it is less probable that already in the first century Christian ideas should have penetrated India. J. Dahlmann (Indische Fahrten, Volume II, 100, 129, 152; The Thomas legend) would have it that the Acts of Thomas rest on a historical basis, that already in the first century a Christian mission was operating in northern India and that the Mahayanistic Buddhism developed under Christian influences. Winternitz is inclined as little to agree with that argument as with that of Garbe (Deutsche Rund Buddhismus, 38, p. 76.)

According to Winternitz the Acts of Thomas only demonstrate that at the time of their composition, *i. e.*, the third century A. D., Christians had penetrated to Gandhara.

Bergh van Eysinga, p. 64, and Garbe Contributions, p. 19. Already in 1762 the Augustine monk Georgias indicated that there were reports about the Buddha in Tibet similar to those relating to the five year old Jesus in the Gospel of Thomas, see L. Conrady, the Gospel of Thomas, Theological Studies and Criticism, Gotha 1903, (p. 403.)

Max Muller, Essays III, p. 538, (Foucaux Lalitavistara II, 43) cites a few passages from which it would appear that the author had received the stories not only from the mouths of the people who had brought them from India but that he had even the text of the Lalitavistara before him.

Already in 1612 the Portuguese Diogo do Conto compared the Barlam-Josephat legend with the Buddha legend (Indian Antiquary XII, p. 288). But Laboulaye in the Journal des Debats, July 16, 1859, asserted for the first time the Buddhist origin of the legend. The entire history of the romance has been studied by E. Kuhn, Munich 1897. Kuhn is of opinion that the author utilises in a free way the general Buddhist tradition and not the principal texts like the Lalitavistara. See V, Chauvin Bibliographic des ouvrages Arabs, volume III, 1898, (p. 83.)

That it was not the Christians but Manichians who first brought the Buddha legend into Europe is surmised by LeCoq. (SBA, 1909, p. 1205), but the real author of the romance must have been only a Christian since the doctrines contained in the book are Christian. The Christians could as well have gathered the material as the Manichians.

The Prince is called in Greek Joaseph, in Arabic Judsaf, which goes back to Budasaf, *i.e.*, Bodhisattva. In Arabic, Syriac and Palhavi j and b are easily confused. The sage Barlam is called in Arabic Balauhar which according to Kuhn is traceable to Bhagavan. Barlam and Josaphet already appear as saints in the Catalogus Sanctorum of Peter de Natalibus who died about 1370.

Angelo de Gubernatis and A. Oblonsky (Le Prince Siddhartha, a drama in five acts, 1899) have dramatised the life of the Buddha. Max Koch, Studies in comparative literary history, volume III, p. 412. Most remarkable are Buddhist tales by Paul Dahlke, 1904.—Winternitz.

---

**Note to p. 130.**

A note on Balauhar wa Budasef by G. K. Nariman, Ind. Ant. 1913, 252.—N.

---

**Appendix I, p. 162.**

To Professor Hermann Oldenberg we owe a Study in the History of the Buddhist Canon (Gottingen 1912) in which the comparative value of Pali and Sanskrit sources is examined in most minute detail, parallels between the two being instituted at every step. He admits that the Pali text is a translation from the Magadhi original (p. 61). He examines the Divyavadana, Avadanashataka and the recently discovered fragments of the Sanskrit Canon. He is unable to decide whether some of the divergences manifest between the several recensions go back to the Pali redactors of the Magadhi original.

Although Oldenberg is inclined to the Pali school and his two masterly dissertations are partly directed against Sylvain Levi's essay, he impartially indicates the passages where Pali is corrected by the Sanskrit-Chinese tradition. An instructive illustration is given at p. 172. It is a question of the four Brahmana-saccani. The Pali has "all the creatures are ignorant hence the compassion," the Chinese on the other hand gives "do harm to no creature." The Pali text is *Sabbe panna Avijja*. Evidently we see that the correct text should be Avajjha; and as a matter of fact this reading is to be found in the Siamese edition as against the edition of the Pali Text Society. Further, on the basis of the Chinese translation by Levi he corrects the Sanskrit of the recently discovered fragments (pp. 176, 177). The conclusion to which Oldenberg arrives is that the Northern texts in their contents and in their form approach right near to the Pali texts, partly they coincide with them, but in other places there are wide divergences. "If the infallibility of the Pali tradition cannot be asserted in every set of circumstances, still it is evidently on the whole essentially the more ancient one" (p. 179). The artists of Bharhut and Sanchi to all appearances were acquainted with the legend of the Buddha's life in a more modern form than we meet with in the great Pitaka texts. The latter do not contain the miraculous descent of the Buddha from the heavens of the thirty-three gods which is represented both at Bharhut and Sanchi; nor do these Pali texts contain the miracle of Shashravasti which is delineated at Bharhut (p. 202). "It goes without saying that the original canon was composed in Magadhi."—N.

---

**Note to p. 172.**

Walleser is inclined also to identify the Questions of Upatishya (Upatisa-pasine) of the Bairat inscription with the Dhammasangani, and the latter to his mind is the Southern equivalent of the Dharma Skhandha, since Upatishya is only another name for Shariputra whom we know to be the author of the Dharma Skhandha (p. 25). To sum up, "in the title of

Upatisa-pasine, the sixth among the tracts recommended by Asoka to his Buddhist subjects, we find the oldest designation of the scripture which was called Dhammasangani, or Dharma Skhanda, or Dharma Sangraha after the tradition was committed to writing (p. 26).—N.

---

### Note to p. 174.

### PRATIMOKSHA.

Although it was published so long ago as 1869 with translation and commentary in Russian it is of standing importance because of the use which Minayeff makes of the Pali commentaries. The Pali text is edited in the Nagari character.—N.

---

For Sanskrit Pratimoksha of the Sarvastivadi school. See Finot & Huber, J. A 1913 (p. 465.)

---

Tokharian Pratimoksha JRRS, (p. 109, 1913.)

---

### Note to Appendix II.

### SOME CRITICAL NOTES ON SUTRALANKARA OF ASHVAGHOSHA.

From the Sutralankara Sylvain Levi traces to the Chinese version of the Tripitaka a number of passages and produces from the Pali canon their exact parallels. There are thus identified in the Pali canon seven passages from the Anguttara Nikaya, two from the Digha, nine from Majhima, seventeen from the Samyutta, two from Pali Vinaya, two from Pali Apadana, two from the Dhammapada, six from the Jataka, two from the sutta nipata, three from the Theragatha.

To the original Sanskrit now surviving only in Chinese the same savant traces four passages, one to Dirgha, seven to Madhyama, eight to Samyukta, eleven to the Sanskrit (Chinese) Mulasarvastivadi Vinaya, three to the Sarvastivadi Vinaya, one to the Mahasanghika Vinaya, seven to the Divyavadana, three to the Tibetan Dulva, four to the Chinese of original Sanskrit Buddha Carita, one to the Chinese of the original Sanskrit Dharmapada, one to the Tibetan of the original Sanskrit Karmashataka, six to the Sanskrit Mahavastu, and several passages to various other Sanskrit, Pali, Chinese and Tibetan extant scriptures.

We shall glance at only the most important of these.

The 3rd story, or sermon, has several parallels. It represents a *sutta* which is given in its entirety in the Chinese Samyuktagama. It is transmitted broken up in the Pali canon.

In the 9th sermon the text, so to say, is well known: "Absence of all desires is the basis of conduct of a Shramana." This is to be found in the 40th *sutta* of Majjhima nikaya, "Yassa kassaci bhikkhuno abhijjhaluna abhijjha pahina hoti samana samici pati padam patipannoti vadami."

The Dharmapada *shloka* 204 is the text of the 10th sermon.

The 16th sermon is in fact in the original Sanskrit as surviving in the Divyavadana (BEFEO 1904, p. 194).

The 18th sermon contains the story of Koti-karna. A study of it shows that Kshemendra, the compiler of *Avadana kalpalata*, had for his source the document of the Mulasarvastivadi school. Parenthetically it may be noted that the Svayambhu Purana is closely connected with the Divyavadana. The text of the *sutra* quoted in the 19th story refers to the Samyuklanikaya, (Vol. V. p. 91.)

The 35th story has a parallel in the *Mahavastu* (Vol. III, pp. 50-52). A parallel passage is to be found in the *Samyukta nikaya* (Vol. 21, p. 219). The Sanskrit redaction of the Samyuktagama has been lost, but a portion of it has been discovered in Chinese Turkestan by the Grunwedel mission (Toung pao, July 1904). From this story Prof. Sylvain Levi comes to the conclusion that Ashvaghosha preferred the canonical text of the Sanskrit redaction to the Pali.

The 42nd story contains a hymn to Shariputra sung by two monks, which is of historical importance. An almost verbal identity of expression is to be found with Divyavadana (p. 394).

The story of Panthaka appears in the 43rd story. The sermon is a highly interesting tale of the Divyavadana. This story also mentions a number of names which have been traced through the Chinese to their original Hindu shape.

The 48th story has its reflex in the Sanskrit Dharmapada. It is the story of Shura whose proper name was misunderstood by previous scholars.

The stanzas collected in the 49th story are to be found in the Samyutta Nikaya, Vol. I, (p. 57).

The simile of the four varieties of mangoes as given in the 58th story is to be found in the Anguttara Nikaya, Vol. II, p. 106. (Cattarome ambupama puggala).

The 51st story gives interesting account regarding the details of the life of the Buddha and the quarrels which some monks were notorious in exciting. At times the sage had to quit his turbulent disciples and seek retreat to a forest. The Majjhimana nikaya has two *suttas* on the principle of establishing harmony among the brethren. (Vol. I, 320, Vol. III, 152). We have corresponding Suttras in the Chinese version though the differences between Pali and Chinese are quite palpable.

The 52nd story is perhaps the most instructive in the whole collection. Here the author refers directly to the discourse, or the Buddhistic *sutra*, on which his sermon is based. It is the 65th of the Majjhim nikaya (Vol. I, 435). The Sanskrit Madhyamagama has the same identical Sutra. A careful comparative study of the Pali and Sanskrit sources as represented by the Chinese translation leads Sylvain Levi to the conclusion that while there is order and regularity in the arrangement of the Madhyamagama there is disorder in the corresponding Majjhim nikaya of Pali. This sutta conclusively shows that Ashvaghosha materially followed the Sanskrit collection.

The 53rd story is also popular, and has been utilised by Kshemendra in his Avadana kalpalata. He agrees entirely with the Sutralankara. Hence it is once more clear that Kshemendra worked on the materials provided by the Sarvastivadi school.

The 54th story has its counterpart in the Divyavadana as has been exhaustively shown by M. Huber (B E F E O 1904).

For the purposes of a comparative study of the various sources of Buddhism the 61st story is of peculiar significance.

It is based on the text which we find in the Anguttara Nikaya, (Vol. V, 437). Here ten qualifications of the Bhikshu are compared to the ten qualities of the ox.

In the 62nd story there is a reference to the contents of the Theri Gathas (verses 236-251) which are illustrated in the Apadana.

A detailed study of the 68th story leads Levi to the conclusion that the Pali *apadana* has utilised a passage of the Sanskrit Sutralankara.

The 73rd story presents verbal identity with the Pali. The shloka in Huber's book at p. 423 is a faithful presentation of Anguttaranikaya, (Vol. II, 275).

" Gunnam ce taramananam ujum gacchati pungavo,
Sabbata ujum gacchanti nette uju gate sati,
Evam eva manussesu yo hoti settha sammato,
So ceva dhammam carati pag eva itara paja.

The Sutralankara contains, as a work of aggressive Buddhism may be expected to do, many flings at the Brahmanic institutes and their ritual, their castes, and their general habits, which are totally opposed to the Buddhistic principles. The 77th story illustrates this.—N.

---

**Note to Appendix III. p. 207.**

Grierson holds that the Paishaci prakrit was a vernacular language of the country around Taxilla and that it is closely allied to Pali. We have a strong reason for holding that literary Pali is the literary form of the Magadhi language which was used as a medium of literary instruction in the Takshashila University. (Bhandarkar's Commemorative Essays, Home of Pali).

### Note to Appendix V, p. 224.

An important contribution to the Iranian influence on Central Asia in general is by Paul Pelliot, see Revue d' Historie et de Litterature Religieuses, March-April 1912, (p. 97).—N.

---

Central Asian Studies by Sylvain Levi, (p. 953 JRAS, 1914).

---

MO-NI ET MANICHBENS, by Paul Pelliot, J. A., 1914, 461, proves Moni to be Mani; he says:

> " il ya des textes chinois aseez nombreaux on Mazdeens.
>
> When shall we get these Zoroastrian texts in Chinese in a European translation?

---

### Note to p. 227.

BULLETIN DE L'ACADEMIE DES SCIENCES.

ST. PETERSBURG.

*Ist March, 1909.*

Fragments of the manuscripts discovered by Berazovshi at Kucha,(p. 547).—N.

---

### Note to p. 227.

Khotan is derived by Sylvain Levi from Gostana. BEFEO, 1905.—N.

Note to p. 229.

BULLETIN DE L'ACADEMIE DES SCIENCES.

ST. PETERSBURG.

*1st April, 1909.*

Tokharian and language I, by Baron A. von Stael-Holstein, p. 479.—N.

---

Note to p. 229.

BULLETIN DE L'ACADEMIE DES SCIENCES.

ST. PETERSBURG.

*December 15, 1908.*

Tokharian and language II, by Baron A. von Stael-Holstein.—N.

---

Note to p. 229.

For a Tokharian Pratimoksha see JRAS, p. 109, 1913. On Uddyotakara a contemporary of Dharmakirti see Vidyabhushana JRAS p. 601, 1914.—N.

---

Note to p. 235

For references to the Magians see Uigurica by T. W. K. Muller, (p. 9).—N.

---

Note to p. 248.

HAND BOOK TO THE SCULPTURES IN THE PESHAWAR MUSEUM.

(BY B. D. SPOONER.)

In the Peshawar Museum there are sculptures in which the young Buddha is represented as at school where he astonished his teacher by enumerating more scripts and modes of writing than the teacher knew (p. 9).

Sculpture No. 152 in the Peshawar Museum depicts the scene of the ordination of Nanda and half brother of the Buddha against his will. Most people will agree in hoping with Dr. Spooner that there is a story of forced conversion somewhere but certainly at present it is obscured if at all existing. It may be that the extraordinary love and pity of the Buddha urged him to save humanity even at the price of being temporarily cruel (p. 23).

Gandhara is the present Peshawar district with some adjoining territories (p. 34).

The art represented by the Gandhara sculptures according to Dr. Spooner is the result of the union of the older Indian or Perso-Indian art and Hellenistic art as it was known in Baktria (p. 34).

The older Indian monuments never show any representation of the Master, his presence in any good composition being indicated by some sacred symbol (p. 37).

The delineation of the first writing lesson in sculpture No. 347 at Peshawar had an added interest in that the writing board shows a few Kharoshthi characters, which the infant Buddha is supposed to have written (p. 54).—N.

---

**Note to p. 274.**

## STUDIES OF BUDDHISM IN JAPAN

(By A. Lloyd.)

Kanishka became a convert to Buddhism after a period of religious hesitation and vacillation which may have been the cause of the sending of the Magi. Kanishka puts on his coins sometimes Hindu and sometimes Zoroastrian symbols. His conversion to Buddhism is said to have been due to an accidental meeting with an aged sage who, supposing St. Luke's story to be historical, may very well have been one of the Wise Men (p. 6). The Japanese name for the Saddharmapundarika is Hokke or Hoke (p. 7).

The Chinese text translated from Sanskrit often represents an earlier version than the Pali (p. 8). It is curious that the true Buddhist propaganda in China was headed by a prince from Parthia in 148 A. D. who had resigned his throne in order to become a monk (p. 37). It is noteworthy that of the earlier Buddhist missionaries to China nearly all came not from India but from Central Asia, from Parthia and Afghanistan and that India proper took no share in the work until much later (p. 38).

According to Lloyd the Shingon doctrine is simply Manichaeism (p. 43). When a Manichaean became a Christian he was required to make the following abjuration:

"I anathematise Terebinthus who is called the Buddha, Zoroaster whom Manes called a god who had, so he said, appeared in former times to the Indians and Persians and whom he named the sun, etc." (p. 44). St. Augustine was himself at one time a Manichaean (p. 45). According to Lloyd, Saddharma pundarika, so strangely Christian in every point as well as in its imagery, was inspired by Alexandrian thought and lay at the basis of the Manichaean heresy (p. 113). The name of the Parthian prince was Anshikao who was apparently a nephew of Khosroes and who resided at Rome as a hostage for several years until released by Hadrian (p. 126).—N.

### Note to Appendix X, p 279.

## RESEARCHES SUR BOUDHISME.

(By Minayeff.)

According to the Kathavathu the law was expounded by Ananda and not by the Buddha (p. 24). Satire against Buddhists (p. 48).—N.

---

### Note to Appendix X p. 279.

Bendall, (Catalogue of Buddhist Manuscripts p. 25) describing the Cambridge Manuscript of Abhidharma kosha Vyakhya by Yashomitra says that it is an accurate copy. The accuracy and the great value of the work may be judged from the fact that firstly it was the only copy of the work existing in Nepal, and secondly that the owner before parting with it had a copy made for himself. Yashomitra mentions two of his predecessors Gunamati and Vasumitra.

The Abhidharma Kosha was translated into Chinese in 563, and again in 654.

According to Waddell (proceedings Asiatic Bengal 1899 p. 70) Tissa Moggaliputta described by the Pali chroniclers of the Mahavamsa is identical with Upagupta of the Northern tradition (p. 22).—N.

---

### Note to Appendix X, p. 279.

On the Vibhasha shastra drawn up by Kanishka see BEFEO, 1905, (p. 286).—N.

**Note to Appendix p. 279.**

J. R. A. S. 1910.

Vallee Poussin evidently shows that vedanta so far from refuting Buddhism in its entirety has been itself influenced by the latter. According to Sukhtankar Shankar himself is indebted to Nagarjuna (p. 129).—N.

---

**Note to Appendix XI, p. 287.**

**BULLETIN DE L'ACADEMIE IMPERIALE DES SCIENCES.**

St. Petersburg.

*15th April 1911.*

Jain Notes by M. B. Mironov, p. 501.

J. A. Sur la recitation primitive des textes bouddhiques by Sylvain Levi.

Example of I-tsing's abbreviated Chinese translation of the Mulasarvastivadi (p. 412.)

Sylvain Levi proves that the Atthaka vagga which Rhys Davids calls the Book of the Eights (JPTS 1897) is really speaking the equivalent of Sanskrit artha and not attha p. 413.

Vasubandhu in his Abhidharma Kosha refers to the arthavargiyesuktam (p. 414.)

The Arthavarga is quoted as a particular collection by Vasubandhu and Asanga (p. 415.)

The Arthavarga counts among the most ancient portions of Buddhist literature (p. 417.)

The Tibetan corrects the Sanskrit titles of some of the texts mentioned in the Divyavadana (p. 418.)

On Chanda and its meaning (see p. 445).—N.

---

**Note to Appendix XII, p. 293.**

Critical remarks on the text of the Divyavadana, WZKM, volume 16, by J. S. Speyer (p. 104.)

Some of the tales abound in Prakriticisms and a good many of the metrical compositions are obviously Sanskritised reproductions of stanzas in some popular dialect. It is clear, for instance, that in the famous two shlokas which began with arabhadhvam nishkramata and occurring so frequently the genitive mrtyunah rests on an original maccuno and that anadagara, iva kunjarah is a clumsy transposition of the Prakrit nadagarova kunjaro.—N.

# INDEX

## A.

PAGE.

## B.

PAGE.

PAGE.



## D.

PAGE.

## G.

PAGE.



## I.



## J.

## K.

PAGE.

Page.

Page.



## L.

## M.

PAGE.

## O.

PAGE.

## P.

## S.

PAGE.

PAGE.



## T.

PAGE.

# CORRIGENDA

The following corrigenda have been most kindly prepared by Mr. Rustam N. Munshi, Superintendent, Kama Oriental Research Institute, Bombay :—

| For | Read | Line | Page |
|---|---|---|---|
| J. A. R. S. | J R A S | 11 | 8 |
| betrayes | betrays | 12 | 9 |
| Mahavastu V. 1, 1. p. 159–2. | ... | 27–28 | 11 |
| Mahastu | Mahavastu | 5 | 12 |
| JA 1933 | JA 1903 | 19 | 18 |
| Mahayavastu | Mahavastu | last 35 | 18 |
| 850–200 | 850–900 | 4 | 26 |
| principle | principal | 31 | 26 |
| 5153 B.C. | 52–53 B.C. | 28 | 28 |
| SBEV, XLIV, p. IX | Vol. 49, p. 9 | 3 | 30 |
| JASBVV, 1909 | Vol. 5, p. 47 | 8 | 31 |
| Sastr | Sastri | 30 | 35 |
| medicant | mendicant | 33 | 65 |
| tram-carts | toy-carts | 16 | 67 |
| then | than | 17 | 67 |
| principle | principal | last 33 | 86 |
| the | he | 11 | 96 |
| maggnum | magnum | 15 | 97 |
| Biblotheca | Bibliotheca | 8 | 102 |
| practice | practise | 22 | 102 |
| mroe | from | 8 | 108 |
| Bodhein | Bodleian | 6 | 111 |
| ethymology | etymology | 21 | 116 |
| sections | section | 15 | 121 |
| religious | religions | 32 | 128 |
| Thoomas | Thomas | 25 | 152 |
| and | was | 18 | 165 |
| princess | princes | 15 | 174 |
| nivirana | nirvana | 15 | 294 |
| effered | offered | 26 | 295 |
| 20–7–19 | delete | 7 | 297 |
| positive | positive, | 18 | 313 |